PRAISE FOR THE INVISIBLE SOLDIERS

"Why did America's war in Iraq end in failure? One big reason was the decision to outsource so much of the war's conduct to private security firms. Who 'won' the Iraq War? Those very same firms. Flooding the war zone with mercenaries, they walked away with vast riches, while leaving behind a legacy of corruption and ineptitude. Ann Hagedorn's coolly devastating book exposes the causes and assesses the consequences of this travesty."

—Andrew J. Bacevich, author of *Breach of Trust: How Americans Failed Their Soldiers and Their Country*

"The story of how private military security companies came to play a pivotal role in wartime operations is an important one, and Ann Hagedorn, a former reporter for the *Journal,* was right to take it on."

—Linda Robinson, *The Wall Street Journal*

"*The Invisible Soldiers* is fascinating, unbiased, thorough, and doggedly well researched."

—Vick Mickunas, *Dayton Daily News*

"The strength of *Invisible Soldiers* is the impressive depth of Hagedorn's reporting: copious interviews, generous use of sources, and a compelling narrative. . . . *Invisible Soldiers* also reports on the people behind these private companies, some of whom are seemingly the stuff of fiction."

—Tony Perry, *Los Angeles Times*

"Well reported and eye opening. . . . This thoughtful book should kick-start a long overdue debate."

—Alan Cate, *The Plain Dealer* (Cleveland)

"A critique of the United States' fateful turn toward private military and security contractors as a consequence of the Iraq War. . . . Hagedorn deftly handles a complex and sometimes grisly topic."

—*Kirkus Reviews*

"Ms. Hagedorn has accurately and objectively begun what should be a national dialogue on the true costs of our use of a mercenary force structure."

—Delbert Spurlock, U.S. Army general counsel under President Ronald Reagan, 1981–83, and assistant secretary of the U.S. Army 1983–89

"Ann Hagedorn has given us a powerful and urgent analysis of our new military and security reality—the hiring of private warriors by governments and corporations for profit and plunder worldwide. As wars explode on every continent, and as these security companies operate in secrecy, shielded from public scrutiny or accountability, this brilliantly researched and vividly written book is essential reading."

—Blanche Wiesen Cook, Distinguished Professor of History and Women's Studies at John Jay College and The Graduate Center, CUNY, and author of *Eleanor Roosevelt*

"Hagedorn lucidly describes the long-range challenges to democracy caused by the privatization of security."

—*Publishers Weekly* (starred review)

"A book historians might someday say made a big difference. . . . Hagedorn carefully shows why the growing PMSC business is a very big deal."

—Bill Nichols, *Newark Advocate*

Also by Ann Hagedorn

Savage Peace

Beyond the River

Ransom

Wild Ride

THE INVISIBLE SOLDIERS

HOW AMERICA OUTSOURCED OUR SECURITY

ANN HAGEDORN

SIMON & SCHUSTER PAPERBACKS

New York London Toronto Sydney New Delhi

Simon & Schuster Paperbacks
An Imprint of Simon & Schuster, Inc.
1230 Avenue of the Americas
New York, NY 10020

First Simon & Schuster trade paperback edition July 2015

SIMON & SCHUSTER PAPERBACKS and colophon are registered trademarks of Simon & Schuster, Inc.

For information about special discounts for bulk purchases, please contact Simon & Schuster Special Sales at 1-866-506-1949 or business@simonandschuster.com.

The Simon & Schuster Speakers Bureau can bring authors to your live event. For more information or to book an event, contact the Simon & Schuster Speakers Bureau at 1-866-248-3049 or visit our website at www.simonspeakers.com.

Interior design by Aline Pace

Manufactured in the United States of America

10 9 8 7 6 5 4 3 2 1

The Library of Congress has cataloged the hardcover edition as follows:

Hagedorn, Ann.
  The invisible soldiers : how America outsourced our security / Ann Hagedorn.
    pages cm
  Includes bibliographical references and index.
  1. National security—United States. 2. Privatization—United States. 3. Contracting out—United States. 4. Defense industries—Privatization—United States. 5. United States—Military policy. 6. United States—Politics and government. I. Title.
  UA23.H255 2014
  355'.033573—dc23
                                        2014015007

ISBN 978-1-4165-9880-0
ISBN 978-1-4165-9881-7 (pbk)
ISBN 978-1-4391-0161-2 (ebook)

In Memory of
Dwight and Elizabeth

Know your enemy, know yourself, and you can fight a hundred battles without disaster.

—Sun Tzu, *The Art of War*

CONTENTS

PART III:
EXPANSION

THE INVISIBLE SOLDIERS

THE INVISIBLE SOLDIERS

PROLOGUE

What the boy would remember most were the shoes. They were not his shoes and they didn't fit, yet he was forced to wear them for nearly five hours as he crossed a desert in the middle of the night. At first glance, they seemed like ordinary leather shoes, but they were different because the heels were at the front. Shoes with backward heels and soles were the invention of the human smugglers who helped people like the boy and his parents to escape from Iraq into Kuwait. The idea was that if footprints were detected, the path of the journey would appear to be reversed. Although the boy longed to go home that night, what stopped him was his astute understanding that if he did, then his backward footprints would define a trail leading to the Kuwait border and thus expose his family's flight.

Kadhim Desmal Majed Alkanani was fourteen years old when he was forced to leave Iraq in April 1985. His mother awakened him shortly after midnight to tell him that he would soon be going on a "desert adventure." For the third time in a year Kadhim felt the anxiety of sudden change coursing through him like a forced injection. The first time had been eleven months before, when in the middle of the night he heard a rush of rapid pounding on the roof above his bed. In his half-asleep state he had a dreamlike image that it was Gasem, his brother, coming home—Gasem who had fled to Syria months before to avoid fighting for Saddam Hussein in the Iraqi war against Iran. But he knew it was not Gasem when he began to hear the loud cracking sounds of splintering wood followed by his mother screaming. Soldiers in Saddam's security forces had smashed through the front door of his family's home in Basra and, as his mother watched, they dragged away his father, who was suspected of betraying Saddam and was wanted for information about Gasem.

The second shock came in the days and months that followed his father's disappearance, when his teacher, a loyal follower of Saddam, turned against him. School had always been easy for Kadhim, but now each morning began with his teacher's brutal ritual of thrashing his hands with a stick and then whipping his back, in pursuit of facts about his father or brother. This was information that could lead to the teacher's promotion. But the boy insisted he knew nothing and that was the truth. All he really knew was that he hated Saddam, a fact he kept to himself. It was the first stirring of hatred he had ever felt, yet strong enough to shape the rest of his life.

In the aftermath of the abduction, Kadhim's uncle began a search throughout southern Iraq for his brother, while Kadhim's mother sold possessions to pay for the bribes necessary to uncover any leads. Seven months later, Kadhim came home from school to find his father sitting at the kitchen table. The faith that someday he would see his father again was one of Kadhim's mental devices for surviving the beatings. As the stick slashed across his stinging hand, he had rehearsed in his mind, over and over, the day he could tell his father all that the teacher had done. But his father had become so weary and frail that when Kadhim saw him, he knew he could never reveal the beatings. His only thoughts were to work hard at hiding his fears and to excel at school as a way to deflect any negative attention away from his family. His parents also had a plan. They would slowly and discreetly sell the rest of their possessions in order to pay the human smugglers for a safe passage out of Iraq. To protect Kadhim, they did not tell him any part of the plot until the morning of their escape.

When the family arrived in Kuwait, they were considered refugees, and it was hard for Kadhim's father to find any income except through manual labor, despite his years as an oil engineer in Iraq. A few years after their escape when his mother became ill with an incurable respiratory infection, his father was unable to afford the medical care she needed. Kadhim was only seventeen when she died of pneumonia. By then, Kadhim had adjusted to Kuwait and was again excelling in school. Although Kadhim had wanted to quit school to help with the care of his mother, his father would not allow it. Education was the key to Kadhim's ultimate freedom, his father insisted.

When Saddam Hussein invaded Kuwait in 1991, Kadhim and his father were forced to move again, this time to Saudi Arabia. There they lived in a refugee camp for many months until one day Kadhim's father informed his son that he was ill with cancer and that a doctor had informed him he did not have long to live. He told Kadhim that he wanted to return home to Iraq to die, and he urged his son not to accompany him. Instead, he wanted Kadhim to go to America, where he believed his hard work and intelligence would be noticed and respected. He asked Kadhim to promise that he would never return to Iraq as long as Saddam Hussein was alive. People go to war to feel the passion of believing in something, his father said that day. "You have to feel something to win a war," he said. And someday passion would defeat Saddam. Only then should Kadhim return.

When and where his father, Desmal, died, Kadhim would never know. But he did keep his promise. He soon began the long process of seeking asylum in America, and in 1995, he moved from a small town in Saudia Arabia to a Washington, D.C., suburb in Virginia. There he worked for years as a carpenter and did his best to push the past aside. But on April 9, 2003, after glancing up at a TV screen in a Washington restaurant, Kadhim could think only of his family. What he saw were U.S. Marines and a small crowd of Iraqi citizens toppling a 20-foot statue of Saddam Hussein in central Baghdad. Kadhim was spellbound. As the Marines secured the rope around the neck of the statue, Kadhim began to feel the past in a way he had never before allowed, as if sensation had returned to a sleeping limb. The grief of losing his father, his mother, his brother, and his home seemed to be surfacing in one sudden moment. If Saddam Hussein had never lived, his parents might still be alive. His family could be living in Iraq, near to one another, likely in Basra. Perhaps he would be sharing an apartment with his brother. And surely he would have experienced the higher education his father had planned for him. As he watched the statue fall, he knew that he had to return to Iraq. For Kadhim the fallen statue released enough passion within him to win five wars.

By summer, Kadhim had enlisted in the U.S. Army and was quickly sent to Fort Bragg, North Carolina, for Special Forces training. Essential components of counterterrorist strategies, Special Forces soldiers were highly valued assets in the new wars of the twenty-first century. What qualified Kadhim were his language skills, which included fluency in Farsi, Arabic, and English. During his training, rigorous as it was, Kadhim, a muscular, stocky man in excellent physical condition, felt that he had discovered a new universe—one where all that he had endured and learned in the past could be applied to a higher purpose. His helter-skelter background and his unrelenting hatred for Saddam Hussein were useful now. In fact, by the time he was deployed to Iraq, he had begun to believe that his life, plagued as it was by an instinct of endless distrust, was changing. Perhaps his father had been right. Perhaps there was potential for a meaningful life in America, through a dedication to defend it.

In Iraq, Kadhim was determined to prove his value and to return to Fort Bragg for more training to become a Special Forces officer. This was his plan and his dream. During the next year, he earned several military awards, and he indeed showed how useful he could be. He helped to identify locations of defiant enclaves—essential information for devising strategies to counter insurgents—and he became adept at explaining to Iraqi citizens the virtues of the Americans in an effort to combat propaganda against the United States. Often, during interrogations, the Army used him as an interpreter, though more frequently he worked as a cultural translator. Like a sports commentator explaining the plays and strategies of a game to spectators, Kadhim could elucidate the Iraqi culture to his military superiors. Soldiers like Kadhim helped to empower the United States through an enlightened understanding of the Iraqi people. They worked to demystify the innuendos of a foreign culture and to counter damaging propaganda. They were tantamount to weapons. And what an excellent weapon Kadhim had become: An Iraqi-born U.S. citizen trained in the U.S. Army's Special Forces, filled with a need for a sense of purpose, and instilled with enough hatred for

Saddam Hussein to ignite an explosion of American patriotism. It was a perfect match. Unfortunately, events took a disquieting turn.

On June 3, 2005, at around 6:30 P.M., Kadhim was sitting in the passenger seat of a black European sedan leaving Baghdad and headed for the U.S. military facility at Baghdad International Airport. His car was the first in a convoy of three sedans that were transporting a dozen intelligence operatives and one medic. Eight of the soldiers were Special Forces operatives in the U.S. Army; four were from the Iraqi Special Forces. None was in uniform. And all were tired, returning from an intelligence mission that had required hours of interrogations.

From the building in central Baghdad where they had spent their day to the first U.S. inspection post on the way to the airport was a distance of about 16 miles. This was a route fraught with peril, demanding silence as the men listened for the slightest sounds of gunfire or human traps. And until they reached the area beyond the initial checkpoint, which was under the exclusive control of the coalition forces, they were compelled to hold their loaded pistols on their laps. After Kadhim and his fellow soldiers showed their American IDs and were permitted to move ahead into what was considered a safe zone, they drove immediately into the right lane, which was reserved for Department of Defense vehicles only. They then proceeded at about 15 miles per hour toward the main gate, 1.5 miles ahead.

Once through the checkpoint, Kadhim holstered his M-9 pistol. Then as if shedding the tensions of war itself, he took a deep breath and began to feel the usual sense of relief that came at the end of such a day. To be safe in wartime Baghdad, he well knew, was an illusion. Yet he was a Special Forces soldier in the U.S. Army and once again he had left the arcade of danger that was his workplace unharmed. He shut his eyes and allowed his mind to drift beyond the events of that day. No one said a word; the men in the car were still quiet, each perhaps feeling the same relief. But barely a minute later, something—a slight swerve of the car, a comment from his driver, a shout from one of the operatives sitting behind him—snapped him back, causing him to look at the road ahead. And what he saw was the barrel of a rifle, an M4 to be exact, suddenly pushing out of one of the rear doors of the SUV in front of him. Although at least 150 meters away, the shooter appeared to be aiming directly at Kadhim's black sedan.

Kadhim never heard the sound of a gunshot nor did he make the connection between what he had just seen and the pain that suddenly perforated his left foot. In only seconds, he felt the sensation of nails pushing against his heel. And as he held his foot and watched his white socks turn red, his fellow soldiers spilled out of the cars in the convoy waving their arms, holding their military IDs high in the air and shouting, "We are Americans! We are Americans! Stop!"

Struggling to stem the bleeding, Kadhim tried to understand what was happening. Why had his car aroused enough suspicion to cause such aggression? He remembered seeing the SUV at the checkpoint and had watched it as it drove away, as his convoy stopped for the inspection. Later he would say: "The men in the SUV had to have seen us at the checkpoint. They had to have known that our cars were filled with U.S. soldiers. We so easily passed through the checkpoint. We were not speeding; we were going slow as we had just passed the inspection. We were not even close to them. If they were afraid of us for any reason, they should have warned us before shooting."

The bleeding seemed unstoppable as the medic in the convoy tried to restrict the flow of blood. The rest of Kadhim's body felt numb. Could he have prevented this somehow? He was the only Arab in the car. Did the men in the SUV think he was a threat? And who were they? Who were the men who would shoot without warning?

As Kadhim would quickly learn, the man who shot him was an employee of a private military and security company hired by the U.S. government to safeguard Americans in Iraq. In a sudden reckless moment, Kadhim's military experience evolved from commendable to unique, though not quite in the way he had planned. There were no medals of recognition, no awards for this. His legacy would now be that he was the first U.S. Special Forces soldier ever to be shot by an employee of one of the private military companies under contract with the U.S. government.

These were the companies sometimes referred to as the "new dogs of war," "neo-mercenaries," or "corporate warriors." They called themselves PMCs, short for private military companies; PSCs, for private security; or PMSCs, for private military and security, the most commonly used acronym. And they offered a vast range of services, armed and unarmed, from logistics support and intelligence analysis to diplomatic security, air transport, and police training. They were the companies filling the gap between military objectives and troop capacities. Advocates of privatization believed that these companies proved that harnessing private-sector power for national security and defense was more efficient than depending on conventional government support, which in a democracy could entail a long-drawn-out process. If the public sector was failing to fulfill its mandates in defending and securing its citizens, then the private sector should step in. Thus, these were companies that exemplified Ronald Reagan's privatization ideal. They were what Secretary of Defense Donald Rumsfeld had in mind in 2002 when he told military leaders to "behave somewhat less like bureaucrats and more like venture capitalists." The following year, in the aftermath of the Iraqi invasion, the combination of the strength of the insurgents and the miscalculation in troop strength for the occupation started a private-military-contracting bonanza, which, in turn, caused America's Iraq intervention to become a giant laboratory for privatizing war and national security.

By the day of the shooting, Kadhim had paid relatively little attention to the influx of private firms, though there was always talk about them among the soldiers. He had heard that they sometimes paid higher wages than the traditional military and that Americans were becoming somewhat dependent on them. He had seen recruiters trying to persuade soldiers to shift their skills to the private sector when their tours ended. He knew some names, such as Blackwater and DynCorp. And he had heard stories about rogue behavior, including incidents in which contractors had opened fire on Iraqi civilians on the highways surrounding Baghdad. But Kadhim was an American soldier. He never imagined he would be a victim of private security contractors.

While it took barely a second for the bullet to pass from the M4 rifle to Kadhim's foot, what happened in the aftermath of the shooting would send his life on a downward spin for many years. In the same period of time, private military and security companies, including the one that employed Kadhim's shooter, would begin to proliferate and profit beyond expectations. Until the shooting, Kadhim's life was filled with the passion that his father once described, the allegiance to one's nation that inspires dedicated service. "You have to feel something to win a war," his father had said. After the shooting, Kadhim's shattered world represented the demise of such conviction, while the rise of the PMSCs represented the triumph of money and power, and allegiance to the pursuit of profit. As Kadhim would soon know, the privatization of defense and security was evolving into more than a trend, more than a stopgap strategy destined to end when the war ended. PMSCs were becoming a bona fide industry.

In America, with the aid of lobbyists, impressive boards of directors, and billions of dollars in contracts, private military and security contractors were slipping into the folds of counterterrorism strategies and foreign-policy agendas. They would soon become indispensable to the Department of Defense as well as the State Department, the U.S. Agency for International Development, and the Central Intelligence Agency. As one Army general said in a 2009 interview, "The Pentagon has a new map and on it are the PMCs. Or better said perhaps, the family tree has a new branch." In August 2011, a congressional commission that had studied private contractors in Iraq and Afghanistan for three years noted in its final report that government agencies lacked the "organic capacity" to perform all the necessary functions that American foreign policy demanded and thus they were "forced to treat contractors as the default option."

By the second decade of the new century, the list of milestones in the privatization of war and national security was long. A congressional report released in May 2011 revealed a record-breaking surge in the use of private military and security contractors from June 2009 to March 2011 in Iraq and Afghanistan. This resulted in the contractors outnumbering traditional troops in a ratio of 10-to-1, outnumbering State Department personnel 18-to-1 and USAID workers 100-to-1. During that same period, casualty totals for private contractors in both nations had surpassed military losses. And as of May 2011 there were eight Americans still missing in action in Iraq, seven of whom were private contractors.

By then too, private military and security companies were supplying more than 90 percent of diplomatic security. The Department of Homeland Security was spending at least half its budget on private contractors. The United Nations had raised its PMSC expenditures by nearly 300 percent since 2009. And the expanding role of the private sector in American counterterrorism policies was increasingly evident, especially in the numbers of PMSCs working for the CIA, beginning in the aftermath of the September 11, 2001, attack on the U.S. and growing annually ever since. As one scholar noted, "The current conduct of American counterterrorism relies heavily on the private sector. Simply put, America cannot counter terrorism without PMSCs. America now relies extensively on PMSCs to conduct most aspects of statecraft, including defense, diplomacy, development and homeland security."

In his testimony at a congressional hearing in late 2011, author David Isenberg, who had been tracking these companies for more than fifteen years, expressed his deep concern over the extent of such "over reliance." He said, "Although it is not widely recognized, the use of private contractors among the complex of national defense, security and foreign policy departments and agencies is so widespread and so wide in scope that their impact can be strategic, as opposed to the merely operational and tactical." A few weeks later, Isenberg described the U.S. government's dependence on private contractors for defense and security this way: "Think back to the Alien series. The film's about the indescribable alien creature that has entered the bodies of humans. The humans look normal on the outside, but inside the alien has wrapped itself around every organ and has become so entwined that it cannot be excised; the human would die without it. And here? The [PMSCs] are so entwined; the government would collapse without them."

Isenberg was confident that these companies would continue to prosper long after troop withdrawals from both Iraq and Afghanistan. A confluence of twenty-first-century realities would guarantee such longevity, he said, including the ongoing influence of a free-market privatization ideology; tensions between America's global ambitions and its capabilities; and the widening gap between haves and have-nots worldwide, the proven catalyst for conflicts throughout history. Indeed, PMSCs have only added to their portfolios contracts with international humanitarian aid organizations, the U.N., and corporations conducting business in hostile environments. They provide armed security on ships to guard against terrorism at sea, making maritime security one of their fastest-growing businesses. They are moving into the vast new cosmos of drones. And they are working for nations other than America or Britain, their frequent employers—including the new Iraqi government—thus becoming increasingly independent of the nations that funded their immense boost in Iraq.

But how big the industry of private military and security companies has become and how fast it is growing, how many companies there are worldwide and how much money they make—how cost-effective they may or may not be—are questions that still cannot be easily answered. Basic facts such as annual revenue are difficult to assess, with calculations ranging from $50 billion to $250 billion depending on which organizations provide the figures and which kinds of services and companies are included in the calculations. Only a small percentage of firms are publicly held; one study of 585 PMSCs noted that 43 were publicly traded. Though government contracts are a major source of income, PMSCs often hold contracts with private corporations, and the private-to-private transactions are hard to track.

Furthermore, U.S. government figures on this subject have not always been reliable, especially those coming out of the Department of Defense. One congressional study showed that the DOD did not begin to gather data on private security contractors until the second half of 2007. That same report described the data that was collected as "understated" and "approximations at best." One glaring example, uncovered in the August 2011 congressional commission report, was "$38.5 billion recorded for 'miscellaneous foreign contractors.'" Although this was the second-highest category of contracting expenses in Iraq and Afghanistan, including the DOD, USAID, and the State Department, the government could not explain which companies got the money or for what services. And these weren't the only agencies blocking the view of the industry's scope. The CIA, for example, is an agency that falls "outside the normal contract licensing protocols," which means that the agency does not have to report operations conducted by its private contractors to Congress.

Even to estimate the number of PMSCs, whether in America, the U.K., or worldwide, is quite a challenge. New ones pop up as quickly as conflicts erupt, while the well-established firms swallow up smaller ones and add subsidiaries in response to new markets, becoming one-stop shopping for their government and corporate clients. Companies sometimes even change their names. And further complicating the task of assessing the industry, they often have headquarters in several nations. They sell their services to countries and corporations on every continent, and they subcontract jobs to firms and workers worldwide.

For any single U.S. contract, there could be as many as five layers of subcontractors. Such a massive web of subcontracting effectively changes the face of U.S. security forces from national to international, as a large percentage of subcontractors doing defense work in the name of America come from Africa, South Asia, and Latin America—often countries such as India, Sri Lanka, Nepal, the Philippines, Colombia, Chile, and Uganda. As one scholar wrote,

"In the past non-Americans who wanted to serve in the U.S. armed forces had to live in the U.S. and demonstrate some loyalty to the country. Iraq changed that." The Washington, D.C.–based Center for Public Integrity noted in 2010 that because of subcontractors "the U.S. government often doesn't know who it is ultimately paying."

What is most remarkable, though, is how invisible it all seems, and how silent, despite the fact that at least one out of every ten returning U.S. soldiers goes to work for a PMSC. Every few years a scandal surfaces, reminding the world that such companies exist. But when the stories disappear from the headlines and the noise dies down, the companies seem to vanish too. Although inherently governmental functions such as intelligence-gathering and embassy security are now performed by private contractors, few politicians have ever debated such practices. But then, this is a slippery topic without precise figures to define the industry and without battalions of reporters to follow it. And despite the evolving sophistication of private military and security firms—their slick websites, savvy lobbyists, and impressive boards—they can be just as elusive as their shadowy mercenary predecessors.

What is clear, however, is that one of the outcomes of the American wars of the early twenty-first century was the success of the privatization experiment and the ensuing rise of a bold new industry. The quest to privatize defense and security empowered companies now moving beyond their roles in Iraq and Afghanistan to wherever the markets for force might be found and becoming wild cards of global policy. How this happened is one of the more intriguing stories in business and military history—a story that started in England in the aftermath of the Second World War. When former British Army officer Eric Westropp, a respected PMSC industry leader, commented on the recent evolution of private military companies, he said it was "a story straight out of science fiction. There's always the seed, and the Iraqi conflict watered it, big time. Now we have a new crop that will spread globally. Many years from now it may have to be stopped, but for now it will be used and must be closely monitored. Anyone taking a close look will tell you that."

PART I

TRANSFORMATION

1

BEGINNINGS

On a short, winding street in Central London, tucked between a small park of oaks and poplars and a mews of shops and pubs, redbrick row houses five stories high stand like sentinels, as if guarding a world few passersby ever see. All alike, they have bay windows trimmed in white and four front steps leading to tall, wide doors made of fine mahogany. Even the door knockers with the brass floral designs seem to be the same. The shades on the windows go up with synchronicity most mornings and down at dusk, as if uniformity were synonymous with order, and chaos banned. But one of the houses is different and, by some standards, quite remarkable.

The door knocker on this house is the head of a lion, and the shades may be tightly drawn all day. Just to the right of the front door, slightly above a small keypad, is a hole with a diameter no bigger than the tip of a saber that emits a soft clicking sound barely audible even to the visitor close enough to set it off. It allows a clerk on the inside to observe all that occurs on the front stoop. Anyone unable to enter the proper code on the keypad or who doesn't have someone waiting inside will simply be left standing, though under close surveillance.

Inside, day and night a clerk sits behind a wooden counter, answers the phone, and scrutinizes activity outside through hidden cameras positioned above the outside doors and even attached to the upper stories of buildings across the street. The clerk watches screens that scan the outside of the building and a significant portion of the winding street. If a passerby lingers near the façade without ringing the bell or a parked car filled with packages is unattended for too long, the clerk will know what to do. In the building, listening devices are said by some to be concealed among the many books. There is a wall of twenty-four mailboxes labeled A thru XYZ, without names, next to a row of wooden hooks. Above the hooks is a tiny brass plaque with minuscule black letters that reads, "Cloaks and Daggers Only"—a touch of British wit.

The story of this row house is known to very few. Even the highly professional London cab drivers, who take two years of classes to obtain a commercial license and then have to pass a rigorous test to prove they know their way around London's streets, wince with slight embarrassment when they cannot recall the address of the establishment that occupies the building. Some have heard of it and ask if the place is somehow tied to the author Ian Fleming. "Didn't he start it?" Or "Yes, I know it well, it's the one targeted for years by the Irish Republican Army. But where it is? Not supposed to know, I would guess." To be sure, not a cabby in London appears to be taught to take passengers to the headquarters of England's elite Special Forces Club.

Since the club's inception in 1945, the British monarchy has leased the building to the SFC for £1 a year, initially as a gift from King George VI in honor of the work of special agents during the Second World War. As such, it is a place that pays tribute to covert forces and unconventional soldiers—those adept at the clandestine arts of sabotage, espionage, and guerrilla warfare. On its walls is its story—part of it anyhow—beginning in the foyer with a photo of Winston Churchill taken in 1940 during his "Set Europe Ablaze" speech, the passionate directive that set into motion urgent new strategies to counter Hitler's Blitzkrieg, resulting in the formation of the Special Operations Executive, the SOE, Britain's entry into special warfare. That was the start of special forces recruited and trained outside of traditional troops. At least 10,000 men and women enlisted in the new force, from America, Britain, France, Norway, Poland, Russia, and Australia, and hundreds of them are now depicted in photographs and paintings on the walls of the SFC.

Among those depicted is Lieutenant Colonel Sir Archibald David Stirling, who, in response to Churchill, devised a plan to send small infiltration teams of paratrooper spies to work behind enemy lines—a concept that became the highly secretive British Special Air Service, or the SAS. "Who Dares Wins" reads the legend under Stirling's photo—the SAS motto. Nearby is a gold figurine of a winged dagger, the SAS emblem. Also well represented at the SFC is Colonel "Wild Bill" Donovan, who pushed for an American equivalent to Britain's new war tactics, resulting in the Office of Strategic Services (OSS), the forerunner to the Central Intelligence Agency, which sent recruits to work side by side with Britain's special units. The CIA's red, white, and blue seal hangs prominently on the wall above the club's reception desk.

Club members have included Frederick Forsyth, who wrote *The*

Day of the Jackal and *The Dogs of War*, and brothers Peter and Ian Fleming. Most books in the club's collections focus on the Second World War or the Cold War, but some are more recent, like *An Unorthodox Soldier*, the autobiography of a mercenary turned power broker in the private military and security business.

The SFC is not part of the military establishment, though many of its members are former members of the British or American militaries. With a membership spanning the globe, including a strong U.S. presence, it is not even an exclusively British club. And to its credit, because of the female paratrooper agents in the Second World War, unlike many private London clubs, it always has admitted women.

Despite its guarded customs of secrecy, the SFC appears at first to be simply a social club steeped in history, filled with dusty trophies and old photos, and frequented by people who seem to be "up from the country" to meet friends for genial luncheons. Undeniably, there is a certain lightness to it, with its club tie—cobalt blue with mustard-colored parachutes—and its distinctive membership card without an address or phone number. In its drawing room, tea and scones seem more appropriate than hidden recording devices, and its cozy restaurant resembles one that could be found at a small art museum. But the inside of the club might be as deceptive as its façade for the SFC is as much about wars and conflicts in the present as those of the past. It is a place where the old and the new ingredients of war mix like finely blended tea.

The club's highly confidential membership list is proof of that. It is known to include the names of former British and American intelligence agents, from the CIA and from Britain's equivalent, the MI6, as well as professional kidnap negotiators and bomb and weapons experts. There are the elderly members who are veterans of the Second World War—even some Jedburghs, the Special Forces regiment whose mission was to transform the French resistance into an Allied fighting force. There are the younger members, many in the Special Forces and some having been active in the twenty-first-century wars in Iraq and Afghanistan. And there is a large contingent of middle-aged veterans of Special Forces, mainly the SAS, some of whom are or have been among the founders, directors, and CEOs of private military and security companies.

For years, the SFC seemed more about the past than the present, but the new wars and interventions of the late twentieth and early twenty-first centuries changed that. These were conflicts in which the specialized skills of unconventional warfare had become indispensable. Decentralized and more chaotic than traditional wars, unconventional wars had undefined beginnings, protracted durations, and often-unidentifiable endings, despite heads of state sometimes declaring an end to them for political purposes. These were conflicts fought according to the tenets of guerrilla warfare, often involving nonstate adversaries who remained hidden. The majority of casualties were civilians rather than combatants; and the victor remained in place long after the conflict ended to create and secure the conditions for a new regime to take form. In the new wars, symmetry was no longer evident; that is, adversaries were unevenly matched, with traditional forces of nation-states, for example, up against transnational combatants who had no national allegiance and were motivated instead by religion, ethnicity, or money.

Although often called "the new wars," asymmetrical conflicts employing unconventional operatives were not new in the history of warfare. In Africa, low-intensity local intrastate battles have been ongoing—in countries like Angola for thirty years, in Somalia for at least twenty, and in the Sudan for nearly three decades. Even the

French and Indian War in America and the Vietnam War two hundred years later used unconventional soldiers who conducted irregular warfare.

What *was* new was the extent of the global shift to asymmetrical wars and conflicts and the consequential demand for a particular type of military and security forces. During the first decade of the twenty-first century, the ever-widening span of unconventional warfare caused an unprecedented call for experts in special operations, intelligence, and security. At the same time, such a need created an unsettling gap between what the traditional militaries of nation-states could do and were trained to do, and what the new wars required of them. Filling the gap in the marketplace of conflict was a big business opportunity for any company peddling military and security services, both armed and unarmed. This development was part of the inexorable commercialization of warfare and national security, especially in the United States and the United Kingdom.

At the SFC, the new wars and private contractors were more than the stuff of drawing room conversations, as many PMSCs had evolved out of special forces. Decades-old British companies were often models for new firms—so often that the SFC became what one club member called "one of the centers of gravity for the industry," which among insiders in the U.K. was sometimes referred to as "The Circuit." The common ground of the traditional and the privatized military and security forces was the SAS, which, operating outside the established military, was one of the toughest, smartest, and most sophisticated of all special forces. Accountable only to the monarch—not to Parliament—it was, as the British Army handbook described it, "particularly suited, trained and equipped for counter-revolutionary operations," including sabotage, assassinations, and "control of friendly guerrilla forces operating against the common enemy."

Although known for such counterterrorism expertise, the SAS was rarely identified as a pioneer in the privatization of security and defense. Yet former SAS soldiers and officers had been cultivating the marketplace of soldiering services long before other groups and individuals had discovered a glint of opportunity. The firms that laid the groundwork for the corporate evolution of the mercenary trade were, in fact, founded by Special Forces operatives, often from the SAS, who had fought in the Second World War.

Such highly trained, unconventional former soldiers launched a new mercenary era in the early years of the Cold War. The companies they founded, rooted as they were in the covert culture of special forces, were part of an underworld of private security, defense, and aggression. They conjured images of gun-smuggling soldiers of fortune and were especially busy in Africa and Latin America, where the West's domino theory of one nation after another succumbing to Communism prevailed. In the employ of multinational corporations and under the command, at arm's length, of the CIA or MI6, among others, they were well paid for jobs such as toppling regimes, reinstating exiled leaders, or eliminating rebel groups to safeguard their clients' control of highly prized reserves of diamonds, gold, copper, and oil.

These companies were the modern-day representatives of one of the world's oldest and most often deplored professions, the mercenaries. Kings had used mercenaries to defend their kingdoms, dictators to protect their autocracies, churches to guard worldly properties, empires to expand militarily. They had sparked battles and perpetuated wars and when diplomacy failed or the willing warriors of a patriotic citizenry were not strong enough to defend a nation, mercenaries surfaced as an option.

In their new incarnation during the first decades of the Cold War, there were two companies that could qualify as the charter firms, the first of numerous companies founded, led, and directed by former SAS operatives. One was Watchguard International, started by the SAS founder David Stirling, whose photo adorned the wall at the Special Forces Club. The other, Keenie Meenie Services (KMS), was also started by a former SAS lieutenant colonel.

Watchguard's specialties included training teams of bodyguards for heads of state in high-risk places, especially in Africa, and training local military forces to combat and eliminate rebel forces. On its list of clients were most of the rulers of the Gulf nations and the leaders of several African states. Under contract with the Saudis in the 1960s, Watchguard hired the mercenaries who waged a guerrilla war against the left-wing Egyptian-backed North Yemeni government in the Yemen civil war. A few years later, Watchguard personnel planned an elaborate coup to overthrow Libya's Muammar Gaddafi. Shortly after Watchguard folded in the 1970s, Lieutenant Colonel Stirling revealed the firm's mission in a British TV interview: "The organization was designed to tackle really important military objectives which couldn't be tackled officially because of questions [that might be raised] in the House of Commons. The British government wanted a reliable organization without any direct identification. They wanted bodyguards trained for rulers whom they wanted to survive."

Close to the time of Watchguard's inception, Lieutenant Colonel Jim Johnson, then working as a broker at Lloyd's of London, started Keenie Meenie Services. "Keenie Meenie" comes from the Swahili word for the motion of a snake in tall grass. With Johnson's tie to Lloyd's, KMS was the first company to link the insurance business and the private military companies—an occasional partnership that profitably identified dangerous regions and peddled security. At

KMS, which focused on the training of mercenaries and bodyguards, SAS veterans filled the top posts. In the 1980s, it stood out among its peers for its work with the CIA in Nicaragua. KMS, for example, supplied pilots for clandestine airdrops in support of the counter-insurgents known as Contras.

The SAS-Lloyd's connection inspired the creation of yet another firm, Control Risks Group (CRG), founded in the early seventies. At the time, airplane hijackings and kidnappings were on the rise and the word "terrorism" was beginning to appear in the annual reports of natural-resources and oil companies operating in high-risk territories where rebel forces fought long civil wars. Such companies recognized that their own governments were not always equipped to protect them and not always willing to negotiate international kidnappings.

A recent Oxford grad, Julian Radcliffe, with a degree in philosophy and a relatively brief stint in the SAS, designed CRG to fill that gap for businesses venturing into hostile environments. The firm would specialize in kidnap negotiations. At a time when unprecedented numbers of Americans were traveling, working, and living abroad, he defined a niche market destined to grow. His plan was to recruit former SAS men to provide hostage-related services as part of Lloyd's kidnap and ransom insurance package. The K&R policy, as it was called, covered the expense of a ransom payment, if a ransom had to be paid, and included the cost of highly trained SAS experts sent immediately to the location of the kidnapping. Radcliffe's first crew consisted of four former SAS officers.

One of the most renowned offshoots of the SAS, however, was Executive Outcomes, a company that originated in apartheid South Africa and became the model firm in the late twentieth century for the evolving phenomenon of private military companies. "EO," as it was typically referred to, was founded in 1989 by Eeben Barlow, a former officer in the apartheid era's highly decorated combat unit known as the 32 "Buffalo" Battalion. Barlow had also been a leader in South Africa's Civil Cooperation Bureau—notorious for trying to destroy the antiapartheid movement and for assisting apartheid companies in averting the antiapartheid sanctions imposed by the United Nations. Four years after starting EO in South Africa, Barlow collaborated with a former SAS commander and another Special Forces veteran who ran a fast-growing oil business to establish the U.K. Executive Outcomes. The EO logo, used in both nations, was the chessboard knight, which represented the paladin, a freelance warrior for justice and virtue.

Executive Outcomes soon operated in at least ten African nations. The firm would occasionally provide security services to a company or a government trying to defeat rebel groups that had taken over gold mines or oil rigs, and in exchange it would receive a lien on the exportable raw materials, usually mineral wealth, of the client country. At one point in the 1990s, EO employed over 3,000 troops and close to 500 military officers, many from SAS-trained command teams and some from the South African Special Forces. Then after Nelson Mandela's South African government passed an anti-mercenary law in 1998, EO shut down, though only in South Africa.

In the U.K., EO was part of a London-based conglomerate of private military firms, mineral resource businesses, and air charter companies. Among its holdings would soon be a company called Sandline International, run by some of the same ex-military men and businessmen who had backed and operated the U.K. EO. Sandline's CEO, Tim Spicer, would become a highly influential and hugely controversial figure in the PMSC industry.

After the Cold War ended, companies like these grew in size

and services in both the United Kingdom and the United States as the former Soviet Union and the U.S. effectively laid off military specialists, who then sought jobs in the private sector. In the 1990s, companies employing former soldiers, spies, and special agents helped to meet the demands of nations, like the U.S., increasingly involved in regional conflicts that had once been subdued by Cold War alliances. Just two years into the post–Cold War era, as scholar Deborah Avant later wrote, "a rash of smaller-scale conflicts unleashed disorder and demands for intervention. As the clamor for a western response grew just as western militaries were shrinking, nascent [PMSCs] provided a stop-gap tool for meeting greater demands with smaller forces."

During that time, the American PMSC business could be divided into three parts. There were the new firms popping up to meet the post–Cold War demand. There were a few older companies that had been contracted for military services in past wars; these included Booz Allen, which provided training programs for South Vietnamese officers in the 1960s. And there were the large well-established defense contractors, the makers of weapons, airplanes, and defense equipment, which were adapting to the emerging markets by adding services to their manufacturing base. While British PMSCs were rooted in the skills of the military elite and Special Forces, with a strong focus on counterterrorism capabilities, the American firms often came out of the war-products industry, moving into services much later. These were the sort of companies that inspired President Dwight D. Eisenhower's cautionary comments in January 1961 about the dangers of fusing military and corporate agendas into what he referred to as the military-industrial complex. Among them was Brown and Root Services Corporation, the construction and engineering subsidiary of the Houston-based oil services multinational Halliburton. Brown and Root's experience building oil rigs in remote, hostile environments in undeveloped nations laid the groundwork for its role in American foreign policy, a role that grew significantly when it added logistics services to its capabilities.

Crucial to understanding the American push to privatize defense was what was known as LOGCAP, the U.S. Army's Logistics Civil Augmentation Program. While product-based American firms moved into the realm of wartime services partly because of the expanding defense markets in the 1990s, LOGCAP was actually a bigger catalyst. Beginning in 1985, it was effectively the U.S. military's experiment in relying on private firms for logistics services and it was instigated in part to bypass the Abrams Doctrine—officially the Total Force Policy—which had been enacted in 1973 at the behest of Army Chief of Staff Creighton Abrams. As the U.S. commander for the last four years of the Vietnam War, Abrams was devastated by the protests and negative public sentiment when his troops returned home. The Abrams Doctrine was a way to prevent such a disconnect between the public and the military, as it required all reserve military as well as active troops to be treated as a single integrated force. Because reservists would have to leave their jobs to serve the country, the impact of war would cause disruption and thus penetrate more deeply into the nation's psyche. The idea was that this would make it harder for politicians to take the nation to war. And it would make the wars more visible. This in turn would force Congress and politicians to debate and deliberate questions of going to war. As author and commentator Rachel Maddow later put it, "sending the military into war would mean, by definition, sending *the country* into war." LOGCAP was a way to go to war without initiating a public debate.

Though it came into existence in 1985 under Ronald Reagan, LOGCAP did not come into play until the end of the administration of President George H. W. Bush. In 1992, Secretary of Defense Dick Cheney, soon to be Halliburton's CEO, commissioned Halliburton's Brown & Root to study the potential advantages of privatizing more of the duties involved in military support. Brown & Root gave privatization a thumbs-up and then was awarded the first ever five-year LOGCAP contract, allowing the firm to run support operations for the U.S. military in Haiti, Somalia, the Balkans, and Kuwait, among other places. Under the leadership of President Bill Clinton, LOGCAP spurred what could easily be called the first bonanza for the private military business, in the Balkans. And by the end of Clinton's two presidential terms, the private military expenditures would grow from hundreds of millions of dollars to billions.

It was in the Balkans in the 1990s that U.S. politicians from both parties began to fully appreciate the strategic value—that is, political strategy—of utilizing PMSCs. In the aftermath of the Cold War, in what was the former Yugoslavia, a civil war broke out between the Serbs (backed by Russia) and the Croatians and Bosnians. And in April 1992 it erupted into a devastating humanitarian crisis as Serbs slaughtered more than 25,000 Muslims in Bosnia and raped at least 20,000 women and girls. Bill Clinton, as a presidential candidate in 1992, vowed to take action to end what the State Department was defining as "ethnic cleansing" in Bosnia. But, as the new president, Clinton faced a multitude of obstacles to keeping his promise: a downsized and overextended military; a nation interested only in domestic issues; and the 1991 U.N. embargo on arms sales to any of the embattled groups in the Balkans. Although airstrikes were an option, both Senator John McCain and General Colin Powell, the chairman of the Joint Chiefs of Staff, fiercely objected. McCain said airstrikes were useless without ground troops and he drew parallels to what had happened in Vietnam. Polls showed that the American public did not understand what interest the U.S. had in the Balkans, and this echoed what General Powell had been saying all along, which was that Bosnia was a "nonstrategic interest." Adding to the complications were two recent events: America's failed intervention in Somalia in 1993 and the 100 days of genocide in Rwanda in 1994 without U.S. intervention. How was it possible for the United States to make an aggressive move to end the devastation in the Balkans without causing a political maelstrom, both nationally and internationally?

The solution came out of a convergence of influence. In 1994 the minister of defense in Croatia sought help from the U.S. government, and around the same time a cadre of private military executives with pasts in the U.S. military and well connected to the Pentagon during the Clinton years presented former colleagues with what later would seem like an obvious way out of the bind: "enlist" MPRI, or Military Professional Resources Incorporated. This was a company known among insiders at the time as "America's professional army." Author Robert Young Pelton referred to it as "the politically correct version of a private military company." Describing itself as "the greatest corporate assemblage of military expertise in the world," MPRI was one of the first American PMSCs to be founded by retired military officers and to follow the British service-based model. With services ranging from modernizing and training national armies to purchasing arms, it had opened its main office down the road from the Pentagon in 1987. And now, MPRI, as if it had been a weapon hidden in some faraway grotto, would be the solution to Clinton's conundrum in the Balkans. MPRI would supply 46,000 rifles, 1,000 machine guns, and hundreds of armored vehicles to the Croatian Army, which it would also train. With U.S. approval and some backing, MPRI, in early 1995, helped to build the Croatian Army into a force that by the fall of that same year pushed Serbian leader Slobodan Milosevic into peace negotiations.

After the Dayton Peace Accords, Clinton again turned to the private sector—this time because of the U.S. commitment of 20,000 peacekeepers in the international force in Bosnia. By then there had been more analyses, beyond Brown & Root's, showing the advantages of privatizing logistics support as well as other military services. And there was the enthusiasm of Vice President Al Gore, a privatization booster who "held up LOGCAP as a poster child for good governance."

To be sure, the occasion of the U.S.-led NATO forces in Bosnia was the unveiling of LOGCAP as a key solution for every future U.S. president. Instead of calling up thousands of reservists to go to Bosnia and Herzegovina, the U.S. government contracted out the work to Brown & Root and to another U.S. firm, Virginia-based DynCorp. Such a strategy removed the political messiness, allowing the U.S. to continue its presence in the Balkans for eight years with little visibility. Few Americans were aware of it. As author and Brookings Institution fellow Peter W. Singer later wrote, "The privatized effort was one of the quiet triumphs of the war."

LOGCAP was successful enough to prompt strategies of outsourcing a vast array of other services, from intelligence and air transport to armed security and interrogations. And so it was that logistics support jumpstarted the privatization trend at the Pentagon, which helped to push the business of PMSCs on both sides of the Atlantic.

Perhaps as significant to the industry's development in the 1990s was an even less visible drive to rebrand the image of the "dogs of war." As a new age of uncertainty and instability unfolded and markets for private forces grew, some smart players in the neomercenary marketplace—including a few members of the SFC—began to pay closer attention to their public image and thus initiated an unofficial campaign to rid their business of the word "mercenary." It was a subtle transformation that started to surface in the mid-1990s and would later prove to be quite meaningful. It began with unnoticed and seemingly inconsequential events.

2

OUT OF THE SHADOWS

On an autumn day in 1995, three men met for lunch at a small Tuscan restaurant near Kings Road in the Chelsea district of London. In a room of closely placed tables and walls of photos showing generations of the Florentine family that had owned the restaurant for nearly forty years, the men sat and ate and talked for hours, as if they too might be family, though what had brought them together was purely business. One of the men was Anthony Buckingham, the head of a British oil concern that managed more than a dozen subsidiaries engaged in oil drilling, diamond and copper mining, and private military services. Another was Simon Mann, the son of a famous cricket player and a fifth-generation graduate of Eton, the privileged school in England known for educating the nation's elite political class. He was also a former SAS commander, a former lieutenant in the British Army's Scots Guards, and one of Buckingham's partners in bringing

Executive Outcomes to the U.K. The third man was Tim Spicer, a former lieutenant colonel in the Scots Guards. Spicer had known Mann for many years but had never met Buckingham. And Mann, who was in business with Buckingham, wanted the two men to meet, for a variety of reasons.

A few weeks before, a reporter at the *Observer* had exposed ties between Buckingham's parent company, Heritage Oil, and Executive Outcomes. The reporter noted that a high-level British politician—in fact, the former head of the Liberal Party, David Steel—was a nonexecutive director of Heritage and that Heritage owned an enterprise shrouded in mystery. In its earliest embodiment, EO had served as a front company to evade arms embargoes against South Africa and to facilitate the shipment of illegal weapons into South Africa. In recent months, the article reported, some of EO's eager young recruits had been working covertly for the Angolan government to defeat and allegedly to slaughter insurgents who had seized Heritage Oil's installations.

Worse still, at least for Buckingham and Mann, the article alleged that EO bartered its military services in exchange for natural resources—hence, the accumulation of Heritage's mineral subsidiaries. In fact, the suspicions swirling around EO included allegations that, on at least two occasions, employees of the company had provoked conflicts in nations where Heritage was seeking mineral acquisitions. On the morning before the Kings Road gathering, Steel announced his resignation from the Heritage board.

It was not surprising then that part of the conversation at the restaurant that day touched on image, spin, and marketing: How to avoid the quicksand of suspicion in a business typically associated with mercenaries and the brokering of men with guns. How to prevent the exodus of EO's clients. How to rebrand EO. Was the solution to create another company that would use, as one writer later put it, "EO's Rolodex" but start anew with "a superficial sheen of respectable leadership"?

Spicer noted later in his autobiography that he, Buckingham, and Mann discussed the creation of "a properly organized, professional company marketing military skills as a commercial operation." The idea was that this would be a company working only for legitimate governments. It would be more conventional, more public, and less secretive than EO had been. They agreed that there was a sufficient market for such companies. Spicer, as he later wrote, even knew of specific work then available and fitting for the company they were defining. "There were legitimate governments that needed help and when friendly nations refused to supply it they would eventually turn in desperation to the private sector."

The company would have a new name. Though not discussed that day, it would be called Sandline International. Same people, same purpose, new name. They also discussed retaining a public relations firm in London to etch out a savvy professional look for the new company. And they talked about fresh ways to describe the business in general, ways that might not call to mind a mercenary history. No more "soldiers of fortune" or "hired guns." The new label for what EO had been and Sandline was about to become would be "private military company."

There was no official name change that day and no announcement to the press. Still, this was a critical step in the process of building an industry. That day on Kings Road three men peered over the horizon, took notes and came up with a concept that could gradually move their business closer to respectability by repositioning a company too tarnished to prosper in its current embodiment. They were going to transform a decades-old mercenary image into a crisp new reputable look, using Sandline as their model. London public relations consultant Sara Pearson, who would work for Spicer at Sandline, said later that the new term "private military company" "took a lot of emotion out of the situation."

In the years to come, the significance of the name change would become more evident. The first use of the term "private military company" in the press occurred barely a month after the Chelsea meeting in an article from a French news agency reporting on the civil war in Angola and referring to Executive Outcomes. Later, after Mann and Buckingham were no longer involved in the business, Spicer would be credited in the British press as the man behind the change. He would become, as British journalist Stephen Armstrong later wrote, "the public face of a PR campaign soon selling political elites and the media, especially in America, on the concept of the private military company."

For a business that had defined itself in a tradition of secrecy, bringing in public relations experts to describe a company's services to the public and even to distribute press releases announcing a firm's latest news was as revolutionary as the industry's new name—and just as crucial to marketing its services to governments and multinationals. It was brilliant, as the years ahead would show. Soon former special ops known for mounting coups or running sabotage maneuvers would appear to be business professionals simply securing and developing the commerce of a global economy. Their industry group would be called the International Peace Operations Association, promoting its services in the name of peacemaking. Their origins in Special Forces and covert armies would be obscured by a swirl of big money and new wars, fading as inauspiciously as the Old World term "mercenary."

In the early years of the new century, however, despite the privatization push in the Balkans, the industry was still barely visible. To be sure, the September 11, 2001, attacks on the World Trade Center and the Pentagon instigated a rush of contracts out of the Department of Defense and the Central Intelligence Agency as part of their counterterrorism strategies in Afghanistan and Pakistan. And as early as 2002, the soon-to-be-notorious American firm Blackwater was assisting the CIA in Afghanistan, at first protecting its bases, then directly participating in CIA missions. But the unveiling of the PMSCs would occur in Iraq.

By the time of the Iraq invasion on March 20, 2003, the U.S. government was devising security and defense strategies dependent on the products and services of private contractors. And because of the vast opportunities for work, thanks to an overstretched military caused by miscalculated troop needs for the occupation and an underestimated number of insurgents, the Iraq War would prove to be a vital turning point in the evolution of PMSCs.

A few months before the invasion, in December 2002, two dozen or more specialists in military strategy, diplomacy, and intelligence convened at the Army's War College at the behest of the Pentagon to discuss Iraq's fragile economy, its years of misrule, and the potential impact of an invasion on such conditions, including expansion of insurgent forces. "The possibility of the United States winning the war and losing the peace is real and serious," their subsequent report stated. "Thinking about the war now and the occupations later is not an acceptable solution." Consistent with such reasoning, Army Chief of Staff General Eric Shinseki said in February 2003 that to occupy Iraq would require several hundred thousand soldiers—a figure he later put at 400,000. Although Shinseki's estimate was largely based on models and analyses from Kosovo and Bosnia, Deputy Secretary of Defense Paul

Wolfowitz adamantly disagreed. While Wolfowitz had demanded 250,000 troops for the invasion, he insisted that only 75,000 would be required for the occupation. Key figures in the administration of President George W. Bush supported Wolfowitz and disavowed Shinseki's estimate.

By May 1, 2003, when President Bush stood on the deck of an aircraft carrier and announced to the world that the invasion of Iraq was a success, the possibility of losing the peace was looming. Rampant looting and street violence were escalating, and so were the numbers of insurgents. Then later in May, Paul Bremer, the head of the Coalition Provisional Authority (CPA), which was the new governing body in Iraq following the overthrow of Saddam Hussein, issued several orders that would worsen the situation. The first was the "De-Baathification of Iraqi Society" order, meaning that top-level members of Saddam Hussein's Baath Party would be banned from the new Iraqi government. This was a move that affected at least 85,000 Iraqis who, having been adherents to Saddam's regime, would now be without work. (Included were about 40,000 school-teachers who had joined the Party simply to keep their jobs.) Bremer signed the order on May 16.

Then one week later, he signed Order 2, which called for the dissolution of Saddam's security and intelligence forces, including armed forces (385,000), the Interior Ministry (285,000), and the presidential security units (50,000). Although the plan was to train thousands of the demobilized soldiers for the New Iraqi Army, Order 2 would add hundreds of thousands of Iraqi citizens to the nation's already large roster of the unemployed, many of them military trained and armed. Humiliated and angry, they could easily turn against their U.S. occupiers, who had forced them out of work. The deputy chief of planning at the Pentagon's Central Command would later say that on the day Order 2 was issued (May 23), "we snatched defeat from the jaws of victory and created an insurgency."

The decisions for both orders were made over the objections of high-ranking intelligence and military officers. Later there would be considerable buck-passing in the quest to establish exactly who issued the commands for the orders. But in Bremer's memoir, *My Year in Iraq*, he wrote that on his last day before leaving for Iraq, Rumsfeld sent him a memo stressing that "the coalition will actively oppose Saddam Hussein's old enforcers. . . . We will make clear that the Coalition will eliminate the remnants of Saddam's regime." That same morning, according to Bremer, the Under Secretary of Defense Douglas Feith showed him a draft for Order 1. The provenance of Order 2 was a bit more slippery, though from Bremer's account the demobilization decision appeared to have come from Wolfowitz, Feith, and Bremer himself. But whoever had been the source of the commands, the impact was quite clear: an insurgency far larger than any Western analyst had predicted.

The implementation of Orders 1 and 2 would prove to be a key moment in the PMSC story. After all, at the intersection of too few troops and too many insurgents, what were the options? To ask Congress for more troops would have been irrefutable evidence that the invasion of Iraq was not well planned—political suicide. Other than leaving the country, the only alternative was to turn to the private sector. And thus a silent strategy was set into motion. Soon PMSCs would be in greater demand in Iraq than ever before in any conflict.

Iraq would be known as "the first contractors' war." Even Bremer, as head of the legislative, judicial, and executive authority in Iraq, was a civilian contractor. This was another first: a private contractor running the military occupation of a nation. And before the CPA shut down, Bremer would initiate more orders, including one at the very end of his regime: Order 17, which gave all foreign contractors operating in Iraq immunity from the Iraqi legal process, meaning immunity from any kind of suit, civil or criminal, for their actions. While Orders 1 and 2 created the need for the private sector to come to the rescue, a need so great that there was no viable alternative, Order 17 reduced the risks for going to Iraq.

In the Balkans, the ratio of traditional military to privatized defense had been 50-to-1, unprecedented at the time. But in Iraq the ratio would soon go from 10-to-1 to 1-to-1. Eventually the number of contractors would exceed the conventional military, as it would in Afghanistan. "In a matter of months, private security in Iraq went from a fledgling cottage industry to a multibillion-dollar endeavor," wrote journalist Robert Young Pelton.

At first, the most lucrative contracts went to an inner circle of American companies, among them several well-established players and a few aggressive newcomers. There was Vice President Dick Cheney's former employer, Halliburton, whose subsidiary KBR, Inc. (formerly Kellogg, Brown & Root) would eventually earn more than $40 billion in Iraq. And there was MPRI, which, by the time of the invasion, had five divisions all headed by retired generals and former Department of Defense officials. There was also Vinnell Corporation, owned by the big defense contractor Northrop Grumman. Most recently having trained the Saudi Arabian National Guard, Vinnell would now be in charge of training the Iraqi Army and would subcontract to several other companies, including MPRI. And there was DynCorp, a firm that got its start in the air cargo business in the 1940s and later developed a reputation for serving America "in areas too dangerous for orthodox diplomacy." DynCorp had supplied former police officers for the international police force, where it drew attention when a U.S. Army investigation revealed that a number of DynCorp's private contractors were holding women and girls as sex slaves—some only twelve years old. DynCorp was best known, though, for running U.S.-authorized paramilitary operations in Colombia to fumigate coca crops. In Iraq, the DOD contracted it to train the Iraqi police. DynCorp was also under contract with the State Department for security needs in Afghanistan, among other hot spots; and it subcontracted its Iraq work for the State Department to Blackwater.

There were several newer American firms, including Triple Canopy and Custer Battles, which both came out of Special Forces, following the British model. Triple Canopy was a 2003 start-up founded in Chicago by Special Forces veterans and initially staffed by former SEALs, Rangers, and Delta Forces. Custer Battles, which supplied the armed guards to secure the Baghdad airport, was one of the several firms that began shortly after 9/11. Its founders were a former Army Ranger and a former CIA intelligence officer.

But the most visible of the newcomers would be Blackwater, which would easily qualify as a bona fide mercenary company. Seven years before the Iraqi invasion, it was founded by former Navy SEAL Erik Prince, heir to a large fortune based in a Michigan auto-parts business. Blackwater was located on a 7,000-acre training base in Moyock, North Carolina. It was not like any of the other American firms, old or new. It was more in the footprint of Executive Outcomes, the former South African company, and it was a company composed of many parts: Blackwater Airships, Blackwater Canine, Blackwater Aviation, Blackwater Target Systems, and Blackwater Grizzly, a customized large armored truck. In 2002, Blackwater's federal contracts from the U.S. totaled $3.4 million. Two years into the Iraqi occupation, its contracts would exceed $350 million, on the way to billions. At least $20 million of that was for the job of guarding Bremer, a detail comprising gunners, helicopters, two canine teams, three dozen armed guards, armored trucks with swivel mounts for machine guns, and more.

From the start in Iraq, a large percentage of contracts were for logistics support, which freed the traditional troops for combat duties. Because of big names like Halliburton, this was typically what the media noticed during the early years of the occupation. But what would make Iraq stand out was that nearly every function of a contingency operation would eventually be outsourced—that is, armed as well as unarmed operational support and training. In fact, private-sector personnel in Iraq would undertake the broadest range of tasks in military history, including gathering intelligence, training soldiers and police, escorting convoys, flying planes, repairing weapons, conducting risk analyses, and, of course, armed security.

And indeed it was largely the immense demand for armed security that would cause the unprecedented expansion of PMSCs in Iraq. Every company involved in the reconstruction of Iraq had to protect its employees, and many subcontractors had to hire their own armed security. Most DOD contracts for logistics, reconstruction work, and a wide range of jobs required the U.S. Army to provide protection for the employees of contractors. But subcontractors were not always covered. Considering that large jobs were sometimes executed through several layers of subcontractors, this was potentially big business for hired guns.

By late 2003, the historic shift in defense operations to the private sector was already underway. There were at least 60 military and security companies in Iraq with as many as 20,000 employees. But equally groundbreaking was the transition from a national to an international force, with contractors and subcontractors from South Asia, Latin America, and Africa. PMSCs were often founded by former military officers and run by them, and some of the more sophisticated high-risk military work—including intelligence, interrogations, VIP security details—was performed by highly trained experts from America, Britain, Israel, or South Africa. But there were two other classes of contractors: host-country nationals and third-country nationals. Ex-pats, typically mentioned in the media, were at the top level of the hierarchy and had salaries about five or six times larger than traditional troops. Host-country nationals were cheaper to employ and often worked as translators or guides of some sort because of their familiarity with the occupied nation. But they also were less appealing to the companies because of security concerns and because they were accountable to local laws. To save money and to diminish legal liability and accountability, companies frequently hired third-country nationals. The scope of their work was vast, from truck drivers and cooks to armed protection of convoys to high-risk air-transport missions. Yet, they were paid the least and could most easily vanish if trouble ensued. They also were sometimes victims of poor living conditions while on the job.

Like floodwaters forcing shorelines to change, the Iraqi occupation would alter not only the face of war but also the nature of the American and British military and security firms. American companies—the new and the established—would now more frequently follow the British model for capitalizing on the expertise of special forces. And the U.K. companies, which in 2003 still reaped most of their profits through commercial clients, would add more government contracts than ever before to their revenue base. Despite such shifts, however, by the end of the first year of the occupation, the British had a relatively minor presence in Iraq. To be sure, the British were getting crumbs from the bountiful feast in the military and security business—until the spring of 2004. It was then that the U.S. government awarded a small, little-known London-based firm the biggest security contract in Iraq—what the *Boston Globe* described as "the largest single piece of the private security pie in Iraq so far handed out by Washington." This was a contract that would one day be seen as central to the new military privatization, making 2004 a defining year for the PMSCs. And because of the company that won it, the contract would also represent a milestone in the modern history of mercenaries and perhaps the best proof of the power of the rebranding that Tim Spicer and his cohorts had undertaken.

3

A WATERSHED YEAR

In every month of the spring and summer of 2004, the U.S. government issued terror alerts, beginning in March with the potential for "a catastrophic attack within the U.S." and the warning "to maintain a high level of vigilance." Then came the April announcement that terrorists "may try to bomb buses and rail lines in major U.S. cities this summer," followed by the May alert, in which U.S. officials claimed they had information "suggesting" a terrorist attack planned for the summer. Potential targets included the Memorial Day dedication of the National World War II Memorial on the National Mall in Washington; the G8 economic summit at Sea Island, Georgia; Fourth of July celebrations across the nation; the Democratic National Convention in Boston; and the Republican convention in New York.

There would be more. In August, Homeland Security Secretary Tom Ridge would tell the nation about specific targets for terror in

Newark, New Jersey; New York City; and Washington, D.C., most of them financial institutions. The intelligence came from "multiple locations, multiple sources." What was extraordinary, the Secretary said, was "the considerable detail and quality of information regarding those sites. We have no specific information that says an attack is imminent, but given the specificity and quality of information around these sites, obviously one would conclude, if you were considering the potential attack, these might be among the targets." The next day, however, the *New York Times* revealed that the bulk of the information for this latest alert had been gathered in 2000 and 2001: "Reports That Led to Terror Alert Were Years Old, Officials Say."

Whether new or old, the alerts added to an already fearful collective consciousness that year, especially in the spring when, for example, there were alarming forecasts about piracy and terrorism at sea. These had dramatically escalated after the February bombing of a ferry in the Philippines in which more than 100 people were killed. "Maritime terrorism is a ticking time bomb," read a report out of Lloyd's of London, which was studying the threats and risks to the shipping industry. Such studies indicated that oil and gas tankers as well as cruise ships could be prime targets for Al Qaeda guerrillas and that piracy attacks were surging. Although there was some confusion about who was a pirate and who was a terrorist, the number of terror attacks at sea, including piracy, had risen by 20 percent annually in 2003, according to several of the reports. "We believe al Qaeda and its associates may be planning a maritime 'spectacular,'" an analyst from the British firm Aegis Defence Services told Reuters in February. "We think there are enough indications now that al Qaeda would like to do this, is thinking hard about it, and is probably beginning to prepare for it. Piracy is the perfect mask for maritime terrorism."

Indeed, by spring, anxiety seemed to permeate the globe—especially in Iraq. There news broke about the abuse of Iraqi prisoners at Abu Ghraib, once a notorious prison and torture center during the rule of Saddam Hussein. It was then that the word "waterboarding," as a method of torture—or, as some preferred, "harsh interrogation"—entered the popular lexicon of American warfare. And a twenty-six-year-old American contractor named Nicholas Berg, from West Chester, Pennsylvania, was beheaded in retaliation for the treatment of the Abu Ghraib inmates. Berg's killers videotaped the decapitation and distributed it on the Internet.

Equally dark and startling was what happened in Fallujah, a city west of Baghdad considered to be dangerous and off-limits because of the activities of insurgent Jihadi groups. There, on March 31, an Iraqi mob shot, killed, and mutilated 4 American civilians working as contractors for a company virtually unknown in America at the time, Blackwater USA. For days, horrifying scenes flashed across TV screens worldwide and ran above the fold of every major newspaper. After torching the victims' bodies, the Iraqis tied their remains to the end of a car bumper and dragged the desecrated bodies through town to a bridge over the Euphrates River, where they hanged what was left of the charred bodies. The insurgents videotaped the carnage and posted it on the Internet. When the U.S. media broadcast it, the world became aware for the first time of the Pentagon's use of armed civilians employed by private military companies in the Iraq War—and of the fact that private contractors as well as traditional troops were risking their lives. In the days that followed, President Bush ordered a major assault on the city of Fallujah—Operation Vigilant Resolve—a bloody street-by-street revenge that resulted in the deaths of at least 600 Iraqi civilians and over 200 insurgents as well as 36 U.S. military.

In the weeks after Fallujah, the news surfaced that at least 22 of the interrogators accused of torturing the inmates at Abu Ghraib were private military contractors. Such news again escalated the violence in Iraq, and soon the number of Iraqi attacks on American forces would reach an average of 87 a day, the highest level since the beginning of the war—a figure that did not include attacks against PMSCs, which also increased. More violence led to more fear, which led to more demands for armed security.

Among the shocking details about the Fallujah tragedy was the fact that contractors working for another private military company had warned the victims' supervisors not to send workers on the road through Fallujah on that day. It was a route always fraught with danger, and earlier that morning there had been intelligence about cells of insurgents gathering in Fallujah to ambush Americans. There was a safer though slower route. But the warning never reached the four young men who chose the road through Fallujah to save time. Thus, one of the immediate ramifications of the tragedy, coming out of the U.S. government, was the concept of establishing a coordination hub for all the security contractors that would be responsible for gathering and disseminating information about where contractors were going and when, with whom, why, and how.

That idea developed into the 2004 contract known as Project Matrix. Jointly devised by the Pentagon and the Coalition Provisional Authority, Project Matrix required the winner to create and manage a coordination center for more than fifty other private military and security companies throughout Iraq. The company in charge thus had the power to oversee and to coordinate security for the reconstruction of Iraq, including the exchange of military and civilian information between American and British security contractors and armies.

The contract also called for security personnel trained in "mobile vehicle warfare" and "counter-sniping" for its seventy-five Security Escort Teams—each team made up of eight contract employees armed with assault rifles and traveling in armored vehicles. The teams protected members of the U.S. Army Corps of Engineers, which had officially issued the contract, as well as other U.S. staff overseeing reconstruction projects, and officials from companies operating the oil and gas fields and utilities in Iraq. And there was a hidden aspect to the contract. Tucked away in its 700-plus pages was a provision that included intelligence work. The contract specifically called for the analysis of "foreign intelligence services, terrorist organizations, and their surrogates, targeting Department of Defense personnel, resources and facilities" and for the task of advising other contractors in decision-making based on such intelligence.

In short, the job was to safeguard all contractors working on reconstruction beyond the lifespan of the soon-to-be-dismantled Coalition Provisional Authority. The CPA would officially shut down in June, transferring limited sovereignty to the new Iraqi Interim Government, as planned, and also effectively handing over power to the company running this immense web of security. On the surface, the shift in authority to the Iraqi administration would appear to be a positive sign, indicating progress in Iraq's rebuilding and the coalition's plan to turn the nation over to its people. This was what America had promised as Iraq's liberator. But behind the scenes a large complex of PMSCs would soon be in place to help reconstruct Iraq, coordinated by the winner of the Project Matrix contract. This was no small job and no small contract. It was on the winner's shoulders to assure that after the CPA was shut down and the post–Iraq War era began that the nation building could happen. That meant armed contractors and the collection of sensitive information. By some accounts, the contract's importance was that it funded a coordination hub that could prove to be the invisible spine of the new Iraq: the sending and receiving of messages vital to the rebirth of a nation.

Amid the mounting fears and persistent high-profile terror alerts, the call for the Matrix contract went almost unnoticed in America. There were six bidders. Three were based in America: DynCorp, Custer Battles, and Triple Canopy; and three were from the U.K.: ArmorGroup, Erinys, and Aegis Defence Services. Of those six, three were already in Iraq. DynCorp, the long-standing client of the U.S. government, was training the nation's police force; Custer Battles was guarding the Baghdad airport; and Erinys was protecting oil installations in southern Iraq. The winner, though, would be a small British company that had provided security for Disney Cruise Line and did consulting work on maritime security: Aegis Defence Services.

While the company's c.v. was short and unremarkable, and the firm was barely known even in Britain, the resume of its CEO, Tim Spicer, was long and extraordinary, deeply linking the firm to the industry's origins in the mercenary trade. In Britain, Spicer was as well known as his firm was little known. In fact, Spicer and his friend Simon Mann were, by some accounts, two of the world's most notorious mercenaries. And in the spring of 2004, both Mann and Spicer made headlines, though for quite separate events. While Spicer was seeking a lucrative U.S. contract for his latest company, Mann was planning a coup d'état—a juxtaposition that brought down the curtain on Old World mercenaries even as it raised the curtain on the neomercenary age.

In March, a Boeing 727 loaded with more than 60 men, $180,000 in cash, and crates of guns was stopped minutes before taking off on the runway of a military airbase on the outskirts of Harare, the capital of Zimbabwe. The men were mercenaries and their destination was Equatorial Guinea. They had planned to overthrow the government of President Teodoro Obiang Nguema Mbasogo, who had ruled since 1979. Equatorial Guinea was the third-largest oil producer in Africa, and in exchange for orchestrating the coup, leaders of the plot would gain oil concessions from the new regime. Those leaders allegedly were Mann as well as a few coup-plotting colleagues such as Mark Thatcher, the son of former British Prime Minister Margaret Thatcher, and Nick du Toit, legendary for his work in the apartheid South African Special Forces. Several of the hired guns arrested that day on the runway were also former members of pro-apartheid South African military groups.

The plot that catapulted Mann into a jail cell in Zimbabwe was a classic mercenary operation that seemed to be a real-life adaptation of Frederick Forsyth's *Dogs of War*, a 1974 novel set in a fictional West African nation modeled after Equatorial Guinea. In the Forsyth plot, the African nation's extensive platinum deposits lure a mining tycoon to hire a company of mercenaries to eliminate the incumbent president and set up a puppet regime. The mercenary leader is a former military officer from an upper-class background, much like Mann. It was a familiar scenario, in both fact and fiction, and it represented an era that was ending.

Spicer and Mann had been partners and compatriots in the private-military world for many years. But in 2004, as Mann hoped that his connections in high places could get him out of jail, Spicer was using his own connections as he won the $293 million Matrix contract in Iraq.

4

THE FAINT HUM OF SECRECY

"Thanks to the contract signed with the Pentagon and with the blessing of the Iraqi government, Aegis is in a good position to become, to the great displeasure of the big American companies, the most powerful private military contractor in the world," wrote the Paris newspaper *Le Monde* in June 2004. From France to Britain to America, the news that Aegis had won America's largest security contract caused quite a stir. After all, Aegis had no experience in Iraq, it was not on the U.S. government's list of recommended contractors for Iraq, it was the second-highest bidder, and it had been operating under the name Aegis for only about eighteen months. What was known only to those government officials who had evaluated the applications for the contract were the potential limitations of the company's financial condition.

Shortly after Aegis had entered the competition, the Department of Defense's Defense Contract Audit Agency at Fort Eustis, Virginia, sent a letter to the Defence Procurement Agency in London, an executive agency of the Ministry of Defence, asking for financial facts and an assessment of the British firm. On May 11 came this response:

We would draw your attention to the financial strength of this company. This company has been only recently formed (15 month period to 31 December 2003 being the first accounting period) and in that period its operating loss before tax was £170k on a turnover [income] of £542k. It had a negative net worth. The company is wholly supported by a £1 million loan repayable over five years. It is also a holding company for three subsidiaries, the two significant subsidiaries both trading at a loss in the year to 31 December 2003, totaling £91k, on a turnover [income] of 438,000 pounds. The trading results of the third company, whilst in profit were insignificant (turnover below £12k). Whilst the company had £649k of cash at 31-12-03.

Aegis's ability to win a $293 million contract (with the potential for renewal in 2007), despite its financial condition, was hugely impressive and intriguing, instigating a flood of media interest. Some commentary regarded the situation as business as usual for empire builders and nations accustomed to occupying other nations, such as England—same well-connected people, new company name. Aegis, by some accounts, was simply a later version of the private military company known as Sandline International, which itself had been a later version of Executive Outcomes. And all three were reshaped and reintroduced as the privatization of conflict and the market for private force evolved and expanded.

In Britain, coverage of the story revived accounts of Tim Spicer's mercenary past. "Controversial ex-British army officer given key Iraq role," read the headline in the *Financial Times*. The article quoted industry insiders who believed "the contract could prove politically embarrassing for both the UK and US governments." Officials at the Coalition Provisional Authority in Baghdad, who had played a role in Aegis's obtaining the contract, responded by saying they were aware of Spicer's "colourful" past as a mercenary but saw no reason for that to be "a barrier to his qualifying for the contract." The *FT* article ended with a British Foreign Office spokesperson saying that the Foreign Office had nothing to say because the contract had come out of the United States, not the U.K. "The contract in question was awarded by the US government to Aegis and the British government is not a party to the contract nor has it been involved in any way in its negotiation."

But the American response showed far less awareness of Aegis and was more focused on the contract itself than on Spicer. In a June op-ed piece for the *New York Times*, scholar Peter Singer, one of the foremost experts on the topic of privatizing the military, described the contract as "a case study in what not to do." Among Singer's concerns was the fact that a PMSC would be overseeing other PMSCs. "A core problem of the military outsourcing experience has been the lack of coordination, oversight and management from the government side. So outsourcing that very problem to another private company has a logic that would do only Kafka proud," wrote Singer.

Singer, who was the author of the 2002 book *Corporate Warriors*, was also critical of the fact that it was a "cost-plus" contract, which meant that the Pentagon would cover all of the company's expenses, plus a predetermined percentage of whatever the company spent, thus rewarding contractors for spending more. And it was troubling to him that the contract did not go to a company with a long operating history or at least some experience on the ground in Iraq. Singer believed that it was possible that the people awarding the contract might not have known anything about Aegis's past because the responsibility and the funding of private military contracts "is spread out over the government to some of the strangest of places." In quotes to the press, Singer seemed truly confounded by the award and told a *Boston Globe* reporter, "It's an embarrassment for the military. . . . We ended up hiring one of the most notorious individuals in the industry with a record not for success, but failure and controversy."

Aegis's competitors for the contract wasted no time in elaborating on the causes for such skepticism. On June 22, DynCorp submitted a formal protest to the Government Accountability Office (GAO), the audit arm of the U.S. Congress. As the watchdog of government spending, the GAO reviews contract protests. Beyond urging the GAO to investigate all aspects of the contract award process, DynCorp hoped the government would reopen the competition. In its complaint, the firm said it was "shockingly" rejected, despite the fact that its bid was at least $80 million lower than Aegis's. Further, DynCorp asserted that Aegis did not have enough personnel on the ground to fulfill the requirements of the contract. "Any reasonable assessment would have to conclude that Aegis is not responsible," claimed DynCorp in its protest. It labeled the award to Aegis "improper."

DynCorp enlisted Texas Republican congressman Pete Sessions to speak up on its behalf, and in his letter to Secretary of Defense Donald Rumsfeld Sessions wrote, "It is inconceivable that the firm charged with the responsibility for coordinating all security firms and individuals performing reconstruction has never even been in the country." Responding to the DynCorp complaint, the GAO announced it would review the contract and report the results by the end of September.

Around the time of the DynCorp filing, Senators Ted Kennedy of Massachusetts, Hillary Clinton and Charles Schumer of New York, and Chris Dodd of Connecticut also sent a letter to Secretary Rumsfeld requesting an investigation by the Pentagon's inspector general, who was responsible for overseeing Iraq's multibillion-dollar reconstruction contracts. Several weeks later, Senator John Kerry endorsed their letter, which spelled out details of Spicer's dubious past.

Dear Secretary Rumsfeld:

We are writing to request you to ask the Inspector General to investigate a $293 million Iraq security contract given troubling concerns that recently have come to light.

The contract, which we understand is the largest yet awarded for security in postwar Iraq, was granted to a British company, Aegis Defense [sic] Services Ltd., in May to provide security teams for the Project and Contracting Office [sic], the body responsible for overseeing $18.4 billion in U.S. reconstruction funds for Iraq.

The company is led by Tim Spicer, a former lieutenant colonel in the Scots Guards. The Boston Globe has reported that Mr. Spicer has "a reputation for illicit arms deals in Africa and for commanding a murderous military unit in Northern Ireland." Two soldiers in the unit shot and killed Peter McBride, a Catholic teenager in Belfast in 1992 while under Mr. Spicer's command. The two soldiers were convicted of murder. Even after he retired from the military, Mr. Spicer defended the two soldiers who shot Mr. McBride in the back. [Spicer] argued for their release, which occurred in 1998, and the soldiers were inexplicably reinstated in the British Army.

The United States Government requires all contractors to be "responsible bidders." Contractors have to "have a satisfactory record of integrity and business ethics" (48 CFR 9.104-1(d)). We would like to know whether the government considered human rights abuses—or an individual who vigorously defends them—as part of this record.

Additionally, the United States Government requires consideration of the contractor's "past performance" (48 CFR 15.304(c) (3)). We would like to know whether the contracting team adequately reviewed the contractor's record, identified past human rights abuses or defense of abuses, and whether the contractor received a poor past performance rating on that basis.

We would also like to know the extent to which these factors were evaluated in awarding this contract to Aegis. If they were evaluated, we would like to know the rationale for awarding the contract.

In light of the recent revelations of abuses of detainees in Iraq, it is important that U.S. actions, whether by military personnel or contractors, have respect for the law. It is troubling that the Government would award a contract to an individual with a history of supporting excessive use of force against a civilian population.

Certainly we understand the urgent need to establish a secure environment, but the United States Government is also working to create a democracy in Iraq in which respect for fundamental human rights is guaranteed.

We appreciate your consideration of this request, and we look forward to the results of the Inspector General's review.

Voices of protest came also from Northern Ireland and the Irish-American lobby, growing louder by the day. Within hours of the government's announcement of the contract, the Washington-based Irish National Caucus had pressed the U.S. government not only to review the contract from a human rights perspective but also to terminate it. "Tear up that contract, Mr. Bush. It has Irish blood on it—that of innocent, unarmed Peter McBride. This could undo any credit you gained from Irish-Americans," Sean McManus, who headed the Caucus, told a number of American, British, and Irish publications.

Aegis spokespersons responded to the contract protests and dissonance with confidence and aplomb. Early in the summer, the company's official comment was that the "tender process [the evaluation of contract proposals] was exemplary and the company was successful." By August, the spokesperson for Aegis told the press, "The awarding of the contract was extremely rigorous and all relevant facts were obviously known by the authorities. We have nothing further to add to that." Spicer made a perfunctory statement: "I am pleased to confirm that we've been awarded a contract to assist the Project [Program] Management Office in Iraq by the United States Department of Defense. The Contract involves coordination of security support for reconstruction contractors and for the protection of PMO personnel." After that, he was quiet and apparently out of the country for much of the summer. The British Foreign Office stuck with its no-comment comment.

"It's like a blast from the past, like I took a leap back into the time-machine to the late '90s," Peter Singer said in an interview. "To be honest, though, I am doubtful that the folks awarding the contract had any sense of Spicer's spicier history." And a *Boston Globe* journalist wrote, "The Army never even bothered to Google this guy to find out" who he was. Backing up such notions were the comments of a U.S. Army spokesman who said that Spicer's résumé as submitted in the proposal showed that he had had a successful career in the British Army and that he had done "security work in Africa and SE Asia." In response to the question of whether the Army knew that Spicer had been a mercenary, the spokesman said, "My understanding is that they [Aegis] met all the requirements," and that it was "not part of the process to look into the backgrounds of the principals." He also said, "Aegis met the criteria and we don't know what else to say."

Others disagreed and believed that the government knew exactly what it was doing.

Supporting that theory, a former EO contractor with experience in Africa, mainly Sierra Leone, in the 1990s, wrote in an email, "The USG [US government] needs an organ that is from outside the U.S., far less accountable [to the U.S.] and already tainted, albeit slightly, with a whiff of dirty tricks. And that is the crux of the matter. The powers that be want mercenaries, for mercenary activity." The email recipient was Deborah Avant, then a scholar at George Washington University who had been studying the private-military phenomenon for several years and who agreed that the government knew exactly what it was doing when it awarded this contract. She believed that Spicer's past was likely viewed as an asset for the work needed in

Iraq. "Some people have suggested that this showed that the U.S. was clueless about contracting," Avant said in 2004. "[But] there is no reason for his company to have gotten the contract, other than Tim Spicer's reputation."

Whether the government was aware of what it was getting may have been discussed for a hot second in 2004, but such concerns would eventually fade away as Aegis became more valuable to the entities that employed it and as its industry became more established. Ambivalence about PMSCs, however, would be a recurring theme. This was, after all, a business dependent on conflict and instability and yet marketed as a force for peace and stability.

In the summer of 2004, Spicer kept a low profile. By then he seemed already different from the infamous mercenary depicted by his critics and rivals. There were hints of respectability, though the media spotlight was scanning every inch of his shadowy past.

In 2004, it seemed that Spicer—perhaps the most important figure in the transition from the Old World mercenaries to the new PMSCs—had already lived several lives. He was a graduate of Sandhurst, Britain's elite training academy for British Army officers, had served as a lieutenant colonel in the Scots Guards, worked as assistant to the U.K.'s director of Special Forces, commanded his own battalion in Northern Ireland, and had managed public relations for the British Army in Bosnia. After retiring from the army, he became a marketing director at one of London's most venerable investment firms, a job that required travel regularly to the Middle East. By the time in the 1990s when he headed Sandline International, he had connections with British generals, high-level Special Forces officers, MI6 agents, Arab sheiks, and a wide range of entrepreneurs. He knew the power of PR and perception management in building the success of any endeavor that involved the general public. He knew what it was like to be lambasted and despised in public, as in the Peter McBride case in Northern Ireland. And, what might be most important in the years ahead, he was tough and tenacious and always seemed to know how to flip a failure into a success. Much like the industry he was helping to shape, he seemed unstoppable, as his years at Sandline had demonstrated.

In the evolution of the private military and security sector, Sandline was a conceptual bridge between Executive Outcomes and Aegis. Playing corporate leapfrog, Sandline started about eighteen months before Executive Outcomes shut down and it would fold about eighteen months after the launch of Aegis. It was conceived by the same cadre of entrepreneurs who had created the rebranded notions of the mercenary business, it had rules that Executive Outcomes did not, and it enlisted the sentinels of public relations to shield its image. What was most intriguing perhaps was that in its short life, Sandline landed in the middle of two scandals, one of which nearly brought down the British government.

The first scandal involved Papua New Guinea, the Australian protectorate that declared its independence in 1975. So did the nearby island of Bougainville, the site of one of the largest copper mines in the world. Because of the mine, the newly independent government of PNG quickly took over Bougainville. Years later, however, the local landowners rebelled and shut down the mine. This became a problem for the PNG government, which depended on revenue from the mine for nearly half of its annual budget. So in early 1997 the PNG government offered Sandline a $36 million contract to push out the Bougainvilleans.

Claiming that the government should be paying the nation's own troops—not mercenaries—the PNG military denounced the Sandline contract. The prime minister fired the military commander. And the soldiers, showing their devotion to the commander and their anger toward their government, began antigovernment protests that quickly escalated to nationwide riots. The Sandline contractors were arrested and deported, while Spicer ended up in a nine-by-nine jail cell in PNG. The prime minister was forced to resign and eventually Spicer was released.

The next year, the second Sandline scandal occurred in Sierra Leone. This one was labeled by the media as the "Arms for Africa" affair, and by most accounts, it caused a considerable stir during Tony Blair's first year as British prime minister. This was the incident that Aegis's competitors, including DynCorp, referred to in their protests of Spicer's 2004 Project Matrix contract victory. In brief, Sandline allegedly violated a U.N. arms embargo when it supplied a thousand AK-47s, as well as mortars, light machine guns, and ammunition to coup-plotters favoring the return of Sierra Leone's exiled leader, Ahmed Tejan Kabbah. The weapons, purchased in Bulgaria, were paid for by a Canadian-based Thai businessman who represented a group of investors with mining interests in Sierra Leone who, in turn, had a deal with the ousted Kabbah regarding mineral rights, mostly diamonds, to be awarded in the aftermath of a successful coup. Spicer claimed that Sandline had proceeded with the approval of the British government, which was true. Members of the British Foreign Office, however, disputed his claim, and investigations, reports, and heated disputes would ensue for years.

In 1999, Spicer resigned from Sandline. For the next few years, until the founding of Aegis, he started and ran several small enterprises, some smartly trying to capture the niche market of maritime and antipiracy security and some fizzling within months of their inception. Journalist Robert Young Pelton reported in his book *Licensed to Kill* that before Aegis, Spicer had started a series of companies, "each of which achieved something between a limited degree of success and total failure. Even so, Spicer forged ahead." In 2002, the director of a New Jersey–based company that did "emergency response" work for the shipping business—for example, working on the *Exxon Valdez* oil spill—won a Homeland Security contract to assess security at American seaports and brought in Spicer as a partner. "Some people in the insurance business in London gave me Spicer's name," the director later said. "I knew he had a rather colorful reputation but he knows the sharp end of security, so we set up a joint venture together." Spicer then brought two more partners into the mix. One was a former military compatriot who had left the British Army for a banking career at the Hong Kong–based bank Jardine Fleming. This was a merchant bank rooted in the Fleming family, of which Ian Fleming was a part, and was rumored for years to be a front for British intelligence. The other Spicer colleague was that banker's star researcher, also at Jardine.

A few months later, in December 2002, while the New Jersey project continued, Spicer, the two men from Jardine Fleming, and one more Jardine banker, who was a big backer, launched Aegis. On the list of Aegis's early investors was author Frederick Forsyth, who said later that he had seen Spicer in London one day and asked him what he was up to. "He told me he was setting up a new company and asked if I fancied a flutter [investment] and I thought: Why not?" said Forsyth. Also on the list was Saad Investments Company, the international finance arm of the Saudi Arabia–based Saad Group, with offices in Bahrain, Geneva, London, and the Cayman Islands.

At first, Aegis was a discreet entity, staying in the same London offices at Piccadilly as the maritime security firm Trident Maritime, one of Spicer's earlier companies, and even using Trident's phone exchanges. But in the late spring of 2003, the new firm stepped out of the past and moved subtly and tenaciously into the public arena of the present, marketing a specialty in piracy and terrorism at sea. Piracy incidents were on the rise in Southeast Asia—37 percent higher in the first half of 2003 than in the previous year—stirring suspicions about terrorists taking to the high seas, and arousing a demand for maritime security. Aegis responded, and became an expert on one of the more notorious incidents of piracy that year in the Strait of Malacca, the channel separating the Malay Peninsula from the Indonesian island of Sumatra.

On March 26, off the coast of Sumatra, ten pirates in a speedboat stopped an Indonesian chemical tanker called the *Dewi Madrim* and, armed with machetes and one machine gun, boarded it. They smashed radio equipment, forced the captain to open the safe, stole the $21,000 it contained, and ransacked the crew cabins, taking cash, cigarettes, watches, and other personal belongings. After collecting the loot, they left, without taking anyone from the boat with them. In the international media, however, there were conflicting accounts about what took place on the *Dewi Madrim,* some reporting that the captain and first officer had been kidnapped and later returned, though no ransom was mentioned, and some that the pirates abducted no one and stole nothing. If they didn't steal anything, they must be terrorists, but if so, what was their motive? Often the differences between pirates and terrorists were debated.

Later in the year, Aegis published a study about the *Dewi Madrim* and, in reporting on the study, *The Economist* magazine wrote: "According to a new study by Aegis Defence Services, a London defence and security consultancy, these attacks represent something altogether more sinister. The temporary hijacking of the *Dewi Madrim* was by terrorists learning to drive a ship, and the kidnapping (without any attempt to ransom the officers) was aimed at acquiring expertise to help the terrorists mount a maritime attack. In other words, attacks like that on the *Dewi Madrim* are the equivalent of the al-Qaeda hijackers who perpetrated the September 11th attacks going to flying school in Florida." *The Economist* then quoted Spicer as saying that tankers carrying liquefied petroleum gas, which is easier to explode than natural gas, were the likeliest targets for terrorists on the high seas. "He [Spicer] fears that hijacked gas and oil tankers could be used to block the Malacca Strait, or the Panama or Suez Canals," the magazine reported.

A star was born. Aegis was one of the first companies to discuss publicly the need for protecting the commercial shipping industry from the risk of terrorist attacks. In the months ahead, the press continued to write about the subject with headlines such as "Terror at Sea: The World's Lifelines Are at Risk" and "Terrorists May Be Rehearsing at Sea." Meanwhile, the Aegis report was expensive to buy, with a price tag of at least £1,500.

By the end of the summer of 2004, Aegis had more authority and attention than it had had when it first applied for the contract in Iraq. It was even quoted in several news sources that August about the terror alert in the United States regarding certain financial agencies and firms in Washington and New York, the one that raised the nation's security to the second-highest level and was exposed by the *New York Times* as based on old intelligence. "It is very easy for those unfamiliar with the world of counter-terrorism, such as the press, to assume that new, specific information about terrorist attacks is automatically urgent. Similarly, it is easy to assume that old information is irrelevant to the current threat climate," said an Aegis spokesperson. "The threat will not disappear, and the trick will be in maintaining defenses over a prolonged period."

In early September 2004, *Lateline,* a popular Australian ABC-TV show, asked Spicer to appear on a segment about maritime security. He declined and instead a senior analyst at Aegis represented the firm. The host of the show, ABC correspondent Thom Cookes, said that "analyzing the nature of the marine terror threat has become a growth industry, and London, as the home of marine insurance, is where many new players are popping up." His focus was on Aegis and its head, Spicer, whom he referred to as "the mercenary thrown out of Papua, New Guinea."

"These days," said Cookes, "[Spicer's] company will now sell you a £1,500 report on why you should be concerned about a marine terrorism attack." In his line of questions about the new company, Cookes asked, "You haven't had any baggage from your [Aegis's] previous incarnations?"

"We haven't found any, no," said the Aegis analyst.

On September 13, the Government Accountability Office rejected the complaints that the Project Matrix contract was improperly awarded to Aegis. And the parallel probe by the Pentagon's special inspector general concluded that the Aegis award was indeed legitimate. This time there was little public reaction, though Sean McManus of the Irish National Caucus told the media: "I am hoping that President Bush will show some basic decency and some sensitivity to the feelings of Irish Americans—and do the right thing and cancel this outrageous contract." But he did not.

"Why Aegis?" From vicious and fantastic to plausible and logical, rumors filled the atmosphere that September. The most commonly expressed opinion was that Tony Blair pressured the Bush administration to hand over a piece of the privatization pie to the British. But if so, why was Aegis the chosen British company? One answer was that Spicer was well connected in high places. A commonly held belief among the British was that Spicer had been part of MI6 for years. This fit with the long-lived suspicions that Jardine Fleming banks, tethered to Aegis's earliest days, may too have had a connection with British intelligence. And that might have explained why Spicer was able to escape relatively unscathed from otherwise scandalous and perilous incidents. "Tony Blair's Pet Bulldog?" was the headline of one journalist's effort to unravel the mystery.

Those were the rumors based on the assumption that the U.S. did not know about Spicer's past and that the hastened quest in the spring of 2004 for a PMSC to coordinate security in reconstruction-era Iraq in combination with Blair's plea for equal opportunity in the privatization bonanza had precluded careful vetting of the company's CEO. But as Deborah Avant had observed, it was entirely possible that U.S. officials knew exactly what they were getting.

The man in charge of writing the specifications for the U.S. contract proposal at the Coalition Provisional Authority in Baghdad, Tony Hunter-Choate, was familiar with both Aegis and Spicer. He had worked with Spicer during the 1990s Balkan war when Hunter-Choate had been part of the British U.N. contingent while Spicer was the spokesman for the U.N. Protection Force, which comprised troops from half a dozen nations. A former commanding officer in the SAS, a former French Foreign Legionnaire, former leader of the Sultan's Special Force in Oman, and former security chief for the Aga Khan, Hunter-Choate in 2004 was the security director for the U.S. Program Management Office in Iraq. Sources within the PMSC industry seemed confident that he formulated specifications with Aegis in mind, partly based on his confidence in Spicer.

"What really happened," said Aegis senior advisor Dominick Donald in a later interview, "was that the other bidders thought the contract was about protection but it was about coordination of protection. That's different. And Aegis understood that, very well understood what was needed there, what the requirements were, and the others just did not completely understand the requirements of the contract, not in the way that Aegis did. That's all that happened. It was just that we did it best, the most focused, most relevant proposal."

Aegis indeed focused on the coordination aspect of the project when it entered the competition, and this was what the U.S. government wanted and needed. But the government also wanted Spicer's expertise, as Avant suggested. At the time, according to knowledgeable sources, one of the biggest concerns was instability in the Kurdistan oil fields in northern Iraq. Although the security risk was not as great in Iraqi Kurdistan as it was in the rest of Iraq in 2004, it appeared to be, and the United States did not want to take chances. "In the early days of Iraq, many didn't realize that Kurdistan was much lower risk than the rest of Iraq," said a London-based source. "It appeared worse than it was and Spicer had been used to dealing with rebel groups. Look at his background. The US found him useful in that way. He had contacts in Iraq in the contracting office. True. But, I believe, it was Kurdistan and what they thought he could do about the dangers there based on his experience that mattered a lot."

Shortly after the GAO decision to green-light the contract, Spicer moved back into the spotlight. Now he appeared to be an expert not only on maritime security but also on Iraq. And that autumn, he was on Sir David Frost's TV show *Breakfast with Frost*. "Congratulations on this assignment," Frost began. "But at the same time it is so difficult isn't it? I mean you've probably got a better view than almost any other individual of how secure or insecure Iraq is. What's your summary of the situation?"

A few days later, the *Sunday Times*, tracking Spicer like a celebrity, reported that he was looking for a new place to live in London and that his two-bedroom £840,000 dwelling in London's posh neighborhood of Belgravia was up for sale. Then during the last week of 2004, Aegis became the focus of a debate over the issue of maritime security. The clash, between a shipping magnate and an Aegis director, played out in a publication called *Lloyd's List*, a trade daily posting with a substantial circulation. The shipping magnate, Andrew Craig-Bennett, was irritated by a comment from an Aegis executive in an early December 2004 issue of *Lloyd's List* about the possibility that "al-Qaeda may seek to block the Suez Canal." Bennett saw it as an example of what he termed "maritime insecurity, a branch of the Fear Business, the growth industry of the early 21st century." And he wrote: "The insecurity experts depend on a plausible threat in order to make a living from us, and since the terrorists themselves have failed to oblige by doing anything scary in maritime for well over a year now, the masters of insecurity have been reduced to scaring us silly with whatever threats they can dream up."

Responding to Bennett, an Aegis analyst wrote: "The fact that nothing bad has happened for a year doesn't mean it won't happen in the future—al-Qaeda had never hijacked an aircraft before hijacking four and using them to kill nearly 3,000 people on 9/11. Far from acting as merchants of fear, Aegis Defence Services sells awareness of risk."

Much like the Special Forces Club, Aegis was a nexus of past, current, and even future conflicts. In the realm of special ops, there is an old maxim that no one really knows who is on which side until the game ends. It was the perfect environment for the PMSCs.

5

RULES OF ENGAGEMENT

By 2005, the flood of new PMSCs into Baghdad, largely as sub-contractors for companies with big contracts, was unprecedented and unstoppable. New companies were popping up daily, especially small ones forming quickly to capitalize on the subcontracting mania. They might last for the duration of a job or disappear in the middle of a commissioned project or possibly prove to be reliable. This was an industry out of control, and it was Aegis's job as the administrator of the coordination hub to manage the mayhem. And because Aegis's coveted cost-plus Project Matrix contract would be up for renewal in 2007, adding nearly $500 million more to its $293 million, Aegis had to prove itself quickly.

At stake, besides Aegis's future, were both the Coalition's re-construction of a dangerous, obliterated, oil-producing nation and the longevity of the world's new fighting force, the PMSCs. Without these companies, there would be no possibility for reconstruction in Iraq because no nation or alliance of nations had a traditional army large enough to do it, replete with the multitude of services the private sector now provided. At the same time, without Iraq there would be no burgeoning market for the industry. And without some sort of coordination, neither could succeed.

Aegis's "term" began on shaky ground. Not enough armored cars, not enough weapons, not enough soldiers. "When it arrived in Iraq, it was in need of a lot," said one industry insider who requested anonymity. "And those of us who knew how important its job was to the future for us all forgot any resentments we might have had. Control Risks (CRG), for example, was one that understood what was at stake here and loaned it [Aegis] armored vehicles and more. Anyone in the business that had any hint of sophistication knew we had to be in it together by then and Iraq was where it would happen or not. We were another army, the second largest in Iraq, but we could fail. They [Aegis] could fail."

In April 2005, the Office of the Special Inspector General for Iraq Reconstruction, an office created by Congress to oversee the billions of dollars allocated for the rebuilding of Iraq, issued its first audit of Aegis. This was an early assessment to determine whether the company was capable of completing the three-year contract. The audit reported that the firm was fulfilling the contractual requirements for providing security to U.S. officials and other contractors, which clearly was not an easy task. However, the auditors also pointed out serious problems in several key areas, saying that "there is no assurance that Aegis is providing the best possible safety and security for government and reconstruction contractor personnel and facilities." For example, there were serious questions about whether Aegis's armed employees had received proper weapons training. According to the audit, a random survey of 20 Aegis employees showed that they had been issued 30 weapons, including AK-47 and M4 assault rifles, and yet the company did not have the documentation to show that any more than 6 of the 20 employees had been trained to use such weapons.

Another problem the audit pointed to was the vetting of employees. Auditors were concerned that the firm was not adequately documenting background checks, and thus had "failed to verify that employees were properly qualified for the job." The company was supposed to conduct interviews and do detailed background checks to be sure that any hires did not pose "an internal security threat." Again in a random sample of 20 records out of 125 Iraqis employed, 6 had not been interviewed, 18 had not had police checks, and no records at all existed for 2 of them. In response, the company managers explained to the auditors that "police checks are difficult to obtain and largely irrelevant to the vetting process because of the current dysfunctional state of the Iraqi government." There were more criticisms, such as shoddy monitoring of the contract at the government's offices in Iraq. More specifically, the official overseeing the Aegis contract, the auditors said, was not trained in monitoring security or even contracts.

Doug Brooks, the head of the International Peace Operations Association, the industry's trade group in the United States, told the press that he considered the auditors' criticisms "fairly minor," keeping in mind the immense challenges of providing and coordinating security in such a dangerous place. For example, on the very day that the audit was released, six Blackwater employees were killed when their helicopter was shot down north of Baghdad. The next day, the U.S. contractor Halliburton told the media that insurgent attacks were so intense it might have to stop its work restoring Iraqi oil fields. Industry insiders like Brooks believed that there had to be some recognition of the learning curve: that is, how hard it must have been to accomplish all that the company had done thus far, considering how ill equipped it was in the beginning and the demands of its mission.

But others were less forgiving. U.S. Senator Russ Feingold, a Democrat from Wisconsin, issued a statement to the press saying that the audit "is deeply troubling and only reaffirms the desperate need for vigorous, independent oversight of the way taxpayer dollars are being spent in Iraq." In subsequent interviews, he said that there was no excuse for the substandard vetting and that the combination of poor weapons training with employees who may or may not be competent and reliable was "lethal." "Aegis was supposed to be providing security for government and reconstruction contractor personnel in Iraq. Not only does it appear that U.S. dollars were not well spent, but the consequence of the haphazard practices revealed in this report . . . could very well be deadly."

Barely six weeks later, what Feingold had described as "lethal" occurred: the incident in which Special Forces translator Kadhim Alkanani was shot. The story of that shooting never surfaced in America that summer and would not become known for several years. The incident was filed away as a "shot in the line of duty" case resulting in an honorable discharge. In the official paperwork, there was no attention given to the cause of the shooting or the identity of the shooter. Few people in the U.S. Army even knew about it, and those who did know may not have connected the shooting with the company running the coordination hub in Baghdad—Aegis, that is. For Kadhim, the silence would be as tragic as the gunshot itself. For Aegis, it was sheer luck that while its critics and competitors continued to look for evidence of incompetence, they remained unaware of what had happened to Kadhim.

Although Kadhim's shooting was exceptional, random shootings were not uncommon in Iraq in 2005. In later years, a former private security contractor who had worked for a PMSC in Baghdad at that time, in an on-the-record not-for-attribution interview in London, discussed such incidents during the early years in Iraq. The shootings, he said, were a result of the confusion and inconsistencies regarding rules of engagement, which at some companies at that time were not the same as the rules followed by the U.S. military. Private contractors were expected to warn civilian motorists who were approaching convoys and who appeared to present a threat by waving them away or firing warning shots into the air. Only if the motorists did not heed the warnings and were speeding toward the convoy, as a suicide bomber would do, was the armed security employee permitted to open fire. However, he said, in those early years some contractors followed different rules of engagement. Each company seemed to have its own rules, he said. "It was hard on us and I know it's hard to realize and there is no excuse but maybe we were all victims at that time." He told the story of a time when a partner of his opened fire on an SUV that appeared to be approaching his car too fast. "After it happened I wanted to go home. I could not stand what had happened. But then the next day we were out again and it was dangerous and I knew it would probably happen again or at least it could. We were not disobeying anyone when we did that. I want that to be clear. We were following orders. It [the orders] changed later. But you have to understand that we felt threatened and were doing what we thought was right."

In November 2005, an unsettling video appeared on an unofficial website established by Aegis workers (www.aegisiraq.co.uk). It was shot from inside a contractor's vehicle and it showed members of a security team shooting at Iraqi traffic on Route Irish, the main route from the Baghdad Green Zone to the international airport. Barrels of guns extending out from the back of a fast-moving SUV fired live rounds at cars driving toward them on the long stretches of highway behind. Some of the cars were a considerable distance away from the SUV and all apparently were driven and occupied by civilians. In one scene, a spray of bullets forced a Mercedes to swerve wildly and then to ram into a taxi, whose passengers spilled out of all doors, running frantically off the highway to avoid more bullets. In another, bullets hit a car so hard that it careened off the road. Adding a touch of mockery to the scene and making the images seem even more callous, Elvis Presley's "Mystery Train" played in the background.

Exactly who the shooters were and whether or not they worked for Aegis was a mystery, as was the provenance of the video itself. But soon the video was circulating all over the Internet, much to the dismay of Aegis. And the workers' website attracted an array of comments about what was appropriate defensive action when cars were headed toward a security convoy. On November 11, one posting from "Way Out Station" read: "Jesus, it must be bad if all cars that advance towards you at speed get the hell shot out of them. . . . How many cars have been shot up where a husband has been trying to get his wife to the hospital in the process of dropping a sprog? What an existence. . . . How about circulating the names of all the members of the team involved in murdering the Iraqis on the footage to all the [PMSCs] working in Iraq, so we won't have to work alongside these maniacs in the future. . . ." And another, from "Low Profile": "All this plays into the hands of those that see us as mercenaries/baby killers/whatever."

Later in November, an anonymous source sent a copy of the video to the *Times* of London, which, on December 1, published a detailed story in which an Aegis spokesperson said that "all such incidents" were investigated and that the company's staff observed strict rules of engagement that "allow for a structured escalation of force to include opening fire on civilian vehicles under certain circumstances."

The *Times* quoted a British PMSC employee who worked for another company and said that he had witnessed "at least two instances of innocent Iraqis being killed by poorly trained defence contractors who left the bodies by the side of the road and drove off." No one knew of any U.S. or British soldiers shot by accident in similar scenarios. The article reported that the Foreign and Commonwealth Office said that experts had viewed the footage and found no evidence that Aegis staff were involved. A company spokesman told the *Sunday Telegraph* on November 27, "There is nothing to indicate that these film clips are in any way connected to Aegis."

Then on April 6, 2006, the man who claimed he had started the Aegis-Iraq website and had posted the video suddenly surfaced and was interviewed on a British news show. His name was Rod Stoner, and he was a former British soldier and a former Aegis employee. He said that he started the website in 2005, after quitting Aegis. According to Stoner, the shooters never knew whether or not they were aiming at innocent civilians or insurgents. "We don't know because we never stop."

By the end of the following day, Aegis had filed an injunction to prevent Stoner from "speaking to the press or disseminating in any way the company's rules of engagement, or other company-confidential." Stoner continued to talk to some journalists, however, and told them that he was an occupant of the vehicle and neither he nor the others in the SUV that day had been questioned by investigators. A former colleague of Stoner's later said that Stoner was "living underground" for several months after the injunction as "he felt he might be in danger."

In June, Aegis announced that its investigation into the video was complete and that "the incidents and the images published were all taken out of context and were therefore highly misleading in what they represented." The episode had little impact on the company's image, as was clear in the autumn of 2006 when Britain's *Spectator* magazine ran a story with the headline "Men with Guns Are the New Dot.coms" that began with this scene: "Sitting behind his smartly fashioned desk in one of the new, antiseptic office blocks that line London's Victoria Street, Tim Spicer looks the very model of the modern entrepreneur. He talks smoothly about service delivery, market share, and profit margins. If he were running a hedge fund or a new media company, you wouldn't be in the least surprised. In fact, his business supplies tough blokes with guns. And a very lucrative trade it has recently become."

In June 2005, in the minutes immediately after the shooting of Kadhim, when it became clear that the medic in Kadhim's convoy was unable to slow the bleeding from the wounded foot, the convoy turned around, passed the checkpoint again, left the "safe" zone, and drove a quick 10 miles to the Special Forces Hospital, located in one of Saddam Hussein's former palaces. The bleeding was eventually stopped. But removing the bullet required that Kadhim be taken to another military hospital in Baghdad, where he received multiple blood transfusions and where a surgeon was able to extract only half of the bullet. The wound developed a severe infection. That plus the need to take out the remains of the bullet required Kadhim to be flown to a hospital in Germany. There, in Stuttgart, the doctors did not attempt to remove the remains of the bullet because it was lodged so close to the nerves in his ankle that surgery could result in loss of motor capability from his foot to his knee. The infection had become life-threatening and was spreading. Kadhim was flown to Walter Reed, the military hospital in Washington, D.C., where he would have a long stay.

By the autumn of 2006, Kadhim had to adjust to several new realities: the remainder of the bullet could not be removed from his foot, which meant that his foot could never bear much weight without causing him extreme pain. He would soon be discharged from the U.S. Army. And he now had developed hepatitis C, an infectious disease affecting the liver as a result of one of the many blood transfusions he had received. Upon his honorable discharge, Kadhim received $20,000 from the government, with the pledge of a monthly benefit of $112. His situation was unique; there was no precedent and no special benefit. However, what Kadhim wanted most was a job, not a handout. He now had a baby son and a wife, and he needed the work—for his family and also for him, as he longed to somehow reinstate his career.

Considering his training, experience, and language skills, he was confident that finding a decent job would not be a problem. He first sought work as an Arab translator at the U.S. Department of Defense. But he failed the blood test required during the application process because of the hepatitis C. Next, he tried to return to carpentry and the types of jobs he had before enlisting, but his foot ached too often to engage in physical labor. He also had signs of post-trauma stress and suffered frequently from the fatigue associated with hepatitis C.

Throughout 2006, he sought a champion of his cause within the Army, someone who would help him to sort out these challenges. He had phone numbers he was given after his discharge and references from those people to other people. But nothing came of any of it. In his frustration, he sometimes harkened back to his feelings many years before when his father had told him he must go to America. At the time, he had questioned such a decision, partly because he knew so little about America. His instinct then had been that his father's vision may have been based more on hope than reality. And he believed what his brother had told him, that America had assisted Saddam Hussein in the war with Iran, that American banks had loaned the dictator money, and that American companies had sold weapons to Saddam. How could the ally of Saddam Hussein be a safe haven for him? But after he had established his military career, Kadhim believed in the greatness of America. Now his circumstances were tugging at his faith. Who was accountable for Kadhim—the company whose employee had shot him, or the nation that had employed it, or both?

As one attorney who would later represent Kadhim said, "If Kadhim had died, people would have known his story. And the media would have helped to make someone accountable. But as it was, he was like a wounded animal walking into the forest, and the hope among his enemies was that no one would ever hear his calls for help."

6

PRIVATIZED MAYHEM

In the spring of 2007, as the deadline for the contract renewal was drawing near, seven U.S. senators, all Democrats, had signed on as Aegis critics: Hillary Clinton, John Kerry, Charles Schumer, Chris Dodd, Ted Kennedy, Russ Feingold, and Barack Obama. And among the most outspoken of the U.S. representatives, at that time, was Ohio's Marcy Kaptur, a Democrat in office for nearly twenty-five years. As a member of the House Appropriations Committee's Subcommittee on Defense, Kaptur had traveled to Iraq that February and after her return became an ardent advocate for diminishing the private military forces, if not banning them altogether. She was more than just a little concerned about the money: how many contractors there were, how hard it was to track the funds, how quickly privatization was happening. "We're in the wake of a speedboat," she said that spring, and later added, "[Congress] can't even begin to catch up to the contracts."

One of Kaptur's colleagues, Representative Henry Waxman, a California Democrat, shared her concerns. Waxman, as a member of the House Committee on Oversight and Government Reform, had initiated a study in 2006 that showed the cost of federal contracts growing twice as fast as other discretionary federal spending. The study noted 118 contracts with overcharges and wasteful spending and it outlined problems with specific contracts related to Pentagon programs and the Iraq War, including "$292 million [*sic*] to Aegis Defence Services Ltd., for Iraq reconstruction services."

Aegis was of particular interest to Representative Kaptur because of the upcoming contract renewal. The first contract Aegis had signed had totaled $293 million. Add to that additional costs for overtime and extended tasks and the total came to $548 million. The upcoming contract was for $475 million. Knowing that Aegis could end up with at least $1 billion of American taxpayers' dollars, Kaptur initiated her own probe to learn more about the company. But as she told the press, the endeavor was harder than she had anticipated. "When the [Department of Defense] refuses to provide information that should be public, I am—what's the word?—incensed."

By 2007, however, the watchdogs of Congress and the Pentagon were beginning to claim that the probes, audits, studies, and reports were accomplishing little toward addressing the impact of the growing numbers of "mercenaries" working for America. No one was taking a stand, stressed Jeremy Scahill, a journalist who at the time was writing a book about Blackwater. Both Republicans and Democrats, with a few exceptions, were "selling out," he wrote. Even shutting down the wars would not stop the PMSCs, he observed. "Until Congress reins in these massive corporate forces and the whopping federal funding that goes into their coffers, partially withdrawing

U.S. troops may only set the stage for the increased use of private military companies (and their rent-a-guns) which stand to profit from any kind of privatized future 'surge' in Iraq. . . . It's making them unstoppable, if they are not already."

By the contract renewal year, the larger firms like Aegis were indeed becoming more embedded in American strategies, more entrenched and more established, with their lucrative contracts, prestigious boards, new subsidiaries, sophisticated websites, media connections, lobbying, and PR firms. While Aegis may not have been the largest or most powerful PMSC in the world by 2007, it likely had had one of the biggest increases in profits since the beginning of the Iraq War. In its first accounting for the year ending December 31, 2003, its income was £542,000. By year's end 2006, its income had grown to £70.9 million.

Aegis was becoming the best example among the PMSCs of the trajectory from covert and infamous to acceptable and indispensable. Between 2004 and 2007, as the industry began to consolidate, Aegis expanded and diversified. In 2005, for instance, it purchased Rubicon International Services, a rival firm specializing in security risk assessment, also known for its intelligence work, with clients in dozens of nations. And it was adding new members to its board and its Advisory Council, including Robert McFarlane, who had served as President Reagan's chief advisor on national security and had been implicated in the Iran-Contra scandal of 1986. More recently, McFarlane had started companies in the international energy industry. He was also vice chair of the U.N.'s Energy Security Forum as well as a director of the Washington Institute for Near East Policy—a man with many connections useful to a budding PMSC.

Another influential figure new to Aegis's board of directors was the grandson of Winston Churchill, the Honorable Nicholas Soames, who had most recently served as Britain's minister for the armed forces and had been a Conservative Member of Parliament since 1983. Other newcomers to the board included a former head of the British Army; a highly regarded, top-drawer London attorney; and a former British Army officer who was also a former senior advisor to the Coalition Provisional Authority in Iraq. After the announcement of new board members, one of Aegis's managing directors told the press, "This is only just becoming an industry and there has been a question mark over how respectable it is. Certainly the reassurance of the [board of directors] names offers an endorsement of our company and points of reference for people not used to dealing with the [private military and security] sector."

In 2006, Aegis established an American branch, Aegis Defense Services LLC, on K Street in Washington, D.C. Soon its website would list offices in Washington, D.C., Baghdad, and Kabul as well as Nairobi, Kathmandu, and Manama in the Kingdom of Bahrain. The American entity, however, was especially important to the growth of the business. The firm's new roost in Washington would assist in gaining connections crucial to winning additional U.S. contracts.

With the Matrix renewal coming up, lobbying and networking were essential components to Aegis's image-building in Washington. Helping with that was Global Policy Group, which in 2007 was under contract to several private intelligence concerns and security firms to help them secure contracts with the U.S. government. Also, Aegis LLC's CEO Kristi Clemens had run public relations for Paul Bremer, the former head of the CPA in Iraq, and had been a Bush appointee in the Department of Homeland Security's Customs and Border Protection bureau. Aegis had also become an official advisor of Lloyd's of London, specializing in threats and risks in the shipping industry. And it had won a major new contract for €3.348 million from the Italian Ministry of Foreign Affairs to protect Italian aid workers in southern Iraq. But that was nothing compared to the Project Matrix renewal.

In January 2007, after the Joint Contracting Command Iraq/Afghanistan of the U.S. Army issued the Request for Proposals for the $475 million contract, Blackwater USA, Erinys, ArmorGroup, DynCorp, Control Risks Group, and Aegis entered the competition. On April 1, the Army announced that the competition had been narrowed to ArmorGroup and Aegis. But then while the two firms awaited the government's decision, a former U.S. Army captain from Colorado, Brian X. Scott, filed a lawsuit in the U.S. Court of Federal Claims to try to stop all government hiring of private military companies. A federal judge thus ordered an extension of Aegis's current contract for six months, delaying the final choice for the Matrix contract.

Scott based his protest on what he believed was a violation of an 1893 law. Each time the government contracted "a PMC," he claimed, it was in direct violation of what was known as the Anti-Pinkerton Act, originally passed to stop the government from hiring mercenaries as strikebreakers. Pinkerton's armed employees were best known for their role in trying to crush trade unions, mainly in the steel and coal industries, by working as armed security for strikebreakers and as spies and provocateurs.

Scott, who had served thirteen years of active duty in the U.S. Army, had filed at least a dozen protests against the use of private military companies, and all had been dismissed—as this one would be too. And by mid-September, Aegis was awarded the contract, this time for two years. It was the largest single security contract awarded by the DOD.

Once again Aegis was not the lowest bidder and once again the refrain "Why Aegis?" could be heard, though not as loudly as in

2004. The *Washington Post*, which had called the bidding war "a high-stakes derby," reported that over the past several months Aegis had "worked to show the military that it had a strong track record, stressing that none of its U.S. military clients had been killed in three years while traveling more than three million miles in Iraq" and conducting over 20,000 missions. To change the leadership of such a complex security operation in the midst of reconstruction and counterinsurgency, Aegis had emphasized, could threaten the security that three years of work by Aegis had established.

That September, however, the security of the citizens of the occupied nation—not the occupiers—was under a blinding spotlight for on the 16th, Blackwater contractors opened fire with automatic weapons and grenade launchers on a busy street west of central Baghdad, killing 17 Iraqi civilians, including women and children, and wounding at least 20. Many were shot while inside their cars as they frantically tried to drive away from the violence.

The incident happened at around noon on Nisour Square, a traffic circle outside the fortified area of Baghdad known as the International Zone or the Green Zone. A convoy of four heavily armored trucks filled with 19 Blackwater contractors and using the code name "Raven 23" was responding to the detonation of a bomb in the vicinity of another Blackwater personal security detail located about a mile from Nisour Square. That detail was in charge of transporting U.S. diplomats to a meeting that day in western Baghdad with officials of the U.S. Agency for International Development. Raven 23's job typically was to provide backup fire support for other Blackwater personal security details. When they reached Nisour Square, they were traveling on the east side of the circle, against the flow of traffic. There they positioned themselves in a line on the southern half of the circle with the purpose of blocking traffic from entering the circle from the south or the west, to protect the U.S. diplomats from any danger possibly following the bombing.

Within seconds of the convoy forming the blockade, the contractors in the third of the four vehicles opened fire on a white Kia sedan that was approaching the circle from the south. In the passenger seat was a forty-six-year-old female physician. The driver was her twenty-year-old son, a medical student. The initial shots killed the son while wounding his mother. Then an Iraqi policeman rushed to the car, apparently in an effort to assist the wounded woman who, according to some witnesses later, was frantically waving her arms. But in that second, another contractor, also from the third vehicle in the convoy, fired multiple rounds from his M4 assault rifle into the windshield on the passenger's side. Deciding that the policeman's uniform could be an insurgent's disguise, at least one member of the convoy launched an M203 grenade, which exploded under the passenger seat, causing the Kia to erupt into flames. At the same time, another contractor fired rounds into the hood, front grille, and whatever was left of the sedan's windshield. Seconds after the Iraqi policeman was killed, other police began firing at the Blackwater guards, as a battle within the war ensued.

Among the dead were:

Ahmed Haithem Ahmed Al Rubia'y, age 20, a medical student, and his mother, Mahassin Mohssen Kadhum Al-Khazali, age 46, a physician.

Ali Khalaf Salman Mansour, the police officer who rushed to the aid of the doctor and her son.

Sarhan Thiab Abdulmounem, another police officer who tried to stop the killings.

Ali Mohammed Hafedh Abdul Razzaq, age 9.

Qasim Mohamed Abbas Mahmoud, age 12, killed while riding in a car with his father, Mohamed Abbas Mahmoud.

Mushtaq Karim Abd Al-Razzaq, age 19.

Uday Ismail Ibrahim, father of two girls and a boy.

Hamoud Sa'eed Abttan, father of three boys and four girls, including a newborn girl.

Ghaniyah Hassan Ali, age 55, shot in the head while riding in a bus with her daughter, Affrahn Sattah Ghafil, whom she tried to shield from an unstoppable spray of bullets.

Affrahn Sattah Ghafil, age 28, killed while riding on the bus with her mother.

Jassim Mohammed Hashim, age 30, shot in the head while standing on the Square.

Sa'Adoon Lateef Majeed, age 56, shot while riding a bus from which he had to watch his son Haider Sa'Adon La Teef being shot multiple times in the legs.

Within ten minutes, Nisour Square had become a scene of death and despair as grim as any in Iraq since the invasion. As the Raven 23 convoy drove away, moving against the flow of traffic to the north of the circle, turret gunners in the convoy continued to fire their machine guns at civilian vehicles. As one of the gunners, Jeremy P. Ridgeway, would later testify, these were vehicles that "posed no threat to the convoy."

Ridgeway was the contractor who had fired rounds into the

windshield on the mother's side of the Kia. He also shot at least three rounds from his M4 into the roof of a white Chevrolet Celebrity sedan, sending bullet fragments into the driver's legs. Later, Ridgeway would testify that he intended to kill the driver of the Chevy sedan. Under oath, he would also say that there had been no attempt on the part of the convoy to provide reasonable warnings to the driver of the Kia to come to a complete stop prior to the use of Raven 23's deadly force. There were no hand or verbal warnings, no firing of flares and no pointing of weapons at the vehicle without firing.

As a condition of all State Department contractors, Ridgeway and his Raven 23 colleagues had signed what was called the use-of-force policy, or the State Department Mission Firearms Policy for Iraq. It specified that deadly force was permitted only when all other means for protecting the individuals the contractor was hired to guard had failed or "would be likely to fail." This meant, the policy acknowledged, that the contractor on the scene "may often be forced to make split-second decisions." In this particular case, the critical decision was made by the "shift leader" of the convoy, who ordered the Raven 23 contractors to set up the blockade at Nisour Square.

In the aftermath of the massacre, the industry braced for a storm of criticism. The International Peace Operations Association in Washington shifted into high gear, as did the companies savvy enough to be working with public relations firms. In a London *Times* piece a few weeks after the incident, Tim Spicer, for example, noted that his company was a contractor to the U.S. Department of Defense—unlike Blackwater, which was contracted by the State Department—and this meant that Aegis had to adhere to "about 15 layers of regulatory control and constraint to ensure that it is fully accountable."

Still, no public relations wand could wave away the damage of such an incident to an industry trying to persuade the world that it was about peace and security, not uncontrollable violence. The murders at Nisour Square exposed what could best be described as privatized mayhem.

PART II

REACTION

7

SOUNDING THE ALARM

Although few Americans would ever know the names of the men, women, and children who died or were injured at Nisour Square—17 dead and 24 wounded—this tragedy, the latest atrocity of war, drew more attention than ever before to the consequences of privatizing wars. And while the incident at Fallujah in 2004 had earned Blackwater the sobriquet "Bush's private army," what happened at Nisour Square made urgent the need to control those companies operating in Iraq, especially Blackwater. This was war, some would say, but was this really what the Coalition of the Willing went to Iraq to do? Had the U.S. government enabled such a fiasco? And had Congress allowed it to happen?

In the weeks ahead, meetings to discuss the Nisour Square massacre were held at the United Nations, Amnesty International, the International Red Cross, Human Rights First, and at the top levels of the governments of Switzerland, Great Britain, and the United States. One such meeting convened on October 2 at the Rayburn House Office Building in Washington, D.C. The House Committee on Oversight and Government Reform met to interrogate Blackwater's CEO Erik Prince and to discuss the burning issue of oversight.

If there was ever a time when Congress could have stopped or at least tamed and controlled the new mercenaries, it was then, in the autumn months of 2007. For a while, it appeared that the privatizing of defense and security, once inherently governmental functions, was an issue of such deep significance in a democratic nation that it might bring together members of both parties. At various sessions of the 110th Congress that fall there were hopeful signs that the gap between the existing legal framework and the much-needed oversight would narrow considerably.

The October 2 hearing lasted five hours. In attendance were 40 members of the committee—22 Democrats and 18 Republicans—plus one other concerned legislator, Illinois Representative Jan Schakowsky, who was not a member of the committee. Also present were the widows, children, siblings, and parents of the four Blackwater employees murdered in Fallujah in 2004 and the families of soldiers who died in November 2004 when a Blackwater Aviation plane took an unauthorized route through a mountain valley in Afghanistan and crashed into the wall of a canyon.

Committee chair Henry A. Waxman made his opening statement:

> Over the past 25 years, a sophisticated campaign has been waged to privatize Government services. The theory is that corporations can deliver Government services better and at a lower cost than the Government. Over the last 6 years, this theory has been put into practice. The result is that privatization has exploded. For

every taxpayer dollar spent on Federal programs, over 40 cents now goes to private contractors. Our Government now outsources even the oversight of the outsourcing. Today we will examine the impact of privatization on our military forces. We will focus on a specific example, the outsourcing of military functions to Blackwater, a private military contractor providing protective services to U.S. officials in Iraq.

Blackwater, Waxman noted, was founded in 1997 by its current CEO, former Navy SEAL Erik Prince, whom Waxman, alluding to Prince's family fortune, commended. "We thank you for that service. As a general rule, children from wealthy and politically connected families no longer serve in the military." Waxman then quoted Prince's own explanation for the creation of Blackwater, which was, "We are trying to do for the national security apparatus what FedEx did for the Postal Service." And then he went on to quote the amount of money Blackwater was making. Since the year 2000, he said, its government contracts had grown from $204,000 to more than $1 billion, more than half awarded without full and open competition. And he noted that privatizing was working "exceptionally well" for Blackwater.

The question was, Waxman said, whether it was working well for the American military, for the security of the American public, and for the American counterinsurgency policy in Iraq to win the hearts and minds of citizens and thus discourage Iraqis from joining forces with America's enemies. Is Blackwater helping or hurting efforts in Iraq? Is the government doing enough to hold Blackwater accountable for alleged misconduct?

"In recent days, military leaders have said that Blackwater's missteps in Iraq are going to hurt us badly," Waxman noted. "One senior U.S. military official said Blackwater's actions are creating re-sentiment among Iraqis. If such observations are true, they mean that our reliance on a private military contractor is backfiring." He then recounted incidents that most committee members were not aware of, including the shooting of the guard of the Iraqi vice president by a drunken Blackwater contractor on Christmas Eve 2006.

"This didn't happen out on a mission protecting diplomats," said Waxman.

It occurred inside the protected Green Zone. And if this had happened in the United States, the contractor would have been arrested and a criminal investigation launched. If a drunken U.S. soldier had killed an Iraqi guard, the soldier would have faced a court martial, but all that has happened to the Blackwater contractor is that he has lost his job. And the State Department advised Blackwater how much to pay the family [of the murdered guard] to make the problem go away and then allowed the contractor to leave Iraq just 36 hours after the shooting. Incredibly, internal emails document a debate over the size of the payment. The chargé d'affaires recommended a $250,000 payment, but this was cut to $15,000 because the Diplomatic Security Service said Iraqis would try to get themselves killed for such a large payout. Well, it is hard to read these emails and not come to the conclusion that the State Department is acting as Blackwater's enabler. If Blackwater and other companies in this industry are really providing better service at a lower cost, the experiment of privatizing is working. But if the costs are higher and performance is worse, then I don't understand why we are doing this.

Before opening the floor to the committee, Waxman issued two caveats: that facts and not ideology should guide any judgment of Blackwater and its industry on the part of Congress and that there should be no questions directly related to the Nisour Square incident, which the FBI was currently investigating. Then beginning with ranking member Tom Davis, a Republican from Virginia, the hearing would slowly develop into a battle between those who firmly believed in the importance of the private military contractors and had no intentions of regulating them and those who thought the opposite. By the end of the day, it would be evident that there was very little middle ground: liberals wanted to rid the world of PMSCs and conservatives wanted to use them to bolster the status quo. Although Democrats and Republicans were equally responsible for the privatization of America's defense and security, a political divide had opened. In his opening statement, Representative Davis said that PMSCs had:

> become an inescapable fact of modern life. They provide everything from logistics and engineering services to food preparation, laundry, housing, construction, and of course, security. They offer invaluable surge capacity and contingent capabilities Federal agencies can't afford to keep in-house. To paraphrase the title of one recent study of the phenomena [sic], Iraqis fear they can't live with private security contractors. U.S. personnel believe they can't live without them. However you define success in Iraq, from stay the course to immediate withdrawal and every scenario in between, security contractors are going to play an integral part. The inevitable redeployment of U.S. military units out of the current urban battle space will only increase the need for well trained and well managed private security forces to fill that vacuum and protect diplomatic and reconstruction efforts.

Davis then stated his objection to the hearing and praised the work of Blackwater: "Blackwater has protected dozens, if not hundreds, of members of Congress including myself and members of this committee when they travel to Afghanistan and Iraq. I, for one, am grateful for their service. Not one single member of Congress has been injured or killed under Blackwater protection, and for that I am grateful."

Republican John Mica of Florida also spoke for his party when he declared that the hearing was a political ploy to discredit the Bush administration. He moved that the committee adjourn within the first hour of testimony. Mica's colleague Patrick T. McHenry, of North Carolina, called the issue of contracting and oversight "the liberal cause du jour." And Ohio Republican Michael Turner was concerned that the hearing looked like an "our team/their team" scenario and that by quizzing Prince, Blackwater appeared to be an adversary, on the other team. However, Blackwater "is on our team," he said. "They are our team working the trenches and in a war zone."

The Democrats seemed less inclined to respond to the Republicans' accusations than to shake some truths out of Prince and to identify reasons for more congressional oversight of PMSCs. Blackwater was not the only problem. It was simply the proof that privatization of defense and security was growing faster than the government could keep up with, and that war itself was changing in a way to which the American system had not yet adjusted. While the Republicans stressed that there had been over 3,000 missions by PMSCs in the previous nine months alone and that the ratio of bad incidents to missions was low, the Democrats were guided by the old adage that one unnecessary death is enough to raise concerns.

Elijah Cummings, a Democrat from Maryland, told his colleagues that Blackwater had been involved in at least 195 escalation-of-force incidents since 2005, an average of 1.4 shootings per week. He said that such behavior was not only undermining the U.S. mission in Iraq but also affecting U.S. foreign relations in the Middle East in general. Dennis Kucinich of Ohio agreed, calling Blackwater's behavior nothing less than "outrageous." "Eighty-four percent of the shooting incidents involving Blackwater are where they fired first," Kucinich told the committee, "and Blackwater did not remain at the scene. So Blackwater's shoot first and don't ask questions later approach most definitely undermines the U.S. position in Iraq and jeopardizes the safety of our soldiers." Kucinich also lambasted the State Department for attempting "to cover up Blackwater's killings rather than seek appropriate remedies." And he concluded his two-minute statement by saying that "if war is privatized and private contractors have a vested interest in keeping the war going, the longer the war goes on, the more money they make."

Throughout the hearing, Democrats asked Prince about a number of those incidents. On June 25, 2005, for example, Blackwater guards shot and killed an innocent man who was standing by the side of a street in Baghdad. The incident orphaned six children and was never officially reported by Blackwater. In fact, the State Department described the death as "the random death of an innocent Iraqi." Other such incidents were cited by other committee members. Perhaps the most moving was the story of the November 27, 2004, crash of Blackwater Flight 61, in which three U.S. military personnel were killed—Lieutenant Colonel Michael McMahon, Chief Warrant Officer Travis Grogan, and Specialist Harley Miller—as well as the Blackwater copilots and a mechanic.

When Waxman told the story, the room was as silent as a held breath. The crash—into the wall of a canyon in Afghanistan—was investigated by a joint Army and Air Force task force and by the National Transportation Safety Board. The NTSB report, Waxman said, found that the Blackwater copilots behaved unprofessionally and were deliberately flying a nonstandard route low through the valley just for fun. The pilots were unfamiliar with the route, deviated almost immediately after takeoff, and failed to maintain adequate terrain clearance. Waxman read the cockpit voice recording of the plane's crew out loud.

"You are an X-wing fighter Star Wars man and you are [expletive] right. This is fun," said one crew member.

"I swear to God they wouldn't pay me if they knew how much fun this was," said one of the pilots.

Investigators, according to Waxman, later found that Blackwater failed to follow standard precautions to track flights, failed to file a flight plan, and failed to maintain emergency communications in case of an accident. Worse still, there was a sole survivor of the crash, one of the three military men whom the U.S. government was paying Blackwater to escort and transport. And he was alive for at least ten hours after the crash. Though he suffered internal injuries, he was able to leave the plane, to smoke a cigarette, and to roll out a sleeping bag. He died from exposure to cold sometime during the first night. Because of the wayward flight path, it took rescuers too long to locate the plane to save him.

Equally startling was the fact that sixteen days before the crash Blackwater's Afghanistan site manager sent an email to the VP for operations at Blackwater Aviation saying that the initial group of Blackwater pilots hired to support the Afghanistan operation had some "background and experience shortfalls, overlooked in favor of getting the requisite number of personnel on board to start up the contract."

As Waxman pointed out, one of the greatest tragedies and ironies of the crash was that while the Blackwater pilot was inexperienced, one of the passengers, Lieutenant Colonel McMahon, was a skilled military pilot with an exemplary safety record. Waxman then read to his committee a note he had received from Colonel Jeanette McMahon, the pilot's widow. "Mike, like Mr. Prince, was a CEO of sorts in the military as an aviation commander and as such had amassed a great safety record in his unit. It is ironic and unfortunate that he had to be a passenger on this plane versus one of the people responsible for its safe operation. Some would say it was simply a tragic accident but this accident was due to the gross lack of judgment in managing this company."

Waxman began grilling Prince. "Mr. Prince, Colonel McMahon is asking why the taxpayers should be paying your company millions to conduct military transport missions over dangerous terrain when the military's own pilots are better trained and a lot less expensive. How do you respond?"

Prince answered that his company was hired by the U.S. government to fill a void. The American air fleet used by U.S. troops was designed to support large conventional battles but was not suitable to the terrain and the demands of missions in Afghanistan. What was needed were air transports capable of quick takeoffs and landings on short strips. Blackwater had them. This, after all, was what private military companies were doing: filling gaps between what the American military was trained and equipped to do—fight conventional wars—and what was needed in current unconventional wars.

Prince's calm, confident responses seemed to agitate Waxman, who wanted answers and was most concerned about accountability. "Were any sanctions placed on the company after the investigative reports that were so critical of Blackwater were released?" he asked.

"Anytime there is an accident, a company also should be introspective and look back and see what can be done to make sure that it doesn't happen again," said Prince.

"Aside from your introspection, were you ever penalized in any way? Were you ever fined or suspended or reprimanded or placed on probation?" asked Waxman.

"I believe the Air Force investigated the incident, and they found that it was, it was pilot error. It was not due to corporate error that caused the mistake or that crashed the aircraft," Prince replied.

Waxman commented, "The corporation hired inexperienced pilots. They sent them on a route they didn't know about. They didn't even follow your own rules. It seems to me that it is more than pilot error. There ought to be corporate responsibility and Blackwater was the corporation involved. Aside from your introspection, you have just been awarded a new contract for almost $92 million. I want to see whether you are getting a stick as well as all these carrots."

But Prince was unflappable. When Representative Diane Watson, from California, asked him why the military couldn't do the jobs outsourced to PMSCs, he said, "The U.S. military can't be all things to all people all the time."

"And why not?" she asked.

"The tyranny of shortage of time and distance," said Prince. "I mean you can't have an anti-air missile guy also be doing armed security and knowing how to be an aviation mechanic too. It is too broad of a base of skill requirement."

"We need more people, then," said Watson.

"Okay, fine, then reinstate the draft."

Prince observed that the percentage of bad incidents compared to the large numbers of missions was low. He often used the figure of 6,500 missions for the year 2006 and said that "weapons were discharged in less than 1 percent of those missions." But most Americans didn't know that, he pointed out. Years later, in his book *Civilian Warriors*, Prince would blame the U.S. government for

Blackwater's skewed public image. "Everything Blackwater's men did in Iraq was by State's direct command," he wrote. The State Department "got its 100 percent survival rate. And yet somehow by doing exactly what the department demanded—regardless of how miscalculated its strategy was—Blackwater got the PR nightmare."

At the hearing, Prince argued that Blackwater operated in danger-ous, high-risk areas and thus shootings were sometimes unavoidable. His personnel, he said, were subject to regular attacks by terrorists "and other nefarious forces within Iraq." And he said, "We are the targets of the same ruthless enemies that have killed more than 3,800 American military personnel and thousands of innocent Iraqis. Any incident where Americans are attacked serves as a reminder of the hostile environments in which our professionals work."

At least twice, Prince reminded his audience that there were other markets for PMSCs than the U.S. government, despite the fact that his company had won more than $1 billion in contracts from that particular source. His was a lucrative business that could now survive without its help. "If the [U.S.] government doesn't want us to do this," he told the committee, "we will go do something else."

The Republicans agreed with Prince and the Democrats did not. In Congress, there was clearly no consensus about the privatization of American security and there was no analysis about what the larger picture might be, such as the PMSCs as part of a rising international industry, evidence of a shift in the conduct of wars worldwide, and by some accounts proof of the slow decline of the nation-state. And despite the questions at the hearing, few legislators were willing to fight for accountability of PMSCs. Their constituents knew little or nothing about the topic, and it was immensely complicated. Also, as the testimony of the Blackwater CEO showed and the response of some committee members revealed, PMSCs were successfully cultivating relationships with lawmakers. For only a few legislators in either party would PMSCs become a cause. Among them was Jan Schakowsky, the guest legislator that day.

Schakowsky had come to the hearing that day to proclaim her opposition to Prince and his company as well as all other companies like his. She wanted to meet the man whom she considered a modern-day mercenary and whose methods represented a trend that she believed was destructive to democracy. Schakowsky would be the legislative nemesis to the PMSCs, especially to Prince. And she would be the only one who had come to the hearing with a plan of action. Her idea for oversight was simple: Ban the PMSCs. In her opening statement, she said: "I want to let everyone know that I am shortly going to be introducing legislation to carefully phase out the use of private security contractors. These are the for-profit companies that carry out sensitive missions that have repeatedly and dramatically affected our missions. I want now to recognize the mother of Jerry Zovko, who is here today. Jerry was an Army Ranger before becoming a Blackwater employee. He died in Fallujah in an infamous mission, fraught with mistakes on the part of his Blackwater supervisors. That was over three and a half years ago, and led to the Battle of Fallujah during which many of our U.S. forces lost their lives. We need a conversation in this Congress and I am hoping that my legislation will provide that."

8

"A REMARKABLY UNPRECEDENTED EXPERIMENT"

Jan Schakowsky was sixty-four years old when she unveiled her plan to end America's new dependence on PMSCs. She had been in politics for fifteen years, eight in the Illinois General Assembly and seven representing Illinois' 9th Congressional District in Washington. This was a career she began when she was nearly fifty years old, after she had raised three children. As a housewife, she had led the national campaign to put expiration dates on food products and as a congresswoman her causes ranged from prochoice and gay marriage to comprehensive immigration reform and patient rights. Schakowsky was a petite woman of Russian Jewish descent who was considered to be one of the most progressive politicians in Congress. She was also known for her spunk and determination and could be described as unflappable and unstoppable.

Her first encounter with private military companies came in February 2001 when she and Jim McGovern, a Democratic representative from Massachusetts, spent six days in Colombia investigating a $1.3 billion U.S. operation called Plan Colombia. This was supposed to be a counternarcotics program focusing on the fumigation of drug crops. But because a large part of the operation was conducted by former military men working for DynCorp, Plan Colombia was effectively free from public scrutiny, though paid for by American taxpayers. That was what most concerned both Schakowsky and McGovern.

Estimates at the time were that there were 200 U.S. military personnel in Colombia, mostly working on bases as trainers, and 170 American contractors, many of whom were on the front lines of Colombia's war on drugs. Few in Congress were aware of Plan Colombia, and those who were—including Schakowsky—believed that the United States, by way of DynCorp, was engaged in a counterinsurgency on behalf of Colombia's government as well as a counternarcotics program, effectively funding a private war with private soldiers. At that time, a reporter covering the drug war called DynCorp one of the new "privateer mercenaries" engaged in a U.S. policy that was outsourcing wars. "Like the old English 'privateer' pirates of the Caribbean five hundred years ago," he wrote, "Washington now employs hundreds of contract employees through U.S. corporations to carry out its policies in Colombia and other countries. While the new privateers are underwritten through U.S. taxes, they are technically 'contract employees.' Like the sixteenth-century pirates, if they get caught in an embarrassing crime, or are killed, the U.S. government can deny responsibility for their actions."

Schakowsky worried about what she had discovered on the trip, and after returning home she told that same reporter, "American taxpayers already pay $300 billion per year to fund the world's most powerful military. Why should they have to pay a second time in order to privatize our operations? How is the public to know what their tax dollars are being used for? If there is a potential for a privatized Gulf of Tonkin incident, then the American people deserve to have a full and open debate before this policy goes any farther."

She asked, "Are we outsourcing in order to avoid public scrutiny, controversy or embarrassment? Is it to hide body bags from the media and thus shield them from public opinion? Or is it to provide deniability because these private contractors are not covered by the same rules as active duty U.S. service persons?"

Then in April a private contractor working for the CIA in Peru identified a group of U.S. missionaries flying in a plane as suspected drug dealers, and the Peruvian Air Force shot down the plane, killing everyone, including a woman and her seven-month-old daughter. The February visit and the Peruvian tragedy inspired Schakowsky to introduce House bill 1591, the Andean Region Contractor Accountability Act, intended to prohibit the U.S. from funding contracts with PMSCs in the Andean region of South America.

HR 1591 never emerged from committee, a fact that would soon typify a pattern: a shocking event spawns media attention and legislative action but no legislative results; then a few years later, another shocking event draws the public's attention to the fact that the same companies and strategies are still active, though out of sight, and accountability issues have not been resolved, followed by legislative proposals again without results; and so on. This was the pattern prior to Nisour Square.

In May 2004, following the tortures at Abu Ghraib and the Fallujah disaster, Schakowsky wrote a letter to President Bush to demand the suspension of any private contractors' involvement in the super-

vision and interrogation of prisoners. Also that summer, Schakowsky, like several of her colleagues, viewed the Matrix contract as an
unsettling step in the evolving relationship between PMSCs and the
U.S. government. Handing over the job of coordination and oversight of private contractors to a private contractor showed an advanc-
ing dependence on PMSCs. Schakowsky believed that privatization
of defense and security seemed to be an ongoing process that no one
was trying to stop. "There were wake-up calls before Nisour Square,
especially Fallujah and Abu Ghraib, but the gap [between the companies and oversight] was never closed," she said in later years. "In
2004, everyone informed about it was certain there would be another
incident. And unfortunately there was."

One major obstacle to closing the gap was that the laws that existed by the autumn of 2007 did not deter bad contractor behavior
nor did they protect the victims of such behavior. Civilians employed
for defense and security jobs in Iraq who committed crimes could
not be brought to justice. Typically, if an American civilian committed a crime in a foreign nation, that nation would have jurisdiction
to prosecute the American. But the decree granting private contractors immunity from Iraqi law, Order 17, that Paul Bremer had
enacted before leaving Iraq in 2004 was still in place. And although
the Uniform Code of Military Justice was applicable to civilians in
combat areas outside U.S. borders at that time, it could be applied
only to wars declared by Congress. The last time Congress officially
declared war was 1941. PMSCs were operating in unconventional,
undeclared wars.

In an attempt to resolve the problem, Congress passed the Military Extraterritorial Jurisdictional Act (MEJA) in 2000, in the aftermath of the sex-trafficking scandal in Bosnia. MEJA authorized U.S.
laws to apply to American military contractors living abroad. Thus,

an employee of a PMSC could be charged with a felony offense and be brought back to the United States for trial. However, MEJA applied only to Department of Defense employees and contractors, excluding all other contractors even if they worked directly in support of military operations. For example, the civilian interrogators implicated in several of the cases of torture in the Abu Ghraib scandal had contracts with the CIA, which MEJA did not cover.

To fill the hole, two congressmen, David Price, a Democrat from North Carolina, and Chris Shays, a Republican from Connecticut, introduced the Contractor Accountability bill in May 2004, which would expand MEJA to include all private contractors in support of the DOD's missions, including non-U.S. citizens contracted for work with the U.S. government. Although the Price-Shays bill failed to pass, the Department of Defense Authorization Act that year would include a new provision that extended MEJA's reach, as Price and Shays had proposed. Once again, however, there would be a problem: the new DOD provision did not define what constituted the support of a mission of the Department of Defense. Thus, if private contractors opened fire on Iraqi civilians and were under contract with the State Department, they could be legally accountable only if their work for that agency could be defined as directly in support of the DOD's mission.

The accountability challenge seemed never-ending. In February 2007, Schakowsky worked with Price on a bill called "The Iraq and Afghanistan Contractors Sunshine Act," which required the secretaries of defense, state, and interior and the administrator of USAID to provide to Congress copies of all contracts and task orders in excess of $5 million for work to be performed in Iraq and Afghanistan. This bill would die in committee. But months later, in the autumn, after Nisour Square, Schakowsky thought the prospects had improved for such legislation. Thus, at the October 2 Oversight Committee hearing, she announced the Stop Outsourcing Security Act, H.R. 4102, cosponsored with Price, and cosponsored in the Senate as S. 2398 by Vermont Independent Bernie Sanders. The law would "restore the responsibility of the American military to train troops and police, to guard convoys, to repair weapons, to administer military prisons, and to perform military intelligence," Schakowsky told the media. It would require that only employees of the U.S. government could guard diplomats, and by January 1, 2009, the U.S. president must report to Congress on the status of planning for the use of government and military personnel instead of private contractors for critical missions or emergency functions in all conflict zones where Congress had authorized the use of force. Further, the bill demanded that government agencies with military and security contractors on the payroll file reports of the cost of each contract as well as the number of contractors employed and any disciplinary actions against them.

Schakowsky saw no reason to accommodate the PMSCs. This was not an ordinary industry acquiring power. These were companies often employing men with guns without any strong legal authority to answer to, and from her point of view to appease them would be regrettable. Although industry leaders often referred to Blackwater as an aberration, Schakowsky believed that Blackwater was a warning that one day PMSCs could be more powerful than the government that had given their industry its biggest boost.

From her point of view, the risks to a democracy in hiring private contractors for U.S. defense and security were too great and thus they should be "phased out," as she said. Representing a more centrist viewpoint was Representative Price, who acknowledged the possible permanence of the PMSCs and thus wanted to shape laws to enhance the nation's ability to control them. At the other end of the spectrum from Schakowsky were the ardent defenders of the PMSCs, who promoted the viewpoint that the industry played a crucial role in American and international security. This was the laissez-faire approach: Leave the PMSCs alone and let them do whatever the government and corporate America need them to do.

At the October 2 Committee hearing, Schakowsky's questions for Prince focused on one of her gravest concerns. To whom did America's private contractors outsource their own work? Who was really providing the armed security for America? In other words, who were the subcontractors? If Blackwater saved money by hiring workers from Third World nations where the military had conducted assassinations or genocides, did the United States have any knowledge of this or any control over it? What did that mean for American security?

Schakowsky: Mr. Prince, in your testimony you stated Blackwater personnel supporting our country's overseas missions are all military and law enforcement veterans. You did not state that they were all Americans, all American military and law enforcement veterans. Is it true that Blackwater hires foreign security personnel?

Prince: One of your colleagues previously asked that question. Yes. Some of the camp guards, gate guards, static locations are indeed third country national soldiers.

Schakowsky: And in 2004, Gary Jackson, the President of Blackwater USA, admitted that your company had hired former commandos from Chile to work in Iraq, many of which served under General Augusto Pinochet, the former dictator of Chile. As you must know, his forces perpetrated widespread human rights abuses, including torture and murder of over 3,000 people. Did Blackwater or any of its affiliated companies at that time, at any time, use any Chilean contractors with ties to Pinochet?

Prince: Well, I can say Mr. Jackson did not admit to hiring some commandos. Yes, we did hire some Chileans. Any foreign national soldier that works for us now, for the State Department, has to have a high public trust clearance. It is basically a security clearance for a third country national soldier where you take their name, it goes back through the U.S. embassy in that country and their name is run, kind of like a national agency check here, which is what someone does for a security clearance. That way we can ensure that they have no criminal record, ma'am.

Schakowsky: I understand that one of your business associates was indicted in Chile for his role in supplying commandos to serve Blackwater. Is that correct?

Prince: He was not an associate. He might have been a vendor to us.

Schakowsky: In your written statement today, you state that Blackwater mandates that its security professionals have a security clearance of at least the secret level. Did any Chilean contractors who worked for Blackwater ever get a security clearance?

Prince: I believe what I said is the [Worldwide Protective Services contract out of the State Department], the Americans working on that doing the PSC mission are required to have a security clearance.

Schakowsky: Did any Chilean contractors get a security clearance?

Prince: I don't know, ma'am.

Schakowsky: Because if yes, they were provided with classified information, if no, then it is not true that all Blackwater personnel in

Iraq have security clearances. On your web site, I don't know if it is still there, there was a recent one, there was a jobs fair advertised in Bucharest. And we have heard allegations that Blackwater recruited Serbians and former Yugoslavs with combat experience from the Balkan wars, some linked to atrocities committed in Croatia and Kosovo and in Bosnia and associates of Milosevic. I am wondering if you could talk to me about that for a minute.

Prince: To my knowledge, we have never employed anyone out of those countries.

Schakowsky: Would you know?

Prince: There are some Rumanians that were on a contract that we took over from a previous vendor, competitor. But we phased them out and we use guys out of Latin America now.

Schakowsky: Would you know if people have been associated with Pinochet or Milosevic before you hired them? Is this part of your inquiry?

Prince: Again, as I said before, for the State Department, for the static guards that were utilized, third country national soldiers, a high public trust clearance is required. . . .

Schakowsky: I heard you say that.

Schakowsky was the last of the legislators to question Prince. When she was done, Chairman Waxman closed the questioning by expressing gratitude to Prince for his patience and endurance. Then he said, "In closing let me just say that we really have a remarkably unprecedented experiment going on in the United States today by having private military contractors. It raises a lot of issues. It raises issues about costs and it raises issues about whether it interferes with our military objectives. I think this hearing will help us continue to sort through what that means for our Nation. We have never had anything of this magnitude before where we have turned so much of our military activity and security over to private firms that used to be, for the most part, provided by the U.S. military itself."

Prince ended the hearing in his own way, with a gesture that apparently went unnoticed: He grabbed the "MR. PRINCE" nameplate from in front of him and stuffed it in his pocket. "I'm no hero," Prince later wrote. "The world knows all too well about my mistakes. But I was never meant to play the villain. I take some solace knowing that, in the end, history will judge me and all that we accomplished at Blackwater. Perhaps children someday will read about us the way I read about cowboys, and battling pirates on the high seas."

Undoubtedly, the October 2 hearing caused a surge of interest in the topic, both in the media and in Congress. There would be more hearings in at least seven other congressional committees (though none would interrogate Prince). And on October 4, the House passed legislation that required the Department of Justice to report to Congress all charges against contractors in Iraq and Afghanistan and that extended MEJA's legal oversight to all contractors in all war zones. This meant that employees of companies contracted by the U.S. government to work in Iraq or any other combat zone worldwide would be under the jurisdiction of U.S. law. David Price sponsored it and the vote was 389 to 30—all 30 nays being Republicans.

When the bill went to the Senate, Bush administration officials expressed "grave concerns." They said that the amended MEJA could complicate national security activities, for while it broadened the scope of U.S. law and thus assisted victims of the violent acts of private contractors, it also opened courtroom doors to those who wanted to stop the work of some American contractors abroad. The Bush administration said it feared a potential barrage of litigation, especially regarding its current methods of what it called harsh interrogation and others called torture. The bill did not pass in the Senate. In subsequent years, another "new MEJA," the Civilian Extraterritorial Jurisdiction Act, sponsored by Representative Price in the House and Senator Patrick Leahy in the Senate, would die in both chambers.

In December 2007, there would be one more legal attempt at oversight: an extension of the reach of the Uniform Military Code. The National Defense Authorization Act that year took the Code beyond the limits of a declared war to "a contingency operation," defining a military operation "designated by the Secretary of Defense as an operation in which members of the armed forces are or may become involved in military actions, operations or hostilities against an enemy of the U.S. or against an opposing military force." And by the end of the year, the State Department and the DOD would issue a document—the December 2007 Memorandum of Agreement (MOA)—defining operating procedures, oversight, and monitoring on an interagency level, to "prevent a situation in which [PMSCs] working for different elements of the US government follow differing policies and regulations." It was, however, limited to Iraq. No similar agreement was ever drawn up for Afghanistan.

Then in January 2008, there was another action prompted by the October hearing and the Nisour Square massacre: the launch of the Commission on Wartime Contracting, a congressional investigation of federal contracting in the reconstruction and security of Iraq and Afghanistan. Authorized by the National Defense Authorization Act that year, the commission would be composed of eight members: two appointed by the president, two by the Senate majority leader, two by the Speaker of the House, one by the House minority leader, and one by the minority leader of the Senate. Their immense mission was for the next three years to assess the scope of the government's reliance on private contractors in war zones, the extent of waste and fraud, the misuse of force, and the level of legal and financial accountability.

But despite the Nisour Square massacre and the investigative commissions, there was no determination to regulate the industry. Regulation was costly and complicated, especially for such an international business. This would not be a cause taken on by Congress. It was, however, a matter of deep concern to the government of Switzerland and to the International Red Cross, which in 2006 launched a joint initiative to explore strategies for international control of the private military and security sector. The Swiss Initiative, as it was called, was motivated by the industry's bad track record for human rights abuses and by the belief that the industry had already passed through the portal of permanence. If indeed there could be no turning back, certain realities had to be faced, and one was that nations would be slow to regulate PMSCs, if at all. Thus from 2006 to 2008, experts in such areas as humanitarian law, international treaties, armed security, and unconventional warfare convened in the Swiss cities of Montreux, Zurich, and Geneva. And at the spring 2008 meeting, representatives from the industry itself were invited to attend and engage in the problem-solving dialogues.

By this time, industry leaders were beginning to agree to work on ways to improve accountability through regulation—self-regulation, that is. This meant offering their own suggestions for ways to regulate and volunteering to serve on commissions to oversee such regulation, to coordinate it, and to enforce it. Just as some of the companies had employed public relations, image-shaping, and name changes to work their way into the establishment, some now were savvy enough to recognize the benefits of self-regulation. After all, if such regulations were to be accepted internationally, then the companies would become further entrenched. Banning them would not be an option. Perhaps this was the time for a chess move. To be sure, the Nisour Square tragedy accelerated the pace of what had begun in Switzerland.

9

CONQUERING CHAOS

The Eden Palace au Lac sits on the palm-lined shores of Lake Geneva in Montreux, a town on the "Swiss Riviera" known for its jazz festivals and casino nightlife. Built in the late nineteenth century, the seven-story hotel, with its colossal marble columns and eighteenth-century tapestries, exudes Old World grandeur, like the palaces of the past where strategies of war and peace were the talk of the day. In September 2008, government officials from seventeen nations gathered in the lobby of the Eden Palace along with human rights advocates, military experts, and representatives of military and security companies to endorse a document that might help resolve one of the most challenging issues of the new century: how to control a growing international industry brokering men with guns.

It was September 17, one year and a day after the Nisour Square massacre, and what transpired, though largely unnoticed in the media, could prove to be a milestone in both the evolution of an industry and the history of global security. There was no fanfare: this was an event focusing on the signing of a document that had been discussed and debated in relative seclusion for the previous two years. Yet the document was part of a strategy to put into place what some participants were calling "a new archetype in response to global change." Henceforth called the Montreux Document and referred to by its drafters variously as a "toolkit," "bible," "milestone," or "stepping-stone," it was the first step in the Swiss Initiative, which was the first serious global attempt to monitor the private military and security industry.

There would be three steps: first, the Montreux Document, which would show how existing international laws could be used by nations to oversee PMSCs; then, the International Code of Conduct to be endorsed by PMSCs; and the third step, a new global enforcement body to certify companies and rule on allegations of human rights abuses and other transgressions. Such a system of oversight would have to include a database of PMSCs globally approved for contracts, with each company's track record for bad or good behavior and for financial responsibility. At the same time, there would have to be a roster of rulers for whom no company could work without jeopardizing its potential for future contracts. Other plans included a directive that nations, corporations, and any entity contracting with PMSCs would require each contracted firm to post a bond to be forfeited in the event of misconduct, malfeasance, or noncompliance.

In a world saturated with conflict and a fast-growing market for force, the Swiss Initiative could literally save lives—if it could achieve what its participants hoped it would. The ultimate hope was to eliminate the security threats posed by the very people hired to provide security. To do this, the document's drafters had sifted through international decrees, charters, and treaties to examine and cull laws that were applicable to privatized defense and armed security, rather than draft new laws, which could take years to put in place. For example, the Geneva Conventions, a compendium of laws for the conduct of war drafted in 1949—some of which were endorsed by almost every country in the world—could be woven into the legal tapestry. Out of this effort would come global norms to shape the relationships between PMSCs, the nations that contracted them, as well as the nations where their businesses were officially based, and the nations from which they hired their workers. As such, the document would inform PMSCs worldwide of their existing legal obligations. It thus repudiated the notion that private military and security contractors operated in a legal vacuum, an assumption that not only gave companies the license to behave recklessly but also gave governments incentives to use such companies to circumvent laws applicable to traditional militaries.

From the earliest meetings in 2006, the drafters grappled with difficult questions. The task was, after all, like nothing ever before attempted. At the first series of meetings in Montreux and Zurich, participants examined studies done by the International Red Cross and the U.N. and they studied laws of the U.K., the U.S., Australia, South Africa, France, and Sierra Leone in search of principles that could be used to monitor the screening and training of employees, to punish bad behavior, and to govern contracts with various nations held by one PMSC. What if, for example, a PMSC with a contract to supply air transport for one nation owned a subsidiary that was contracted to maintain the weapons systems of another nation in conflict with the first? Or what if a government in an increasingly unstable environment hired a PMSC to guard high-level officials or to train security forces for countering rebel groups that the PMSC's own nation supported?

On the day of the endorsements, a representative of the government of Switzerland explained to the press that the thirty-seven-page document gave "expression to the consensus that international law, in particular international humanitarian law and human rights law, does have a bearing on PMSCs." As Anne-Marie Buzatu, an attorney who participated in drafting the document, said later, "[Montreux] was about recognizing the impact of these companies. They are everywhere; they are part of our lives today. And we can't just hide from this and say, 'not in my own backyard.' What we are looking at is an industry that is emblematic of how private actors [PMSCs] have an influence on the world; it's about privatization. And this type of privatization simply cannot be ignored because these are people with guns. I think everyone attending well understood that."

Buzatu, who specialized in international humanitarian law, worked at the Geneva Centre for the Democratic Control of Armed Forces, a foundation known as DCAF and a major player in the Swiss Initiative. From her perspective, what was happening in Switzerland was a groundbreaking response to the largest shift in world order in almost four hundred years, changing from a time when only nations made the laws. More recently, international bodies began to regulate activities among nations. Now, in the twenty-first century, another transition had begun: the fading power of the nation-state. And by some accounts the growth of the PMSCs was a sign of this development. The era of globalization was forcing the need for legal adjustments, and the PMSCs were at the core of the change. Said Buzatu: "It all worked well when it was hard to travel and people stayed and worked in their own nations. Now we have [PMSCs] working two or three borders a day. The laws of states [nations] are being challenged by the new international era."

Buzatu's organization, DCAF, was created by the Swiss government in the autumn of 2000 in Geneva. DCAF, as its name implied, focused on the accountability and democratic oversight of armed forces worldwide, from police to traditional military to private military companies. It emerged from a project initiated by the Swiss government in 1999 to investigate security issues in post–Cold War Europe. A project team conducted hundreds of interviews in nations struggling in the throes of transition, especially in central and Eastern Europe as well as central Asia. What became quickly clear was not only that the end of the Cold War had caused an outbreak of conflicts in nations whose armed forces had shrunk but also that the large supply of displaced and unemployed soldiers, in combination with the rising demand for armed forces and military expertise, had created a new market for mercenaries—and for companies that employed them. Controlling "unleashed and unmonitored armed forces" was becoming an urgent necessity.

Funded by thirty member nations and two Swiss agencies, DCAF sought international solutions for some of the toughest issues of global security and armed forces in the new century, from child soldiers to unaccountable private contractors. At the core of its concerns were transparency, accountability, and democratic control. DCAF members believed that they were fighting for the survival of democracy and in this case wanted to initiate dialogue and end the PMSC industry's deep-rooted conventions of secrecy. "The privatization of military and security services, now occurring on a mass-scale, seriously challenges the traditional notion of the state monopoly on the use of force," one writer noted in a 2006 DCAF publication. "The consequences of this we are only now beginning to grasp. Most serious of these challenges is the lack of quality information and transparency regarding the nature and scope of PMSC personnel, rules and practices."

Buzatu had worked for DCAF only since September 2007, starting in the weeks following the Nisour Square massacre. A soft-spoken Swiss resident and native Texan, Buzatu had a weighty résumé that included a doctorate in law and another advanced degree in international humanitarian and human rights law. But more impressive than her education was how she used it. For human rights advocates like Buzatu, laws were effectively weapons and being a lawyer was more than a livelihood. Her career coincided with the emerging challenges of a new global landscape and shifts in the conduct of war, both of which demanded new legal strategies in the pursuit of human rights and peace.

Buzatu was among those who recognized the challenges that PMSCs posed. Her ultimate incentive for focusing on the transparency of the private security sector was the cause of peace. Sustainable peace was, after all, impossible without controlling the PMSCs, making them answerable to the citizens of the world they supposedly served, beginning with somehow tracking their use, growth, income, and conduct. Thus far, no parliamentary or congressional body had come close to such an achievement. Even before the U.S. Congress addressed the issues prompted by the privatization of war and security, DCAF was dealing with them. And DCAF would continue to focus on transparency and accountability long after PMSCs, such as Blackwater, had disappeared from the headlines.

The Montreux Document was the first international law directly addressing the problem of PMSCs. The nations endorsing the Montreux Document would require the PMSCs they contracted with, or that were contracted to corporations within their borders, to agree to uphold its standards. Then, in the second step of the Swiss Initiative, the International Code of Conduct, the PMSCs themselves would also be signatories. Thus the regulations that would evolve would be in part self-imposed, self-managed, self-regulated.

"What we wanted to do from the start was to make a laudable attempt to clarify a very complex state of affairs," said Buzatu in an interview. "Today's world is a far cry from the 1960s and 1970s when this business usually meant mercenaries of the rather unsavory kind involved in postcolonial and neocolonial conflicts. Today's version is fundamentally different, the critical factor being their modern corporate business form. They are hierarchically organized into incorporated and registered businesses that trade and compete openly on the international market, link to outside financial holdings, recruit more proficiently than their predecessors, and provide a wider range of military and security services—some armed and some unarmed—to a greater variety and number of clients. For obvious reasons, the lines of accountability are convoluted. What we must be aware of in our work is that mercenaries, whatever era, can be an effective tool in ending conflict, and there are good companies today. There really are. But they can also lead to more conflict, further chaos, and long wars, if not part of a long-term plan for control."

What seemed to impress Buzatu most about the Swiss Initiative was that such a diverse group with often contrary interests—from defending human rights to marketing military services—worked so well together. All sides appeared willing to face the reality of a ubiquitous presence of PMSCs, she said, but all sides also acknowledged that the industry had grown without effective monitoring. And there was an unspoken understanding of urgency. After all, no one really knew where the markets would be in the coming years. The wars in Iraq and Afghanistan would one day be over and then where would the PMSCs find work? What would be the developing markets for force?

Whatever one's views of the industry, the Montreux participants agreed that regulation was necessary and that stopping the expansion of the PMSCs was not possible. The companies were already too entrenched in the global structure. Establishing codes and standards would force the industry to sort itself out. The worst companies, the ones guilty of human rights abuses or fraudulent business practices, would not meet standards and would go out of business. Industry representatives saw self-regulation as beneficial partly because it would discourage any governmental efforts to ban PMSCs. In this way, Montreux was a true chess move that could easily give the industry firmer footing in the world. This was a sophisticated step for a business seeking respectability. After all, a regulated group of companies defined an established industry.

Part of the Montreux challenge from the start, however, was actually to define that industry. As Buzatu noted in a 2008 speech, the "confusion among terms, 'private security,' 'private military' and 'mercenaries,'" was a "key challenge" to tackling the issues of transparency and accountability. "These terms are slippery and ill-defined with one easily blending into another creating a fog that clouds and distorts the issues, both from a legal as well as a moral point of view, of how and when such services should be used appropriately. But out of such fog one aspect is clear: actors [PMSCs] working under any of these labels have the potential to use deadly force against other human beings. In these times when the State has relinquished some of its traditional monopoly on the use of force, resulting in its assuming less control on the standards and training of persons authorized to use force, this fog can be—and has been—lethal."

Despite the common usage of the term "mercenary" in the media, the definition of "mercenary" in international conventions of law was limited to individuals and thus so narrow that it did not apply to

PMSCs. They were, in some cases, brokers or middlemen for finding workers who might indeed be legally defined as mercenaries. In an early effort to address the problem, a DCAF group differentiated the tasks of what would be called PMCs and PSCs. They defined PMCs, private military companies, as corporate entities typically contracted for offensive services including military advice and training, operational support and security protection, logistics support, intelligence, policing, drug interdiction, arms procurement, de-mining, and counterterrorism. And PSCs, private security companies, provided defensive services to protect individuals and property, such as multinational companies extracting resources in hostile environments or humanitarian aid agencies in areas of conflict and instability in Africa. However, quite often, as the industry matured, the larger and more sophisticated companies offered a vast array of services that fit both categories. So the Montreux drafters chose "PMSC" as the industry's defining term.

The greatest of all challenges, however, would be establishing the next two steps of the Initiative as soon as possible. Speed was of grave concern because of the many human rights violations occurring each year. Whether it was Blackwater or any number of other firms, PMSCs were shooting civilians, spending excessive amounts of taxpayers' money, failing to screen the backgrounds of their armed employees, smuggling weapons, or drinking and carousing excessively. They were doing everything, it seemed, but promoting peace and stability, which was what their industry spokespersons wanted the world to believe their mission to be. Instead of supplying protection, they were sometimes lures for danger. As the *New York Times* would later observe, "far from providing insurance against sudden death, the easily identifiable, surprisingly vulnerable pickup trucks and SUVs driven by the security companies were magnets for insurgents, militias, disgruntled Iraqis and anyone else in search of a target."

It wasn't always about Blackwater. In early October 2007, a few weeks after the Nisour Square massacre, employees of the big British firm Erinys allegedly opened fire on a taxi in northern Iraq, injuring a twenty-six-year-old Iraqi man, his sister, and a young Iraqi journalist who worked for a major Kurdistan TV station. In that same week there was a tragedy in Baghdad when an employee of a PMSC based in Dubai opened fire on a car filled with four young Iraqis driving home from church. Two were killed. Sitting in the back of the last armored vehicle of a four-car convoy, two shooters fired thirty to forty bullets into the car from a distance of about seventy-five yards.

Some industry advocates blamed such problems on the fact that the industry was "still in the development phase." They also stressed that some companies—DynCorp, for example—were forming ethics committees, hiring compliance officers, and improving background checks of new personnel. Others from within the industry, less confident about the snail's pace of this self-governance, were unabashed about proclaiming the urgent need for more and better oversight.

On board with such views in Montreux were industry representatives from a handful of companies, including Aegis, G4S, and Triple Canopy. One of the key players present from the industry was Eric Westropp, a former director at Control Risks Group (CRG), the British firm well known for its highly skilled kidnap negotiators. Westropp was a former British Army brigadier general who had served in the Middle East, Southeast Asia, Central America, Europe, including Northern Ireland, and had received the award of the Commander of the Order of the British Empire. After leaving the Army, he worked at CRG for more than twenty years and unofficially took a significant role in the unfolding drama of his sometimes notorious industry.

Westropp, who worked often with Buzatu, was a major participant in the Swiss Initiative. Well connected in both political and
military circles, he was a born negotiator, and the type of person
who could articulate the options for a potentially dangerous situation while sipping tea—perhaps in the drawing room of the Special
Forces Club, where he was a longtime member. Although he might
be concerned and know exactly what was at stake, he was typically
calm in the face of contrary winds—calm enough to discern what
was likely the smartest move. As one of his former colleagues put it,
"Eric is the one who is always the most informed. He knows how to
keep a ship on course, even if there's near mutiny on the deck."

By most accounts, what was impressive about Westropp and what
made him useful to his industry was that he had the ability and the
will to move beyond the past to try to envision a future not based on
fear, distortion, or worn-out paradigms. During his years at CRG, he
had expanded the company by seizing opportunities in the borderless
business environment that was evident everywhere. In one instance,
he added a division that would focus on contracts in failed or failing
nations, mostly in Africa. At the time of the Iraq invasion, Westropp
proposed that CRG launch a security business that included armored
vehicles and armed employees. For some CRG staffers at the time,
this was tantamount to asking a Four Seasons hotel to put a McDon-
ald's franchise in the lobby. In their industry, the hierarchy looked
like this: at the top were crisis management consulting, intelligence
work, and kidnap negotiation; in the middle were air transport and
logistics and other services in contingency operations; and at the
bottom was anything having to do with weapons, including carrying
arms to guard clients and training local police. At the time, CRG had
represented the high end of private security firms for decades. But
from Westropp's viewpoint, shifts in the global marketplace, and

especially changes in warfare, required rethinking the firm's range of services. It was this ability to see the future of his industry and to persuade others that made him invaluable in the Swiss Initiative negotiations, which he called "a way to conquer the chaos."

Westropp and most everyone involved had accepted the fact that there would be skeptics who scoffed at such efforts. They would claim that the newly endorsed document was as limp as the paper on which it was written. But in 2008, at the signing of the document, the Swiss Initiative, with the first step in place, sent a message of possibility and determination to all naysayers. On September 17, the Montreux Document was endorsed by representatives of Switzerland, the United States, the United Kingdom, China, Afghanistan, Iraq, Canada, Germany, France, Australia, South Africa, Sweden, Angola, Austria, Poland, Sierra Leone, and Ukraine. Soon dozens more would sign on as more meetings were scheduled for the next step, the International Code of Conduct, to be signed by PMSCs. Then with hundreds of companies and nations on board, the third step, the toughest of all, would be put into place: establishing an authority to enforce the code. "It will happen eventually and it will affect everyone in some way, I assure you," Westropp said in an interview later, "as there will be a time coming up when foreign policies and diplomatic decisions will be made with the [private military and security] industry in mind."

In America that fall, such notions seemed very far away. Only the active members of Human Rights First or Amnesty International would know about the signing of the Montreux Document and the anxious rush to establish a code of conduct. Both organizations released announcements of the event, but no mainstream press picked them up. In September 2008, after all, the media in America was focused on the U.S. presidential campaign. And for those people concerned about PMSCs, the election of Barack Obama seemed at the time to have the potential for making a far bigger impact on controlling privatized defense and security than any slow-moving international pursuit of accountability.

Obama was, after all, one of the few American politicians who had ever questioned the privatization of American military and security operations. He had expressed concern over the Aegis Matrix contract and its CEO's notoriety in 2005. In a letter to a constituent, Senator Obama had written, "The CEO of Aegis Defense Services Tim Spicer has been implicated in a variety of human rights abuses around the globe. Given his history, I agree that the United States should consider rescinding its contract with his company. Several of my colleagues have contacted the Pentagon expressing their concerns about this issue. I will be in touch with their offices to see how I can be of assistance in their efforts." And in 2007 as a U.S. senator, he had introduced the Transparency and Accountability in Security Contracting bill as an amendment to the Defense Authorization Act that year. This bill required federal agencies to report to Congress on the numbers of security contractors employed, wounded, and killed, and to keep track of disciplinary actions taken against them.

Thus, throughout the 2008 campaign those few Americans concerned about the private military trend hoped that the promising young candidate from Illinois would express his views on PMSCs, especially in the context of Iraq and Afghanistan, and his plans for enhancing transparency in the industry. And in fact, during the Democratic primary campaign both Obama and Senator Hillary Clinton commented on "mercenaries" and "private security contractors." Clinton, in a press release in February 2008, had said, "From this war's very beginning, this administration has permitted thousands of heavily-armed military contractors to march through Iraq without any law or court to rein them in or hold them accountable. These private security contractors have been reckless and have compromised our mission in Iraq. The time to show these contractors the door is long past due. We need to stop filling the coffers of contractors in Iraq, and make sure that armed personnel in Iraq are fully accountable to the U.S. government and follow the chain of command." Later that month Clinton would join Senator Bernie Sanders as a cosponsor of the Senate's version of the Stop Outsourcing Security Act, which Representative Jan Schakowsky had introduced in the House a few months before.

While campaigning in July, Obama had shared his thoughts about PMSCs with the editorial board of the *Military Times*, a media group that published weekly papers for each of the branches of the armed forces. "There is room for private contractors to work in the mess hall, providing basic supplies and doing some logistical work that might have been done in-house in the past," he said. "I am troubled by the use of private contractors when it comes to potential armed engagements." After interviewers' questions, he said, "I am not arguing that there are never going to be uses for private contractors in some circumstances. What I am saying is if you start building a military premised on the use of private contractors and you start making decisions on armed engagement based on the availability of private contractors to fill holes and gaps, that over time you are, I believe, eroding the core of our military's relationship to the nation and how accountability is structured. I think you are privatizing something that is what essentially sets a nation-state apart, which is a monopoly on violence. And to set those kinds of precedents, I think, will lead us over the long term into some troubled waters."

On the campaign trail, however, Obama did not publicly discuss the topic except in response to commentator Amy Goodman, host of the television and radio program *Democracy Now!* Goodman cornered him on his way out of New York's Cooper Union after a speech in March. "Would you call for a ban on the private military contractors like Blackwater?" asked Goodman.

"I've actually—I'm the one who sponsored the bill that called for the investigation of Blackwater and those folks, so—" said Obama.

"But would you support the [the Stop Outsourcing Security Act, introduced in Congress in 2007] now?" asked Goodman.

"Here's the problem," said Obama. "We have 140,000 private contractors right there [in Iraq], so unless we want to replace all of or a big chunk of those with US troops, we can't draw down the contractors faster than we can draw down our troops. So what I want to do is draw—I want them out in the same way that we make sure that we draw out our own combat troops. Alright? I mean, I—"

"Not a total ban?" asked Goodman.

"Well, I mean, I don't want to replace those contractors with more US troops, because we don't have them, alright? But this was a speech about the economy," Obama said, referring to the speech he had just given.

"The war is costing $3 trillion," said Goodman.

"That's what—I know, which I made a speech about last week. Thank you," said Obama, and then left.

That was the last time the public would hear much about PMSCs from Obama, despite the fact that shortly after the election, the Pentagon's inspector general reported that the DOD was relying more and more on contractors "bordering on inherently governmental functions, thereby potentially taking on decision-making roles." The Transparency and Accountability in Security Contracting Act died. Reintroduced three years later, it died again. During Obama's first term as president, private military contractors would exceed the number of traditional troops in both Iraq and Afghanistan. Perhaps the Swiss Initiative should have drawn more attention.

In his 2008 book, *The Limits of Power*, historian Andrew J. Bacevich dissected the economic, political, and military crises facing America, arguing that the United States was extending military power to fulfill its imperialistic goals but it did not have the military means to do it. Americans had two choices, he said. One was to endorse its imperial ambitions and thus remain committed to current foreign policy agendas. This would mean reconfiguring the U.S. military and security forces "to specialize in peacemaking, peacekeeping and nation-building—contemporary euphemisms for imperial policing," he wrote. The other was to end the imperial agenda of U.S. foreign policy. Bacevich favored the latter. "Rather than transforming the armed forces of the United States into an imperial constabulary, the imperative of the moment is to examine the possibility of devising a non-imperial foreign policy."

But by the time the book was published, it appeared that the decision had already been made in Washington. The evidence was the growth of the PMSCs, which allowed the United States to proceed with its imperial role. Expanding the U.S. presence globally and reconfiguring U.S. forces required adding more private contractors, who were filling the gap between what America was capable of doing and what its imperial policy demanded. Extend the military or alter the foreign policy? The choice was made without much debate. The American public was not even aware of the options. There was no resistance, not even in the military. After all, Lieutenant General David H. Petraeus, the top commander in Iraq, had told the Senate Armed Services Committee in January 2007 that he considered the "thousands of contract security forces" to be, as the *Washington Post* reported, "assets available to him to supplement the limited number of U.S. and Iraqi troops to be used for dealing with the Iraqi insurgency."

Was it only the Montreux participants who understood what was at stake?

10

THE GENERAL AND KADHIM

At the U.S. Army Command and General Staff College at Fort Leavenworth, Kansas, in the spring of 2009, the deputy commandant, General Edward Cardon, initiated a study into the "unprecedented inclusion of private military companies within U.S. theaters of war." His intent was to awaken his students, who were Army majors engaged in a year of graduate studies, to the "full reality of PMCs." "In a future where the U.S. Army anticipates persistent conflict with limited increases in manning, the trends indicate continued pervasiveness of PMCs on the battlefield [which] compels the U.S. Army to develop an understanding of them," the project description read.

A few weeks before the study began, the U.S. force in Afghanistan had reached a historic marker: 57 percent were private contractors. From the general's viewpoint, the widening scope of PMSC involvement intensified the need for the Army's future leaders to know as much as possible about private contractors, especially how to synchronize with them and not resent or resist them, as the military was sometimes known to do. The growing use of PMSCs also spurred his fears, his worst being an unintended encounter between an American detail and private contractors. "Some nation could hire an American PMC or subcontractors of such a firm and our forces could show up in an intervention. It could take several forms but what would most concern me is that American soldiers could be in potential conflict with employees of a PMC under U.S. contract." The general, however, did not know that a variation of his fear had already been realized. And ironically, later that spring Kadhim Alkanani, the former Special Forces soldier wounded in such an incident in 2005, would be attending classes at Fort Leavenworth as part of his course of study in the Army Civilian University, hoping to reintegrate with the Army as a civilian intelligence agent.

That such a twist of fate occurred at Fort Leavenworth was fitting, as this was, after all, the intellectual center of the U.S. Army, where the conduct of war and dramatic shifts in military tactics and strategies, such as privatization, were studied and where new ideas took shape. As American journalist Robert D. Kaplan wrote, "Leavenworth is where military doctrine is written." For years, crucial and sometimes controversial solutions to national defense challenges had come out of the Fort Leavenworth studies, including the quiet revolution of 2006 when the Vietnam-era strategies of counterinsurgency were reconstituted for Iraq—a project under the direction of General David Petraeus, then the commandant of the Command and General Staff College (CGSC). Leavenworth even looked like a college campus, with its nineteenth-century clock tower and its sprawling red-brick buildings linked by covered walkways to a research library. Roads named after Pershing, Eisenhower, Stimson,

Sherman, Sheridan, and Meade branched off from Grant Avenue, the main thoroughfare, where directional signs noted buildings that housed the Command and General Staff College as well as the School of Advanced Military Studies, the Combat Studies Institute, the Counterinsurgency Center, and the National Simulation Center, among others.

Situated on the western bluffs of the Missouri River, the fort was originally built to facilitate expansion in nineteenth-century America by providing supplies and security for those early explorers daring enough to venture into America's western territories. The gateway to the American West, it was where the Santa Fe Trail began. In the twenty-first century, it was no less significant, though a post of a different sort—this time supplying strategies for America's survival on the conflict-ridden global frontier. In its hundreds of classrooms, extensive lessons on the history of warfare were integrated with the realities of the present in an effort to inspire useful projections for the future.

Much of what happened here was about peering into the future to prepare for potential conflicts and to design ways to negotiate safe ground internationally for American citizens and interests. As the graduate school for U.S. military leaders, its alumni included Dwight D. Eisenhower, Douglas MacArthur, Colin Powell, and Petraeus. Its international officers program had attracted military leaders from nearly every nation in the world in an effort to establish global relationships—ties that sometimes prompted calls from the Pentagon to the fort at the start of U.S. interventions or international crises, in pursuit of the hosts and close associates of the graduates who had become presidents of nations or heads of foreign militaries. After 9/11, for example, calls came in about Pakistan's Army chief, General Ashfaq Parvez Kayani, a 1981 Leavenworth grad.

Leavenworth's military studies were often published in monographic series by the Combat Studies Institute Press. In early 2005, for example, the Press came out with Occasional Paper #12 in the Global War on Terrorism series, entitled *Public War, Private Fight? The United States and Private Military Companies.* It was utterly prescient. Taking the point of view that an increasing reliance on PMSCs "has altered irrevocably the American way of war," the author, Deborah Kidwell, a professor of military history at the CGSC, raised questions about costs and accountability and then zeroed in on a crucial issue for the traditional military: the profound difference between efficiency and effectiveness. The companies promoted their efficiencies—of speed and cost—as they were "on call," she noted. But the military is about effectiveness, she wrote. The best, most effective strategy for a campaign to succeed might not be the quickest. Efficiency is more applicable to economics and politics.

Kidwell stressed that attention must be paid to the impact that private contractors have on American soldiers, sailors, airmen, and marines, a concern that should transcend "political expediency," "cost efficiency," or the fulfillment of a privatization ideal. Did PMCs (her acronym) assist in the effectiveness of military policy? In her opinion: "PMCs lack the exemplary performance record of American military forces in combat; coordinated action and protection is more difficult; costs rise unpredictably; and legal ambiguity often leads to great personal risks to both contractor employees and military units. Thus, a number of significant risks accrue [in] the extensive use of contractors. This increased risk detracts from overall military effectiveness."

In 2005, Kidwell was one of the few Americans asking the crucial question, "Does the current extensive use of private military companies ultimately benefit American society and its citizens?" If the nation loses a personal connection to the military and as a result, fewer members of future generations know what it means to serve the nation, then what? The psychological cost of privatization and its impact on allegiance to the country must be considered, Kidwell said. "Americans may do well to consider the social legacy of participation in World War II," she wrote. "Because American society and its military are mutually reinforcing, leaders must be mindful of the social as well as the financial implications [of PMSCs]. Ultimately, military policy must benefit American society." In the conclusion to her 80-page monograph, Kidwell wrote: "It has been observed that war is too important to be left to the generals; industry analyst Peter Singer adds that 'war is far too important to be left to private industry.' Americans cannot abdicate their responsibility to govern—and wage war—wisely."

Kidwell's work was highly regarded by the participants in the spring 2009 study at the Command and General Staff College. And the students, who would add their findings to Kidwell's, quickly learned that since her assessment PMSCs had moved far beyond being suppliers of logistics support. Some firms had become so large they were beginning to resemble military and security department stores, dubbed by one of the Leavenworth participants as "Walmarts of war." The same company could send armed employees to guard oil rigs in hostile territory and supply unarmed risk consultants to a shipping company concerned about piracy.

One spring day at a meeting on the second floor of the CGSC library, one of the students expressed concern about the issue of citizen awareness and democracy. "Have we circumvented the ability to have a national debate about whether to enter a conflict?" he asked. "When we do that, the political cost goes up. Dialogue, discourse, these are the basics of democracy. Democracies require bureaucracies to slow down decision-making so there can be a dialogue. Privatizing the military obviously averts that; it's good for politicians but what about us, about Americans? And what about *us*? I mean some of us are actually in the military because we believe in this system and want to preserve it. I am willing to work with these contractors as I know I must but will there be limits, I mean some limits in the name of the whole reason we are fighting, for the system, for democracy?"

Another participant added, "What concerns me are the paradoxes and what the general public can't see. We are taught here to be self-critical. At Leavenworth soldiers are self-critical. We are trying to define best paths; we are looking at reality; ironically, we want to figure out ways for peace. But we look like just the opposite, which is what the companies are. They are trying to deflect criticism and to rebrand. We are open and accessible; they are secretive and sometimes have created their own rules of engagement. They make money off of conflict, while we are running studies to find strategies for ways to end conflicts. And now, we are having to learn how to work with them. Do we even have a choice?"

Such questioning was exactly what General Cardon wanted to hear. Four seminars of sixteen students each examined what was clearly a major shift in America's military history. The general himself had studied monographs and books on the topic, ranging from histories about the mercenary trade over the past several centuries to analyses of its latest incarnation. He was impressed with the work of Peter Singer, whose book *Corporate Warriors* he had carefully read; he had even discussed the topic with Singer. During the weeks of the PMC study, he was reading books by the German political scientist Herfried Münkler, who wrote *The New Wars* about the transition from wars that resulted in the formation of nations to recent wars that emerged in conjunction with the failure or collapse of states. It was through his understanding of that shift, from "symmetrical conflicts between states to asymmetrical global relationships of force," that is, from nations to nonstate actors in the theater of war, that General Cardon saw the urgency of understanding and working with private military and security companies.

At the time, Cardon, a brigadier general, was one of the youngest generals in the U.S. Army. The word at Leavenworth that spring was that he would soon receive his second star, thus becoming a major general, and would return to Iraq, where he had already held three command posts. A West Point grad, he had two master's degrees, one in national security and the other in strategic studies. In the 1990s, he had served as an officer for NATO forces in central Europe and Bosnia. And from 2000 to 2002 he was the special assistant to the army chief of staff at the Pentagon, followed by his first tour in Iraq. His career thus far had been extraordinary, but even in ways beyond his résumé. He was serving in Germany on the day the Wall fell; he was working in the Pentagon building during the attack on September 11, 2001; and he was the deputy commanding general for the 3rd Infantry Division during the Surge in Iraq in 2007–2008.

Despite his accomplishments, Cardon exuded an aura of immense humility. A wiry, fit man with an almost stereotypical military appearance, he always put the other person in the spotlight, and with an intense eye-to-eye focus, he listened to every word, as his detailed, carefully worded responses proved. He spoke in low tones in a deliberate style that was predictable for someone with such a visible penchant for order and regimen. But he was also capable of occasional bursts of liveliness, often revealing his deep devotion to the military and the nation. With discretion, he was willing to express observations and concerns.

At Leavenworth, Cardon stood out as one of the best examples of the College's integration of the military and academia. He was a thinker and a man of action. He could lead well because he was not only a good listener but was open-minded and willing to explore ideas and strategies. Within the confines of military discipline, he wanted to know the truth and to use whatever he learned for the benefit of the men and women who worked for him—hence, his concern and interest in the private military sector, which he called "PMCs." Although he had accepted their presence and the notion of the public-private partnership, he wanted to know more and to work through the maze of issues they presented. In one of the meetings that spring, he said that what was happening from the perspective of history was that "the nation state, with its slow ability to act militarily due to political realities, is becoming increasingly vulnerable to easy solutions that avoid the complexity of government. That is a reality and nothing shows that more than the growth of the private military and security businesses. Gradually systems of international security that have been in place for a long time are falling apart and the more anarchy there is then the more these companies offer themselves as the solution."

The advent of the PMSCs, Cardon believed, was a harbinger of the future of warfare. He saw the signs of entrenchment in the form of the companies' revolving-door boards and their astute marketers and lobbyists. There had even been an initiative within the Department of Defense in 2009 to "update the DOD doctrine to incorporate the role of contractors." The strongest evidence of permanence, however, by 2009 may have been the industry's expanding portfolio of profitable firms. But what part of that success was good news for American security and defense, and what part was threatening? Where were the landmines on this new road? These were among the many questions that Cardon knew needed to be studied.

Among the General's deep concerns was the possibility of PMSCs, if not properly trained or accountable, interfering with U.S. missions. He knew about incidents of drunken behavior among private contractors as well as corrupt billing practices and wartime contractor waste. And, as the participants in the CGSC study discussed, there were instances of PMSCs threatening to stop work on the battlefield if not paid on time. There were stories too of private contractors who had judged a situation too dangerous and thus had quit. In that year, 2009, there had also been complaints from military leaders about PMSC-protected convoys "blowing through intersections, or even Iraqi police checkpoints, without bothering to stop." As a CNN producer noted in her 2009 book, "In one sign of stunningly aggressive behavior, an unidentified contractor ran a U.S. military Humvee off the road. Inside the Humvee was a very angry U.S. general."

As Cardon knew, most of the world did not distinguish between public and private-sector security and defense in U.S. military missions. This concerned him, as it did the participants in the Leavenworth study. And although their case study for the project was the privatization that had occurred in Bosnia in the 1990s, their discussion groups frequently touched on recent changes tightening the bonds between the U.S. military and PMSCs—such as AFRICOM, a new Unified Command for American military activity in Africa.

Unified Commands are responsible for running Department of Defense operations for specific territories or functions, and this one, which became operational on October 1, 2008, would mean, among other things, more business for PMSCs. It would be the latest example of a policy partly based on the knowledge that PMSCs were available. Bush had first announced the plan for AFRICOM in February 2007, explaining that its mandate was to guard America's vast spectrum of interests in Africa at a time when the continent's strategic importance was growing, referring in part to China's equally vast array of interests. AFRICOM represented a reconfiguration of a typical Unified Command from a military mission to a security operation, which was an interesting development for anyone well informed about the military. The Department of Defense had laid the groundwork for such change when it issued a directive in 2005 that defined "stability operations" as "core US military missions," to be "given priority comparable to combat operations." At the time, the *New York Times* reported, "This marks an evolution of defense strategy for a military that traditionally has focused on fighting and winning wars."

And, as one of the participants in the privatization study pointed out, for the private military and security industry AFRICOM marked the beginning of a new market. Already stretched militarily, America would have to turn to PMSCs to do a large portion of the work. "Once the Iraq and Afghanistan economic 'bubble' bursts, [PMSCs] will seek new US-sponsored markets involving pre- and post-conflict support, and that market will include AFRICOM," wrote Sean McFate, a U.S. Institute of Peace consultant. "Senior leaders within the Department of Defense have repeatedly assured African nations that AFRICOM will have a 'small footprint' on the continent with no new military units. Yet, its mission remains ambitious, requiring more than staff officers to accomplish it. How will it reconcile the twin mandates of 'small footprint' with large mission? In a word: contractors. And the potential over-utilization of [PMSCs] could create a market for force in Africa, if not checked by meaningful regulation and knowledgeable policy makers."

Within a few weeks of the completion of the general's project, Kadhim Alkanani began his classes at the Army Civilian University. This was the center for what was called the Human Terrain System, a program designed to integrate cultural sensitivity into U.S. military strategy. Kadhim had discovered it in 2008 through his network of Special Forces soldiers who, around the same time, had connected him with an attorney interested in investigating his 2005 shooting. Later, Kadhim would say that both discoveries—the Civilian University and a legal advocate—were like "seeing the sun after many days of darkness."

The attorney, Shereef Akeel, was part of a team out of Washington, D.C., Seattle, and Troy, Michigan, handling a number of the lawsuits involving PMSCs contracted to conduct interrogations at the Abu Ghraib prison. He was distressed to hear Kadhim's story. As he later said, "One of our own gets shot and who is accountable? Out of sight and so, out of mind and out of the reach of justice? We were supposed to ignore this, just because it happened years before? I don't think so."

Soon, the legal team started the process of filing a civil suit in U.S. District Court in Washington, D.C., against Aegis Defense Services, LLC, in Washington, Aegis Defence Services Limited in London, and "unidentified Aegis employees." The suit, filed in the summer of 2009, claimed that the company and its "unidentified agents acted negligently and wrongfully by failing to prevent their employees, agents and/or representatives from engaging in foreseeable and predictable wrongful acts." It defined negligence to include "failing to take due care in hiring, failing to train, failing to supervise, failing to discipline and failing to investigate reports of wrong doing."

The suit could not reinstate Kadhim's military career nor could it reconstruct his shattered dream. He understood that. But at least because of it, he felt visible. And at Fort Leavenworth he had returned to military environs with the hope of once again utilizing his language skills and his experience as a "cultural translator." After several months of training, he would be sent back to Iraq, where his assignment would include the detection of anti-American propaganda in Arab media. To do this, he would travel to cities such as Amman, Damascus, Tripoli, Abu Dhabi, and Cairo. His only concern, besides leaving his family back in America, was his health. No doctor could predict when his fatigue might worsen or when his liver might further weaken from the effects of the hepatitis C.

Kadhim was not aware of the special study of private military companies at the Command and General Staff College that spring, nor did he and General Cardon ever meet. But soon they both would leave Leavenworth for Baghdad, moving from intellectual pursuits into the swirling vortex of military realities and new challenges. Among them, for Kadhim, were the occasional memories of his two previous lives in Iraq—as a child and as a Special Forces soldier. His continuing struggle with chronic fatigue could easily summon an image of the shooting. But there was another reminder he did not anticipate: he had lunch daily at a cafeteria where private contractors, including employees of Aegis, frequently dined. Because of Kadhim's civilian post within the military and Aegis's considerable presence in Iraq, it was not surprising that Kadhim and Aegis would interact in some way. This was something Kadhim had not expected; however, he was not bitter. "I tried not to judge them or to connect them with what had happened to me," he would later say. "There is a saying in Arabic that translates to this: 'The son cannot be blamed for the wrongs of the father.'"

Among Kadhim's few memories of the shooting was the moment immediately after his fellow soldiers jumped out of the sedan and waved their American IDs at the shooters. It was one of those seconds lost in the midst of chaos that later return. In this case, what

Kadhim remembered was someone in the SUV shouting an apology; he believed it was the shooter. Although he always assumed that the shooter had quit his job or was fired and he knew that he would not be able to recognize him, there was the slight possibility that the man was there in Iraq in 2010, even in the cafeteria one day perhaps. Now, though, he sometimes thought about the shooter as a victim too—as if they were both players in a historic epic, both part of a global transition, both collateral damage in the world's latest incarnation of the mercenary trade.

In late spring 2010, a few months after his return to Iraq, Kadhim and his team of lawyers received the first big news about their suit: a federal judge in D.C. district court dismissed the case, ruling that the court did not have jurisdiction over London-based Aegis Defence Services, which under the 2004 contract had employed the shooter. And Virginia-based Aegis Defense Services, LLC, the Aegis subsidiary with offices on K Street in D.C., was not incorporated until the year after the shooting and was not the Aegis under contract with the DOD in June of 2005. Legally, neither the British Aegis nor the American Aegis could be held accountable for the shooting of Kadhim—a fact as solidly grounded as the truth of the shooting itself.

The dismissal of the suit caught the eye of Washington-based writer David Isenberg, in part because none of the facts in the shooting incident were in dispute and partly because nothing had ever appeared in the media about the case. In his column for the Huffington Post, Isenberg juxtaposed the bad news for Kadhim with the good news for Aegis—the double good news, that is. During the same week that the D.C. judge dismissed Kadhim's civil action against Aegis, the firm won a prestigious security contract from the Olympic Delivery Authority for the 2012 Olympics in London. Isenberg wrote: "One wonders if the Olympic [Delivery] Authority was aware that it was Aegis security contractors who shot and permanently disabled U.S. Special Forces sergeant Kadhim Alkanani as he returned to Baghdad International Airport after an intelligence mission in June 2005."

The shooting, Isenberg stressed, occurred at a place where "there were no ongoing hostilities nor credible threats of imminent hostilities." And he ended his column with a skeptic's wit and a word of advice to the Olympic Delivery Authority: "You might want to ensure that the Aegis unit you signed a contract with is officially incorporated and deemed to legally exist."

11

"WHAT'S ALL THE FUSS ABOUT?"

By the second decade of the twenty-first century, the critics and skeptics of this bold new industry seemed like a crowd standing on one side of a deep and widening moat, while on the other side a fortress was under construction to protect the PMSCs. One way the critics sometimes articulated their concerns was to call the PMSCs "the new condottieri," referring to the military companies employed by the ruling nobles of the Italian city-states in the fourteenth and fifteenth centuries. The condottieri were mostly military professionals without national or political alliances. They were in great demand because the city-states frequently went to war with each other or defended themselves from attacks by the armies of the Holy Roman Empire. Bound by intricate legal contracts, these companies gradually offset the balance of military power. And while their contracts required them to protect their employers and their employers' assets and resources, they eventually became so powerful that they effectively held hostage the governments that hired them.

Although there were monumental differences between the Italian city-states of the fourteenth century and the world of the twenty-first century, the story of the condottieri raised crucial questions that deeply concerned the critics and skeptics. Could the "new" privatized military and security forces ever become more powerful than the governments that hired them? And if so, what would be the telling signs? As the military historian Martin van Creveld wrote in his classic 1991 book *The Transformation of War*, "The spread of sporadic small-scale wars will cause regular armed forces themselves to change form, shrink in size, and wither away. As they do, much of the day-to-day burden of defending society against the threat of low-intensity conflict will be transferred to the booming security business; and indeed the time may come when the organizations that comprise that business will, like the condottieri of old, take over the state."

High on the critics' list of fears by 2010 was the real possibility that nations hiring PMSCs could be slowly and irretrievably ceding power. To the critics, the idea of citizens relinquishing the power of national defense and security to private companies was a threat to democracy. They could not accept the notion that the PMSCs had become "too big to ban" or that self-regulation was a solution. After all, the Swiss Initiative, no matter how laudable and hopeful the intentions of its participants, or how practical and innovative their plans, had not yet made a difference.

While industry leaders and other Montreux contributors zeroed in on the Swiss Initiative's second step, which was the International Code of Conduct, the critics believed that no matter how many nations endorsed the Montreux Document and how many companies signed a code of conduct, the industry could not be trusted. And although the Swiss Initiative was motivated in part by human rights lawyers and advocates, the involvement of companies in the studies and negotiations could hinder the potential for true oversight and accountability. Once a mercenary always a mercenary, said the critics, whether carrying a crossbow in the fourteenth century or wearing a suit and conducting shareholder meetings in the twenty-first.

To the advocates of ridding the world of mercenary activity, regulation was a sham. Setting up codes of conduct could require years of negotiations among participating nations and companies. That in turn might lead to enough compromises to result in little more than monitoring mechanisms that would be ineffectual, superficial, and purely political. After all, how could regulations be enforced?

From the critics' viewpoint, whatever controls were established, the PMSCs would always find a way to avoid them. In the United States, for example, PMSCs competing for State Department contracts had to obtain a license. However, if they had something to hide, such as a record of overspending or lawsuits alleging bad behavior or human rights abuses, that they did not want exposed by applying for a license, they could apply through programs that did not require licensing—for instance, the Pentagon's Foreign Military Sales (FMS) program. And contracts for less than $50 million did not require Congress to be notified. Hence a larger contract could be broken into pieces and never attract the scrutiny of legislators, thus effectively avoiding public examination. As author Allison Stanger wrote: "The private military sector is distinctive in that it can easily expand quite rapidly without that growth being properly scrutinized."

Organizations such as Britain's War on Want took a firm stand against self-regulation as a solution. War on Want was a long-standing advocacy group based in London that focused on eliminating the root causes of global poverty—one of those causes being war. From the point of view of War on Want advocates, PMSCs helped to sustain conflict, and thus to achieve peace they had to be eliminated. In 2006, the group published a detailed and lengthy report on what it believed to be the peril at hand. After noting that the PMSCs had "moved from the periphery of international politics into the corporate boardroom, becoming a 'normal' part of the military sector," and that was "so much a part of war efforts that some major Western countries, like the UK and US, would now struggle to wage war without PMSC partners," War on Want demanded that governments "move toward legislation to control the PMSC sector as an urgent priority." The group insisted that "self-regulation by the industry is not an option."

War on Want was joined by the Campaign Against Arms Trade and Amnesty International, among others, in its concern that as PMSCs became more embedded in the military and political establishments, their influence could become more entrenched. The use of well-paid lobbyists and well-connected revolving-door boards of directors—who were not always as dedicated to quality as to profits—would secure more power and independence for PMSCs. With time, self-regulation could become more about *self* (i.e., profits) and less about *regulation*.

The British government, as if testing public sentiment, had announced in 2009 that it was working on a voluntary code of conduct of its own that would allow PMSCs "to police themselves" in the near future. This plan was much like the International Code of Conduct being negotiated in Switzerland. Companies would have to comply with a list of high standards of conduct or the British government would not do business with them. The idea caused a stir on both sides of the Atlantic, though mostly in Britain. A director for Amnesty International told the *Guardian*, "If the government does propose a self-regulatory system it would effectively grant [the companies] impunity to do whatever they like. The arms trade has been poorly regulated for far too long and we have seen the results: weapons getting into the hands of dictators, criminals and child soldiers. We should learn from these mistakes, not repeat them. We need a robust system that is backed-up by legislation."

A spokeswoman for the Campaign Against Arms Trade, based in London, was equally concerned: "The government proposal that mercenary groups should self-regulate is frankly ludicrous. We have all learnt from hard experience that self-regulation, whether in finance or consumer protection, simply doesn't work. It is even more dangerous with corporate mercenaries. Basically, it is a way of letting these companies do exactly as they like, operate where, when and how they want. There is no point in saying that the government would only contract companies which could demonstrate they operate to high standards because there would be no independent standard by which to measure them and, in any case, many are employed by other governments, extractive companies, and others over whom the government has no control. The government is allowing the mercenary companies to legitimize themselves as respectable private military and security corporations, something we are deeply opposed to."

To these critics, shifting the control of force from the public sector to private enterprise undermined the democratic process and threatened state control. The very existence of a military or intelligence organization without effective government oversight enhanced the potential for abuse of power. After all, what could be a greater danger for a democracy than a military and security complex unaccountable to civil authority—or even partly accountable—but not transparent even to the legislative body to which the citizens entrust decisions? What could result other than a defense policy shaped by the profit motives of the well-connected private sector?

Part of the concern for democracy was the issue of empire. To the industry's critics, PMSCs were emblematic of empires. They were imperial tools allowing nations to use security and military forces for more than self-defense. "Behind [this] is the old colonial structure," wrote the American journalist Elizabeth Rubin. "Only now it's dressed up in a multinational corporation, with suits and [cell] phones instead of Jeeps and parasols."

In the United States, PMSCs made it possible to stretch beyond the capacity of the traditional military to fulfill the missions required by our foreign policy, conducting what author Andrew Bacevich referred to as "imperial policing." How else could the nation have engaged in two wars—Iraq and Afghanistan—simultaneously without reinstituting the draft? In the history of empires, military overstretch, for whatever reason, has often led to dependence on private forces, which in turn has allowed the mercenaries to gain power over the nations they were hired to protect, as in the history of the Italian city-states and the condottieri. From the viewpoint of the privatization critics, America's reluctance to admit to being an empire was based on the fact that the motivations of empire ran counter to the ideals of democracy. PMSCs, they believed, allowed the government to maintain the appearance of a democracy while proceeding with expansion that defined it as an empire. Indeed, they would say, the growing presence of PMSCs was the proof that the United States was an empire. Without imperial interests and policies, there would be no need for private-sector support for our national security and defense apparatus.

Whatever their arguments against PMSCs, the skeptics and critics had few models for "leashing" the dogs of war, Old World and New. South Africa was one. The privatization of the military had begun in South Africa during the last years of apartheid. By some accounts, that was a strategy to shrink the size of the state in general before the new government of Nelson Mandela came into power as well as a way to move the best of the apartheid military into private companies so that those forces would not owe their allegiance to the Mandela regime. But President Mandela saw the very existence of PMSCs as a threat to the stability of the government and its foreign policy, which is why his government effectively banned "mercenary activity" in South Africa in 1998.

In the United States, by 2010, the cause to phase out PMSCs continued as Representative Jan Schakowsky teamed with Senator Sanders again to reintroduce the Stop Outsourcing Security Act, first introduced in 2007. For the advocates of banning armed contractors through legislative action, no industry was too big to conquer. And each year it seemed there were more reasons to try. In early 2010, for example, a federal judge in Washington threw out the charges against the Blackwater employees accused of killing the 17 Iraqis at Nisour Square and, as a *New York Times* editorial noted, the judge "highlighted the government's inability to hold mercenaries accountable for crimes they commit." The editorial pointed out that the government had not yet prosecuted any cases of casualties committed by armed contractors overseas. "There are many reasons to oppose the privatization of war. Reliance on contractors allows the government to work under the radar of public scrutiny. And freewheeling contractors can be at cross purposes with the armed forces. Blackwater's under-supervised guards undermined the effort to win Iraqi support," said the *Times*.

But for industry insiders advocating self-regulation, it was a matter of immense frustration that the rest of the world wasn't seeing their business their way. They scoffed at the label "new condottieri." They were certain that the critics and skeptics were not well enough informed to grasp the significance of their companies' roles in the quest for global stability. And they were confident that the naysayers did not understand how deeply entrenched the PMSCs already had become worldwide. PMSCs were not terrorist groups or thug-ridden gangs that could be outlawed. They were part of the establishment. To believe they should or could be abolished was to live in the past, from the point of view of industry leaders. "I have watched the discussions of the issues surrounding the [PMSC] sector—regulatory, ethical, moral, political—with a degree of bafflement," wrote Aegis's Dominick Donald. "All too often, the voice of the sector has seemed to be absent. This is partly because the sector is naturally secretive, to a considerable degree because commercial confidence and concerns about the competition often mean it can be little else. But it is also because the sector gets drowned out. Its explanations and context tend to lose out to a news dynamic that favours the join-the-dots, dogs-of-war take on the issues. This in turn makes the [PMSC] sector yet more secretive. Why explain when it only brings more grief?"

Donald and other insiders saw two ways of looking at defense and security in the geopolitical sphere of the early twenty-first century: through a lens of the past or a lens of the present. In the new century, the world was in flux, moving forward on waves of change in such a way that looking at the present as truthfully as possible was as difficult as it was crucial. Not since the seventeenth century, when the Treaty of Westphalia mapped out the beginning of the sovereignty of states, had the world seemed to be heaving with such ferocity. And to Donald and his compatriots, their companies were essential to any efforts toward stabilization of the world order.

By 2010, there were scholars and experts who agreed with the "here to stay" point of view and could not support efforts to ban the "new condottieri." However, they were not necessarily industry boosters. Allison Stanger, one of the most astute observers of the private-contracting surge in American defense and security, believed it was far too late to try to stop the spread of PMSCs. "Since privatization is intimately connected to globalization, we cannot turn the clock back on privatization without unwittingly undermining some of globalization's gains," wrote Stanger. "Strategic outsourcing done well can advance U.S. interests; uncontrolled outsourcing of the sort on display in Iraq creates more problems than it solves. We need to be able to tell the difference." She noted that American power was "taking on a different shape" in part because of an increasing dependence on private-sector defense and security.

Whatever the pros and cons of PMSCs and whoever the proponents and opponents of reining them in might be, the Swiss Initiative that had begun at Montreux was moving forward. On November 9, 2010, representatives from 58 private military and security companies met in Geneva to sign the International Code of Conduct. The 17-page Code laid out ground rules for the screening and training of personnel and the reporting of incidents as well as the use of force, the illegality of torture, and the banning of human trafficking. Over the next several months, more than 150 companies from 46 nations would sign the Code. By the tenth anniversary of the invasion of Iraq in 2013, there would be more than 700 PMSC signatories.

As with the endorsement of the Montreux Document, the 2010 signing attracted little attention. Yet it was the completion of the second step of an extraordinary process that, if successful, would establish a global regulatory authority for PMSCs. And this in turn would confer the validity that the companies were seeking and the permanence their critics most feared. To succeed, however, the Code would have to be enforced, which was the third step. It would have no value without a mechanism for oversight and governance. On the day of the 2010 signing, the steering committee for developing the oversight system was already in place. It included representatives from the Pentagon, the U.S. Department of State, the U.K. Foreign Office, the Swiss government, DCAF, Human Rights First, the Red Cross, and three PMSCs—G4S, Triple Canopy, and Aegis.

Among the signers representing the many companies that day was Aegis's Spicer—a predictable occurrence considering that Aegis had been actively involved in the Swiss Initiative for several years. Spicer signed on behalf of Aegis Group while Kristi Clemens Rogers signed for Aegis Defense Services, LLC, and Major General Graham Binns signed for Aegis Defence Services, Ltd. The Aegis website that day announced the signing and noted the importance of the Code and the work ahead. "As private security companies face rapidly changing missions and increasingly complex and dangerous operating environments, Aegis contends that regulation such as the Code is necessary to improve accountability, transparency and oversight, as well as to better serve and protect its clients while enabling their missions."

Spicer's presence at such an event and his involvement in the cause to regulate—self-regulate, that is—should not have surprised anyone. In his 1999 autobiography, he had addressed the issues of regulation in detail: "A first step towards regulation must be the setting up of a list of PMCs, a register. Were such a register to exist, it would have to be monitored and PMCs would have to subject themselves to a procedural audit process whereby the registration body—and this should perhaps be a U.N. function—conducts an evaluation of the company's compliance with a predetermined set of internationally defined and accepted operating practices." In his book, he acknowledged the concerns of skeptics, including the potential scenario of PMSCs abusing power to the extent that "the tail wags the dog." He wrote, "If a government employs a PMC, before long it is no longer the client government which calls the shots but the PMC, which, having the control of command and weaponry, is in a position to alter its terms of employment and dictate to the host government." But this, he explained, was not a realistic concern, mainly because of the number of private contractors typically deployed at any given place. "I cannot recall any instance where we have put more than a hundred people on the ground, and it is usually much fewer," he wrote. But that was in the 1990s.

By the time Spicer was signing the International Code of Conduct, he had been in the business of private soldiering long enough that he was becoming a visionary of sorts, although his enemies would have disagreed. Still, it would be hard for anyone to refute the fact that he was among the first to see the sun setting on the old world of Cold War mercenaries, and to witness the sun rising on a new industry of companies usurping the military and security roles of nation-states.

By 2010, Spicer was often quoted in articles about global security, maritime risks, and Iraq. He was interviewed on talk shows, featured at industry conferences, and called into high-level government meetings for security consultations and assessments. Articles about Aegis and its CEO less frequently commented on the shadowy details of the Arms to Africa scandal, the New Guinea jail episode, his tie to coup-plotter Simon Mann, or the controversy over the shooting of Peter McBride. Instead, they dwelled on new information about the PMSC industry's rising star.

The well-known British journalist Stephen Armstrong began an article and a TV interview with the observation: "Tim Spicer is the future of warfare." Another writer described him as "the closest thing to the father of the private security and military industry." And although journalists were still relatively skeptical, the contrast between Spicer's past and his dramatic rise drew them in, as if he had been to a dark kingdom where few dared to go and had learned things that might be useful to know. Or perhaps it was simply that alluring aura of intrigue that so-called mercenaries projected and that lingered long after the shareholders and board members had taken over.

In 2010, Spicer agreed to an interview with the author of this book, a few blocks away from the K Street offices of Aegis LLC in Washington. Tan and well dressed, he looked like an investment banker on holiday. It was hard to imagine him in a Papua New Guinea jail cell or surrounded by rebels in Sierra Leone during a mission to overthrow the government. To be sure, Spicer swinging a nine iron seemed more probable than Spicer toting an AK-47.

Alternately daunting and charming, confident and defensive, witty and somber, he spoke for a long while about the evolution of "the sector," as he called the PMSC industry. "The American companies came later," he said. "The British were earlier, sixties, seventies, eighties, nineties." And why Britain? "History of empire. Part of our past. It's sort of, well, we've been around doing this sort of thing."

Spicer saw the trajectory of PMSCs as analogous to the history of the American railroad industry. "At first, they were accused of everything, but they were essential, as the world was changing and they in turn changed the world," he said. The global frontier was like America's Wild West to him, so the analogy made sense to him. He added yet another analogy, for his industry: "You start off wild and then become part of the establishment. Experimental music becoming mainstream. It's like rap. Took twenty years. And now? What's all the fuss about?"

What should cause a real fuss, from his point of view, was not how the private sector was behaving but rather how the public sector was failing its security and defense mandates, letting citizens down all over the world. It wasn't as much of an issue that the PMSCs were threatening democracy as it was that the democracies were threatened by economic and geopolitical instabilities that the PMSCs could tackle more successfully than the public sector, in his opinion. "You can't have huge standing armies. That is not efficient or economically feasible. You have to be able to draw on a labor pool that is skilled. You pay for the recruitment of soldiers, the training, sustainment, forever. Every twenty-four hours, he costs you money. Health care until he dies. A contractor—hire him for a special purpose and then fire him. You hire him and fire him. Oil. Water. Food. Pirates. Support of future military operations where you want to get involved."

The future for "the sector," he stressed, wasn't about identifying geographical areas and getting work there. It wasn't about Iraq or Afghanistan or Africa. It was about roles and functions, having all services available to go anywhere needed. "Military expeditionary operations wherever that happens," he said. "NGOs, disaster relief, famine, earthquake, you name it. Support to customs control on the Mexican-American border. Training in Mexico."

Spicer was a determined man, with intense blue eyes that could stare down a leopard. Yet there was part of him that always seemed to be somewhere else, as if all the recognition in the world couldn't really satisfy him. He had an aura of restlessness, sending a message that his "unorthodox" adventure was far from over.

Spicer's favorite book was Evelyn Waugh's Sword of Honour trilogy, a classic work about war, religion, and politics set in World War II. Its three volumes—*Men at Arms, Officers and Gentlemen,* and *The End of the Battle*—were mischievous and somber but mostly satirical. What was important, from Spicer's view, was that Waugh modeled the story on the life of commandos and the regimental life in the British Army. The main character, he said, was "much more concerned about his regiment than his nation." The book was meaningful to him because "they were fighting for their friends in the context of a strategic purpose. Tribal identity with your regiment is most important. Group cohesion more than national ideological obligations. He shows that, plus it's terribly funny and well written. And it's so relevant, to now."

12

A THICKET OF IRONIES

In *The Irony of American History*, the eminent American ethicist and theologian Reinhold Niebuhr described irony as the unexpected incongruities in life that upon closer examination are not so incongruous after all. For example, he wrote, "If virtue becomes vice through some hidden defect in the virtue; if strength becomes weakness because of the vanity to which strength may prompt the mighty man or nation; if security is transmuted into insecurity because too much reliance is placed upon it; if wisdom becomes folly because it does not know its own limits—in all such cases the situation is ironic."

In the story of the rise of private military and security companies, irony was abundant. That an industry making its living from instability and conflict called itself "the peace and stability industry" was perhaps the most obvious example. That a soldier in the U.S. Special Forces whose dream of becoming an SF officer was shattered by a bullet shot by a man working for a company employed by the soldier's government, a company that was part of an industry rooted in the history of Special Forces, was another. And the fact that the U.S. State Department defined democracies around the world as those nations in which militaries were accountable to civil authority, while in the United States there were private militaries sometimes legally unaccountable to civil authority, was yet another.

For Aegis and for Spicer, an ironic situation surfaced in August 2010 when Aegis established a new nonoperating holding company in Basel, Switzerland, and newspaper headlines branded the company "a mercenary outfit." In the fourteenth and fifteenth centuries, the Swiss were renowned for their excellent mercenaries; the nation has the oldest mercenary unit still in operation—the Swiss Guards protecting the Vatican. Still, Swiss politicians fretted over the arrival of what they publicly referred to as "the mercenary Aegis." The Swiss foreign minister even commissioned a probe into how the presence of such a firm might affect the world's perception of Swiss military neutrality. Could Aegis truly be called a "mercenary outfit"?

Earlier in the year, at hearings of the bipartisan Commission on Wartime Contracting on Capitol Hill, a University of Maryland professor had asked Aegis LLC's president, Kristi Clemens Rogers, if Tim Spicer was a mercenary. She did not deny that he had been a mercenary in his past, but, she explained, he had acted only on behalf of "governments that were Western-Allied governments." Very soon, however, it wouldn't really matter what the PMSCs were called. "Everyone was busy trying to identify, label, vilify what was really part of the past, the dogs of war," said Congresswoman Marcy Kaptur, "while something big had developed that obviously needed to be dealt with. Whether you called it mercenary or not it was happening."

The mercenary scare in Switzerland that August was an event of minor significance, for, as Kaptur said, things were happening on a grander scale, though unnoticed, and greater ironies were taking shape. While President Obama told Americans about the upcoming drawdown in Iraq, Secretary of Defense Robert Gates announced a 10 percent decrease in the Department of Defense budget for private military contractors. This looked like the action the industry "abolitionists" were hoping for, but that was not the case. Behind the scenes, PMSCs were competing for the State Department's $10 billion Worldwide Protective Services contract. While the DOD was planning to shrink its budget for private contractors, the State Department was raising the WPS contract from $2 billion to $10 billion.

One of the eight companies winning a piece of the $10 billion contract was International Development Solutions, a private security firm recently purchased by Xe, the former Blackwater—"a blandly named cut-out" of Blackwater, as one writer put it. Only a few months earlier, Senate Armed Services Committee Chairman Carl Levin, a Democrat from Michigan, had railed against Blackwater for "setting up shell companies in order to keep winning government security contracts." "Do we check these things out?" asked Levin at a February 24 hearing. "Do we ask for references. They make representations here which are wildly false. It is Blackwater. It is just a shell. It is just the name changed." But the contract was awarded despite presidential candidate Hillary Clinton's pledge in 2008 to ban Blackwater from federal contracts and "to show these contractors the door."

And while the news of withdrawing troops and cutting the defense budget gave Americans the illusion that the need for private military and security support must be ending, the militarization was taking another form. The government was expanding its paramilitary security forces—sending the bill to the State Department—to allow a replacement, task by task, of the jobs necessary to make Iraq a secure place for development. Despite economic recessions and global instability, this industry would actually grow based in part on those very uncertainties, which was one of the biggest ironies of all.

Aegis too was one of the WPS winners, contracted to train private security contractors to replace troops in Iraq and Afghanistan. By now, Aegis was one of the brightest stars in the PMSC galaxy, with its U.S. contract in Iraq twice renewed, having garnered nearly $700 million from work with the Pentagon (on the way to over $1 billion). It operated one national command center and six regional branches across Iraq, out of which it provided daily intelligence for every security firm and the U.S. military, serving as the bridge between the coalition forces and the contractors. Since the 2007 renewal of its Department of Defense contract in Iraq, Aegis had won other sizable contracts, including one from the DOD to oversee private military and security companies in Afghanistan, monitoring their activity, and investigating any "escalation-of-force incidents." The firm was also finding work in Africa, turning its attention to oil and thus following the lead of other PMSCs, such as Control Risks Group, Erinys, Triple Canopy, and ArmorGroup. The Niger Delta, for example, had become a bonanza for such companies, as Nigerian officials hired them to subdue violence in the oil-rich region. There was work too in Algeria and Sudan, as well as Yemen and Djibouti, where Aegis had recently entered negotiations with the governments to set up a control center that would monitor the piracy threat and disseminate risk information to vessels transiting the Gulf of Aden.

In 2010, government contracts were still the most lucrative, and Aegis received a positive evaluation from the Special Inspector

General for Iraq Reconstruction (SIGIR), the watchdog for the Iraq reconstruction contracts, which would surely boost the company's respectability. In the report, the SIGIR commended Aegis's financial record-keeping and control of inventories, and said that the firm adhered to proper personnel screening and selection processes.

On the occasion of the audit, columnist David Isenberg wrote a piece for UPI with the headline "Dogs of War: Contractors Fulfilling a Contract—Imagine That." He began his article with the question of whether it was possible for a "PMC to do a good job, to do what it is contracted to do without waste, fraud, or abuse? Of course, the answer is yes."

For a company with a history like Aegis's to reach this point was monumental. Aegis, wrote Isenberg, was now "considered to be a model contractor." The audit was clearly a defining moment, one that would distance the firm from mercenary images and draw more attention to its strategies and developments as a thriving enterprise. In 2010, the components of its success were becoming apparent—for example, more board members with political connections. That year, Aegis LLC added two former senior CIA officials from the Bush administration to its board of directors. One was Robert Reynolds, who once headed the CIA's procurements office, and the other was the former number-two man in the CIA's National Clandestine Service. Both would help Aegis work with the agency when appropriate.

Crucial to the company's success was its continued focus on public relations, which from the start had been almost revolutionary, especially considering this was a business renowned for its secrecy. Aegis even opened a charity, the Aegis Foundation, to help dispel the image of money-making mercenaries. Its projects, largely in postconflict communities of Iraq and Afghanistan, were mostly grassroots, such as installing water purification systems in schools, donating generators for hospitals, and providing furniture for orphanages. In one case, it teamed up with the oil concern Gulf Region South to spend $450,000 to refurbish a gym in Basra, giving the eighteen and younger children a place to congregate.

Another tactic for escaping the mercenary aura was litigation, or at least the threat of it. The U.S. government used SIGIR as a watchdog, but Aegis had one of London's leading law firms as its pit bull. And in its earlier years when it was trying to shape its image and downplay its founder's colorful past, Aegis had a reputation for being litigious, particularly among journalists. However, as it began to win respectability, the need to protect its CEO lessened. Success became the new armor for Spicer. Ironically, with time, Spicer's wild and unconventional past had become a component of his own success story—the *before* making the *after* all the more impressive.

In late autumn 2010, as the new multibillion-dollar State Department security contract in Iraq revealed a shift from military to security operations reliant on PMSCs, another rather significant irony surfaced. And that was that the president whom the industry feared would curtail its work—especially after Obama's and Clinton's pledges in 2008 to escort the contractors out the door—had made possible an expansion in the number of private military and security forces. This was proof that by 2011 the PMSCs were so embedded they had become a fact of life.

PART III

EXPANSION

13

SHELL GAMES

Three hundred fifty miles southwest of Santa Fe, forty miles north of the Mexican border, and nine miles down the road from an abandoned copper smelter at the edge of the Chihuahuan Desert sits the town of Playas, New Mexico. The smelter and the town, which was built for the smelter workers, were both once owned by the Phelps Dodge Corporation. But in the late 1990s, Phelps Dodge closed the smelter, laid off all but a few workers, and in 2003, put the town up for sale. With its homes and schools, rodeo ring, bowling alley, shooting range, helicopter pad, and even its own zip code, Playas had a price tag of $3.2 million.

Isolated in New Mexico's sparsely populated boot-heel region and situated in a county where nearly 30 percent of the population fell below poverty level, Playas appeared to be a dusty desert town with little appeal. However, the town drew more attention than expected, and in 2004, Phelps Dodge sold it for nearly $5 million. The official buyer was New Mexico Institute of Mining and Technology—New Mexico Tech (NMT), as it was called—based in nearby Socorro, New Mexico. But behind the scenes, the backer of the purchase was the then relatively new U.S. Department of Homeland Security. The remote location and even the poverty were hardly obstacles to the U.S. government. In fact, they were assets, as the government's vision for Playas was to develop it into a counterterrorism training site. If such a transformation prevented Playas from turning into a ghost town and even supplied new jobs, then who among the few who still lived there would object to the sound of helicopters simulating attacks on terrorists or the sight of commandos circling deserted cul-de-sacs of former residential neighborhoods?

The Playas Training and Research Center, as the new facility would be called, would offer coursework such as the analysis of "anarchist literature." But the main feature would be the realistic training facilitated by the layout of the town, which was surrounded by mountainous landscape and desert. One section of it, for example, would become a community populated by 200 or so Afghan-born or first-generation Afghan-Americans hired to help prepare American troops for what they might encounter in Afghanistan. A Santa Fe reporter described it as a combination of "the realistic environment of the FBI's Hogan's Alley, a mock town in Quantico, Virginia, and the classroom strategy of the Western Hemisphere Institute for Security Cooperation (formerly called the School of the Americas) at Fort Benning, Georgia."

The new Playas opened in 2004, and for the next seven years its client base consisted mostly of first responders or U.S. military personnel. Then in March 2011, its clientele shifted to private military and security contractors training to replace the U.S. military in Iraq and eventually in Afghanistan. New Mexico Tech, specifically the Playas Center, had become a subcontractor to Aegis Defense Services, LLC, under Aegis's State Department Worldwide Protective Services contract. As a subcontractor, NMT would receive approximately $27.5 million.

For a private military and security company to have leased or purchased sites for training was not uncommon in the United States in 2011. The sites were, after all, moneymakers. In addition to training their own employees for whatever contracts they had, the companies had clients, often funded by other government contracts, who used the facilities and the staff for such things as weapons training, one-on-one combat, intelligence analysis, Mexican border security, and more. Blackwater had been one of the first to establish its own training center, which was accessible to the military and to law enforcement agencies for combat tactics and weapons training. Located on 7,000 acres in northeastern North Carolina, it started under the Blackwater name but changed to the United States Training Center. Blackwater claimed in its brochures and on its website that this was the largest military training facility in the nation. In 2007, it opened another, smaller facility at an 80-acre site west of Chicago, first called Blackwater North and later renamed the Impact Training Center. This one served law enforcement agencies throughout the Midwest while the bigger facility was under contract to the Pentagon for intelligence analysis specifically for NATO in the Afghan drug war.

Out West where land could be cheap, remote, and plentiful, there were more such sites, in Nevada, Arizona, and three California counties—Riverside, Imperial, and San Diego. The company that boasted the largest facility west of the Mississippi was SOC, Inc., Special Operations Consulting—officially SOC-SMG, or Special Operations

Consulting–Security Management Group. Based in Minden, Nevada, SOC was founded by a former Navy Seal in 2000 and, like Aegis, was one of the winners of the Worldwide Protective Services contract. On its website it spelled its acronym as standing for "Securing Our Country." And it described its property two hours south of Reno and close to the California border as "4,000 dedicated acres of varying terrain, several multi-purpose pneumatic and flat ranges, special purpose training munitions, simulator systems, state-of-the-art classrooms and both field and facility accommodations."

Despite the thousands of acres devoted to private military training, such sites were for the most part known only to the people in nearby communities or to the clients using them. Among the last things most Americans were thinking about in 2011 was the use of land in the United States to train private contractors to help secure Iraq after the troop withdrawals. Private military contractors were as far from the minds of most Americans as they had been when the war began. After all, the war that had watered the mercenary seed and had expanded the crop of military companies worldwide was ending. Wouldn't companies like Blackwater also shut down? The new inhabitants of Playas knew better.

On October 21, 2011, President Obama declared the Iraq War's end and announced a new day for a self-reliant Iraq. "I can report that, as promised, the rest of our troops in Iraq will come home by the end of the year. After nearly nine years, America's war in Iraq will be over. Over the next two months our troops in Iraq, tens of thousands of them, will pack up their gear and board convoys for the journey home," the president told the world. But as U.S. soldiers packed their duffle bags, private contractors were en route to Iraq. Joining the thousands of private contractors already operating in Baghdad would be thousands more arriving by the beginning of the

New Year. Using private forces, as journalist Jeremy Scahill put it, was "a backdoor way of continuing a substantial US presence under the cover of 'diplomatic security.'"

The official end of the war set into motion a political shell game. At an October 12 hearing of the House Committee on Oversight and Government Reform, Subcommittee on National Security, Homeland Defense, and Foreign Operations, Jason Chaffetz, a Utah Republican congressman, told his colleagues, "When President Obama tells the American people the forces will be out of Iraq, I'm not sure the average American will understand that the troops will be replaced with a private army of security contractors."

Indeed, the plan was that after the withdrawal of the troops, the State Department effectively would be taking over the role of the Pentagon in Iraq, funding the contracts for as many as 8,000 PMSCs to work within the walls of the largest embassy in the world. The 104-acre embassy on the Tigris River with its 21 buildings might even have to expand to accommodate its vast community of private contractors. Roughly half of the State Department's diplomatic security budget for 2012 would be slated for the embassy, its staff, and its security. The number of personnel under the authority of the U.S. ambassador was set to increase from 8,000 to about 16,000, half of which would be the PMSCs. Some were contracted to be armed guards, protecting personnel leaving the embassy, including the staff responsible for tasks such as selling the $13 billion in arms used during the war. Others were hired to defuse explosives and still others would be part of armed response teams. Many would be performing quasi-military functions, doing everything expected of soldiers except for going out on patrols to engage the enemy. As an NPR reporter noted in May 2011, the U.S. Army helicopters would be leaving Baghdad in December, but there would still be armed helicopters with pilots and machine gunners employed by DynCorp. "What is clear from the current State Department plan for Iraq is that the United States is going to have armed forces in the country for the foreseeable future," wrote Scahill.

In addition to the embassy in Baghdad, the State Department would be running the "tactical operations center" that deployed armed response teams and at least five military/security posts—called "Enduring Presence Posts"—at military bases in Iraq. To support its private paramilitary force and to prepare for its new responsibilities, during the spring of 2010 the State Department asked Congress and the Pentagon for military equipment that included 24 Black Hawk helicopters and at least 50 special vehicles resistant to mines. Undersecretary of State Patrick Kennedy had explained, in a letter to the Pentagon, that there were "items of equipment only available from the military" and designated as necessary for what would be tasks "of a magnitude and scale of complexity unprecedented in the history of the Department of State." Kennedy defined those jobs contracted to PMSCs as "not military functions."

But some members of Congress present at the October 12 hearing of the House Subcommittee on National Security were more concerned about the specific functions of the PMSCs than the nomenclature, or even the numbers. Whether the contractors were defined as security or military, they were still under contract to the State Department. As Representative John Tierney of Massachusetts said at the hearing: "I understand the department will employ a number of contractors who will be responsible for rapid response to security situations in the field, in addition to the stationary security forces who will be responsible for our protecting the embassy. These rapid response forces will be responsible for emergency response, including security for State Department employees in the case of an attack. In my mind, this situation would almost certainly require the private security contractors to engage in combat." Added Jason Chaffetz, "So, as the defense department winds down, the state department is ramping up. [What could] be more of a political shell game than a drawdown of forces?"

For most Americans, the apparent end of the war implied the end of the private-contractor era—an inference that was easily surmised as evidence of the PMSC presence began to disappear. There had been no recent reports of misconduct. The name Blackwater was no longer visible on newspaper front pages. But there would be ongoing contracts in Iraq, and the soldiers coming home would potentially provide thousands of new PMSC recruits. Whether it was the aftermath of the Hundred Years War in the fourteenth century or the Cold War in the twentieth, the end of wars and the homecoming of troops either spawned private military and security forces or bolstered existing ones. This time, the process was spurred by the White House Joining Forces initiative, a program to help U.S. servicemen and women find jobs after returning home—a good cause for veterans, obviously, and just as good for the PMSCs. DynCorp would soon add more than 7,000 veterans to a workforce composed of about 60 percent veterans.

Long after the troops had returned home, the PMSCs and the diplomatic personnel would be representing America in Iraq and the region. The importance of Iraq to the United States strategically and geopolitically had not diminished, and the stability of Iraq's infrastructure was uncertain. Yet after the troops withdrew, both the security and the image of the United States were entrusted in part to an industry that was not yet officially regulated, that did not have the accountability of the traditional military, and that was not necessarily imbued with national allegiance or love of country. A concerned member of Congress's Commission on Wartime Contracting commented that the presence of such a large force of private contractors would increase the chances that "people acting in the name of the U.S. can get the U.S. involved in perceptions of misconduct."

The strategic importance of the private contractors in the aftermath of the withdrawal showed the entrenchment of the industry. By 2011, the industry seemed to have become an integral part of what Andrew Bacevich in *The Limits of Power* called America's national security state, which consisted of the armed services (including the Joint Chiefs of Staff and the Secretary of Defense), the various intelligence agencies, the staff of the National Security Council, the State Department, and the FBI—and now, it appeared, the private security industry.

The national security state was intended to serve the public and yet, as "a large permanent and ever-expanding" apparatus, it was highly secretive. While the expressed intention of such secrecy was to shield the truth from America's enemies, its actual purpose, wrote Bacevich, was "to control the information provided to the American people, releasing only what a particular agency or administration is eager to make known, while withholding (or providing in sanitized form) information that might embarrass the government or call into question its policies." In place since the end of the Second World War, its objective changed in the aftermath of 9/11 when the U.S. began a policy of preventive war, undertaking a campaign against states posing a potential security threat and targeting not only terrorists but also the states that supported them.

In defining preventive war, historian Arthur Schlesinger, Jr., once said, "If we don't act today, something horrible will happen tomorrow." While most Americans saw force as a last resort and war as something to avoid, the national security state's shift to preventive war, meant, as Bacevich pointed out, that "for the United States war had become a permanent condition." It also meant that unless the draft was reinstituted or the power elite in the national security state was willing to reveal what was needed to pursue such a policy and to ask Congress for the support, there would have to be a way to fill the gap between the vision and its execution. The solution was the PMSCs. Thus, using the industry to secure both Baghdad and Kabul after the military withdrew made perfect sense. And if the president did not reveal the role of the private military and security sector in America's foreign policy, that also was not surprising as it was consistent with the secrecy of the national security state.

President Eisenhower's concern in 1961 about the military-industrial complex was perhaps more applicable than ever. "The potential for the disastrous rise of misplaced power exists and will persist," he had said. However, in the twenty-first century, calling it the military-and-security-industrial or even security-industrial complex was more appropriate. But no president in recent years had dared to warn Americans about it. The words of warning this time came from a congressional commission.

In August 2011, after three years of studying federal contractors in Iraq and Afghanistan, the Commission on Wartime Contracting issued a final report that sent a message of urgency. The 240-page study included assessments of contingency contracting in the State Department and USAID, as well as the DOD. And the foreword began: "Contractors represent more than half of the U.S. presence in the contingency operations in Iraq and Afghanistan, at times employing more than a quarter-million people." It ended with a strident warning: "Delay and denial are not good options. There *will* be a next contingency, whether the crisis takes the form of overseas hostilities or domestic response to a national emergency like a mass-casualty terror attack or natural disaster. Reform will save lives and money, and support U.S. interests. Reform is essential. Now."

When David Isenberg, the Beltway writer who persistently probed the industry, told his readers about the report in his Huffington Post blog, he described the day of its release as "the rubber hits the road day" for those following the saga of the PMSCs. Isenberg praised the hard work of the eight commissioners, who had conducted numerous hearings and hundreds of interviews, had traveled often to Iraq and Afghanistan, and had worked out of offices in Baghdad and Kabul. Using the headline "War and Private Contractors: Can't Live with Them, Can't Live Without Them," he alluded to one of the most important sections of the report, about U.S. dependence on the industry: "Because the heavy reliance on contractors has overwhelmed the government's ability to conduct proper planning, management, and oversight of the contingency-contracting function, the Commission concludes that the government is *over-reliant* on contractors."

For the uninformed reader, parts of the report must have seemed almost like fiction, for some of the facts defied previous assumptions. Other parts just didn't seem possible. For example, the category of spending called "Miscellaneous Foreign Contractors" totaled $38.5 billion out of the $206 billion spent on contracts since 2002. The commissioners could not determine what that category might have been used for or which companies benefited from it. Also, after a thorough analysis of spending, they calculated that from at least $31 billion to as much as $60 billion had been lost to waste and fraud. Isenberg wrote, "Clearly, if one could bring back Willy [*sic*] Sutton from the dead, he would be a private contractor, not a bank robber."

Of grave concern, considering the shift from the Department of

Defense to the State Department for the job of managing the U.S. presence in Iraq and Afghanistan after troop withdrawals, the commissioners claimed that the State Department had not made necessary changes for good governance of the many private contractors it would soon have under its authority. In fact, the State Department had a shaky record of overseeing armed security, they said—a statement that would later prove prescient. An earlier study had shown that many of the contractor abuses in Iraq for the first several years were caused by those working for the State Department, not for the Pentagon. The commissioners stressed that this could result in "significant additional waste and mission degradation to the point of failure."

The report was dark. And it was bold. The commissioners unveiled one shocking detail after another. They even looked at private-contractor casualties, a taboo topic though close to the heart of the reason for America's dependence on PMSCs. Between October 2001 and July 2011, there had been 2,429 contractor deaths in Iraq and Afghanistan, and 6,131 American military deaths. And in the period between June 2009 and March 2011, contractor deaths, including local- and third-country nationals, actually exceeded military casualties in both countries.

Private-contractor casualties were never publicized and thus, after troop withdrawals, the American public would not have any idea about the full human cost of American involvement in Iraq and Afghanistan. No matter where the United States sent PMSCs to represent it, the footprint would be invisible to most Americans, largely because of the silent deaths of private warriors. "The extensive use of contractors obscures the full human cost of war," the commissioners had written. "The full cost includes all casualties, and to neglect contractor deaths hides the political risks of conducting overseas contingency operations. In particular, significant contractor deaths and injuries have largely remained uncounted and unpublicized by the U.S. government and the media." They added that such casualties were "undoubtedly higher" than any reported totals. This was because the government's figures were based on insurance claims, "and many foreign contractors' employees may be unaware of their insurance rights and therefore unlikely to file for compensation."

Of equal concern to the commissioners was the issue of contractors' outsourcing and subcontracting their work, recruiting increasingly from war-torn nations with high levels of poverty and unemployment, such as Namibia, Uganda, Mozambique, and Burundi—an issue that Jan Schakowsky had discussed in 2007. In one of its earlier reports, in 2010, the commission had revealed an array of statistics regarding the nationalities of PMSC employees in Iraq and Afghanistan, including estimates from the South African Foreign Affairs Ministry showing 10,000 South African nationals, mostly former police officers and soldiers, working mostly in Iraq. Other countries supplying workers were Nepal, Colombia, Peru, Chile, Honduras, and the Philippines.

At the Baghdad embassy, the final report noted, roughly 75 percent of the PMSC personnel would be Third World nationals. Triple Canopy, for example, the firm contracted to guard the diplomats, had often employed Ugandans and Peruvians, according to a 2010 State Department audit of the company, noted in the report. And a significant portion of those employees had not been held to what the audit called "English language proficiency standards." If the embassy were to be attacked, the guards would be responsible for telling hundreds of English-speaking occupants what to do. This troubled the commissioners. DynCorp and Erinys also hired workers from Third World nations, especially in Africa.

In their recommendations for reforms, the commissioners suggested more rigorous vetting of subcontractors. They also called for improved coordination among agencies using PMSCs in contingency operations, and they believed that the posts of those civilian officials responsible for contingency contracting at DOD, State, and USAID should be elevated in the government hierarchy. There should also be a permanent inspector general, they wrote, to oversee all contracted contingency operations.

Among the commissioners' numerous discoveries was the fact that out of hundreds of private military and security companies in many countries, only a small percentage won the big governmental contracts. And they likened such elitism to the financial-services industry. "Because the U.S. government relies on only a handful of contractors to provide most of the support for the contingencies in Iraq and Afghanistan, this reliance potentially presents a situation analogous to the U.S. financial industry's 'too big to fail' calamity."

The commission's conclusion was, however, not so surprising. Contractors, they wrote, "will remain a significant element of the U.S. government's total force." Because government agencies lacked the "organic capacity" to perform all the necessary functions American foreign policy demanded, the U.S. government was "forced to treat contractors as the default option." Because of the innumerable flaws thus far in this public-private partnership, "the need for reform is urgent." The last line of the report was "The nation's security demands nothing less than sweeping reform."

Because of the commission's report and all that it revealed about U.S. dependence on PMSCs; because of the U.S. troop withdrawals and the "replacement" role that the companies would play in Iraq; and because of broadening markets for PMSCs worldwide, beyond Iraq and Afghanistan, even beyond war zones, 2011 would prove to be a banner year in the industry's quest to slip into the establishment. It could be called the Year of Entrenchment.

It was the first year since 2004 that there were no shocking headlines drawing worldwide attention to PMSCs. It was the year that the U.K. and the U.S., in response to the work begun at Montreux, would cooperate with industry leaders to lay the groundwork for a self-regulatory authority based in Geneva—a new organization that would serve as a watchdog, granting accreditation or withdrawing it if companies did not respect the International Code of Conduct. And in a year when so many businesses were faltering in the ongoing worldwide economic struggle, it was a time of growth for PMSCs— by some accounts, at rates from 8 percent to 15 percent. After all, economic troubles led to more instability and conflict, which in turn generated more work for these companies.

When New Mexico Tech announced its big new contract with Aegis to use the Playas Center for training private contractors to go to Iraq, the school's vice president of research and development, Dr. Van Romero, assured the public that the school was "not getting into the business of training mercenaries." He explained that the school's training focused on the ability "to peacefully interact with people in their cultural environment. We have role players who are actually Afghanis, we have an Afghan village, and that's what they're learning." Then, as if the trajectory of the rise of the private military industry suddenly flashed before him, he moved on to the core issue of money. "There's unrest in the world," said Dr. Romero. "And that doesn't hurt us."

14

BEYOND IRAQ

By the time President Obama announced the withdrawal of American troops from Iraq, PMSCs were in line to collect billions of dollars in contracts for at least another five years. They included SOC, Inc. (the firm with the extensive training site in Nevada, whose contract to safeguard the Baghdad embassy would bring in nearly $1 billion), Triple Canopy (a five-year $1.53 billion contract for embassy security), ArmorGroup, Control Risks Group, DynCorp, Erinys, and Aegis. And as always, there were many smaller firms working as subcontractors, though these were not listed on the government's Baghdad Embassy website. What was noted on the site, however, was a rather big caveat: "The U.S. government assumes no responsibility for the professional ability or integrity of the persons or firms whose names appear on the list."

These contracts hardly resembled the feeding frenzy of the Iraq

War, but they were lucrative for several firms and resulted in new PMSCs surfacing in Iraq, some without track records and many in search of subcontracts. There were, in fact, enough unknown firms with unfamiliar names popping up in Baghdad that some underwriters at Lloyd's of London were uneasy. Insurers typically demanded that these companies produce what were called security protocols from the military if the companies wanted insurance for operating in unstable environments.

The Iraqi contracts would cushion some of the top firms during the industry's transition from wartime. And while the gold rush in Iraq was ending, the pursuit for the next rush of markets had already begun. Where exactly were these markets? Wherever instability threatened development; wherever the military commitments of states exceeded their capacities; wherever preventive war was a ruling principle; wherever governments were viewed as incapable of supplying defense and security fast enough in times of sudden conflict; wherever maritime terrorists threatened the shipping industry; and wherever kings, dictators, or presidents felt endangered by mass protests, such as the nations involved in what became known as the Arab Spring in 2011.

To be sure, there was plenty of work for PMSCs during the Arab Spring, especially protecting companies trying to operate in the midst of the political unrest. For example, in Bahrain, where Aegis had an office in Manama, the capital, the firm, according to its own release, implemented a "crisis management plan" for an unnamed multinational energy company and evacuated 100 or more people.

A few months after the protests abated, the United Nations released a study showing that the use of "mercenaries in armed conflict" had vastly increased in recent years. Examples included Arab countries during the spring protests. Muammar Gaddafi, it noted, had brought in hired guns from Eastern Europe and from African nations to fight prodemocracy protestors. Although leaders in the PMSC industry argued that the hired guns in the Arab Spring were not the companies that formed the backbone of their industry, there were clearly some mainstream companies acting as brokers of combatants deployed to stop the protests. The U.N. stressed that the presence of private forces, whether employed by companies or self-employed, was growing worldwide without enough control to stop "an onslaught of human rights problems."

But even the United Nations had begun to employ PMSCs. Since its inception, the U.N. had relied on governments to send peacekeepers to guard U.N. personnel in hostile environments. For years, its committees and councils had been critical and watchful of what were often described as "mercenary" operations. What, then, had changed? Mainly, it was the rising number of U.N. relief workers who had been killed or kidnapped in recent years—for example, the Taliban killing five U.N. employees in Pakistan in October 2009. That year, the former head of diplomatic security for the U.S. Department of State, Gregory Starr, became the U.N. top security official. Starr had been a proponent of PMSCs in both Iraq and Afghanistan, and when pressed by a reporter about the possibility of privatized U.N. forces, he declined to comment. A U.N. spokesman then tried to explain the organization's intentions, falling back on definitions and nomenclature. "He [Starr] wanted you to know that our understanding of the current usage of the term 'Private Security Contractors' typically refers to contractors doing close protection work for movement security, such as Blackwater/Xe, Triple Canopy, DynCorp, Aegis and many other companies providing this type of service. However, the U.N. doesn't avail itself of this type of service. We do use some private companies to provide static security guards at some sites in Afghanistan and Pakistan."

This was a controversial move for the United Nations. Using PMSCs instead of government peacekeepers sent the message, as one former U.N. peacekeeping official said, that "we care about you, but not to the point of risking our own boys." But U.N. Secretary-General Ban Ki-moon told the press in early 2010 that the U.N. "will have to turn to the private sector to protect its people." That year, the United Nations had contracted a subsidiary of a London-based PMSC to provide several hundred Nepalese Gurkhas to guard U.N. officials in Afghanistan. And humanitarian organizations were reporting that U.N. peacekeepers had been "quietly turning to private security, particularly in hazardous stations like Somalia and Afghanistan." Private-sector support allowed the U.N. to continue its work in environments that were becoming more and more dangerous, as U.N. officials acknowledged.

In 2010, the U.N. spent $75.7 million for "security services," a 73 percent increase from 2009. That figure rose to $113.8 million in 2011. And in 2012 the total cost for U.N. private security contracts would go even higher, to $124.3 million—an increase of about 300 percent since 2009. In a report entitled "Contracting Insecurity: Private Military and Security Companies and the Future of the United Nations," the Global Policy Forum, which monitors international organizations, including the United Nations, noted the difficulty in defining "security services" and cautioned that the U.N.'s statistics were "not an exact reflection of reality." However, the figures nonetheless showed a "rapid increase in the use of security service firms."

A far bigger market, however, and one of the fastest-growing businesses for PMSCs, was maritime security, which received an immense boost from the U.S. State Department. In late October

2011, U.S. Secretary of State Hillary Clinton sent a memo asking diplomats to promote "the use of privately contracted armed security personnel on merchant vessels to deter or prevent pirating off the Horn of Africa." For the shipping industry, this was a momentous and surprising endorsement of PMSCs. Clinton, after all, had been a strong critic in 2008 of the use of PMSCs in Iraq and Afghanistan. Some of the same players in both wars were entering the burgeoning marketplace for maritime security.

The maritime memo drew little attention in the mainstream media, but the use of armed security on ships had been intensely debated in the shipping industry, which had been reluctant to place armed guards on board. Now the U.S. State Department was not only endorsing the action but encouraging it. This was a major victory for companies like Aegis that were strong in maritime security, and also for the former Blackwater, now called Xe Services and soon to be renamed Academi, which even had a 183-foot vessel outfitted for disaster response and maritime-security training. With the focus on the Gulf of Aden, one of the busiest shipping lanes in the world, this was very big business. Also benefiting—especially if armed security did in fact deter piracy—would be the insurance industry, which had been tightly linked to the private security business since the industry's beginnings. Curbing piracy would save lives and would also save the shipping industry's insurers millions of dollars.

Once again, the government was stepping aside and allowing the private sector to sail right in. And it wasn't just off the coast of Somalia. In early November, Andrew J. Shapiro, the assistant secretary of state in the Bureau of Political-Military Affairs, spoke to the Defense Trade Advisory Group to explain the State Department's thinking. "With so much water to patrol it is difficult for international naval forces in the region to protect every commercial vessel.

Working with the industry, we recently established a national policy encouraging countries to allow commercial ships transiting high-risk waters to have armed security teams on board. The reason for this is simple: to date no ship with an armed security team aboard has been successfully pirated. We believe that the expanded use of armed security teams by commercial vessels is a major reason why we have seen a decline in the number of successful pirate attacks this year. Therefore, we have recently demarched countries to permit the use of privately contracted armed security personnel on commercial vessels. And we are also working with industry and transit countries to make it less onerous for privately contracted security personnel to transit foreign ports with weapons intended for the self-defense of ships."

In America, too, business was picking up for PMSCs. The idea of preventive war at home was seeping into the collective consciousness of Americans, echoing that familiar rationale for using private-sector security when governments appeared unable to come through with mandates to safeguard its citizens. Case in point: the Mexican-American border.

If unstable environments stimulated the market for PMSCs, then the Mexican-American border was a candidate for another bonanza. Capitalizing on such potential in the summer of 2011 was the firm International Security Agency, or ISA. With headquarters in Houston, ISA employed former Special Forces members as well as former police, and told the press that it had done work in thirty-three nations. Its rationale for security work was, as the *Texas Tribune* described it, "If the government cannot protect its citizens, it's up to the individual."

In August 2011, ISA announced that it had received the "required licenses to operate" in McAllen, Texas, on the Mexican border. At the time, ISA President Jerry Brumley told the press: "I love my country. If I were king or emperor of America, I would do exactly what Ronald Reagan did. [Reagan said,] 'You know what? You hurt an American citizen—I don't care where you are—and I am coming after you.' And we're in America."

In its presentation to the McAllen business community that summer, ISA showed a newsreel clip of a car chase along the U.S. border that ended with one car in the river. Another clip displayed the devastation following the explosion of car bombs on the Mexican side of the border, and an animated rendering of Glenn Beck telling the audience that drug dealers were tantamount to terrorists and that the government would not and could not protect Americans from the violence they caused. In its corporate slide show, the company then informed potential clients about the expertise of its employees, who were trained in military skills and who, as the ISA president implied, had aggressive rules of engagement. The presentation harkened back to Iraq in 2004 or 2005.

"Our practice," said Brumley, "is if someone raises a weapon to me and I feel threatened, with my life or the life of my client, I am taking action. I am not going to lose an American because my rules of engagement say 'Well, you know, they have to shoot at you [first].'" The *Texas Tribune* commented, "[The presentation] demonstrates what a military-style 'cadre' is, complete with a photograph of a camouflaged soldier raising a weapon and taking aim."

ISA, according to its website, required its applicants to be "former military with at least four years of service and an honorable discharge, a federal law or civilian law enforcement officer with at least two years of service, a security officer with six years of experience or a personal protection agent with more than three years of experience." Pay scales ranged from $200 a day per agent, to $2,500 a day depending on the work. The firm's overall quest, as presented in its promotional material, was to stop drug-cartel-instigated violence in the United States before it started—the Wild West version of preventive war.

When asked whether it was appropriate to hire private security firms to guard the border and what his concerns for accountability might be, Texas Governor Rick Perry, then a candidate for the Republican nomination for president, said, through his deputy press secretary: "Let's be clear here: It is the federal government's responsibility to protect Americans by securing the international border between the U.S. and Mexico. Since the federal government is not fulfilling that responsibility, it is unfortunate but not surprising that the citizens living along the U.S.-Mexico border feel so unsafe on their own property that they could be looking to hire personal security."

Quelling fears along the Mexican border promised to become a profitable business, and it extended beyond the realm of guarding homes, individuals, and businesses. There was money to be made, for example, in the crackdown on immigration. PMSCs could run and sometimes own detention centers. This was a high-growth market. In 2005, there were 280,000 detentions and by 2011 there were 400,000. The demand was such that the close proximity to the Mexican border of some training sites—for example, Playas, only forty miles from the border—meant they could easily be used as future detention centers. After all, immigration enforcement had become another growing market for PMSCs, especially in the U.S., U.K., and Australia. By 2011, for example, private contractors controlled half of all immigration detention beds in the United States. Although it was a niche market, it was often identified by analysts as one source of potential growth for the PMSC industry. Detention attracted the large multinational firms known for their vast offerings of what were once government services. G4S, with more than 600,000 employees in 125 countries, was one. G4S owned both the British ArmorGroup and the large American security company Wackenhut. It had been one of the corporate participants in the 2008 meetings at Montreux. As part of its immigration work, it was under contract with the U.S. Department of Homeland Security to escort illegal border-crossers back to Mexico.

But despite the Border Patrol work and immigration-related armed security, PMSCs remained nearly invisible to the American public. That they would continue to have a presence and an influence in Iraq or Afghanistan would have surprised most Americans. But that they would play a bigger role back home, within U.S. borders, would have been more surprising. And yet they were establishing a presence on Main Street. By the fall of 2011, there were dozens of municipalities, counties, and townships in the United States that had hired a private military and security company to train their police forces—often Blackwater. Big cities on the list included Atlanta, Washington, New York City, Chicago, and Los Angeles.

There was no law prohibiting the training of police in military methods. Blackwater figured that out, thus identifying the training of domestic police as a potentially lucrative part of its business, and then cornering the market. In the beginning, the market consisted mainly of the Department of Homeland Security, which was in a hurry to improve local police protection in the event of a terror attack. It was quick to utilize Blackwater's police-training services, funding and supporting police departments nationwide to employ Blackwater. In addition, some municipalities were considering contracting PMSCs for special duties, such as patrolling a city's most dangerous neighborhoods. The theory was that this saved the city money, from insurance benefits and retirement packages to bullet-proof vests and uniforms.

The difference between a police officer trained to "keep the peace" and a soldier was quite easy to identify. A policeman was legally required to protect and to serve the citizens of the state, to assume innocence unless there was a reasonable suspicion of illegal activity, and to use weapons against a citizen only as a last resort. A soldier was trained to identify enemies and if necessary to kill them while protecting any nonenemies in the vicinity. "I stand ready to deploy, engage, and destroy the enemies of the United States of America in close combat" was their creed. And although most policemen trained by a private military company would remain dedicated to their oaths to serve and protect the public, there was the possibility of the exception.

Evidence of potential problems bubbled up in autumn 2011 when the Occupy Wall Street movement inspired demonstrations in U.S. cities and towns and on university campuses, as people protested the greed of what they called "the 1 percent" of the U.S. populace. Although there was no direct involvement of PMSCs, as had been the case in New Orleans during Hurricane Katrina when Homeland Security brought in Blackwater, there were clear signs of the militarization trend in policing. The protests began on September 17 in New York with the occupation of a park near Wall Street. These were nonviolent political protesters using their First Amendment rights to express their views, thus inspiring some journalists to refer to "the American Autumn" following "the Arab Spring." But in early October things began to change. In their black full-battle uniforms armed with assault rifles, sometimes even M4s like the ones the military used in Iraq and Afghanistan, some police began to act the way they looked. In Oakland, for example, police kicked and attacked demonstrators, including war veterans, shooting them in the face with tear-gas canisters. An ex-Marine who had spent two tours of duty in Iraq was hit so hard in the head with a police projectile—while he was texting—that he was taken to a hospital in critical condition and for nearly two months lost his ability to speak. As if in a flashback scene from the disaster at Nisour Square, Oakland police threw a "flash-bang grenade" at the people who ran to help the wounded vet.

In November, a former Washington State peace officer who had earned a Bronze Star and Purple Heart while serving in Iraq teamed up with a lawyer from Arlington, Virginia, to warn in the *Atlantic* about the consequences of bringing military-style training to domestic law enforcement: "When police officers are dressed like soldiers, armed like soldiers, and trained like soldiers, it's not surprising that they are beginning to act like soldiers."

It was a potentially shameful situation for the United States, especially when the U.N., the watchdog of human rights violations across the globe, turned its gaze on the nation that considered itself the world's icon of freedom and human rights. In early December, Frank La Rue, the U.N.'s special envoy for protecting free expression, drafted a memo to the U.S. government demanding to know why it was not protecting the rights of the Occupy Wall Street protestors. From his view, as long as they were peaceful nonviolent demonstrators occupying public spaces, the government had an obligation to protect their rights and not to exert excessive force against them. What was at risk, La Rue wrote, was America's credibility as a model democracy.

In late 2011, another affront to democracy was taking shape as the government was outsourcing jobs to design, maintain, and operate cybercapabilities for national security. This included devising defenses against cyberattacks, and even orchestrating offensive cybertactics. In what some government officials were calling the cybercontractor complex, there was a shift in 2011 from internal defense of the infrastructure to offensive strategies, including cybersurveillance sometimes aimed at American citizens—a startling reality that would soon be exposed to the world by former private contractor Edward Snowden. Equally unsettling was the fact that a few of the new surveillance systems operated by companies under contract to the United States had customers other than the United States.

For the industry, it meant yet another market to inspire "the incubation of new and more powerful capabilities from within the industry [of PMSCs]," as a British journalist wrote. At least cybersecurity was not armed security and it was not on the list of usual services offered by most PMSCs—not yet anyhow.

15

RIDING THE WAVE

In early December 2011, six presidential hopefuls from the Republican Party gathered at Drake University in Des Moines, Iowa, to debate the issues of the day. The publicity leading up to the debate, which aired on ABC, made it sound more like a wrestling match than a political contest, as the main attraction appeared to be the anticipated showdown between front-runner Newt Gingrich, former Speaker of the House, and runner-up Mitt Romney, former governor of Massachusetts. Onstage, Romney and Gingrich took the center podiums. Next to them, from left to right, were the former Pennsylvania Senator Rick Santorum, Texas Governor Rick Perry, Texas Representative Ron Paul, and Minnesota Representative Michele Bachmann. Commentators Diane Sawyer and George Stephanopoulos moderated. The questions as well as the answers were somewhat expected—with one exception.

It happened when Diane Sawyer asked the candidates to comment on the payroll-tax cut that was set to expire on December 31 that year. If the tax cut ended, Sawyer said, "it would add as much as $1,000 to the tax burden of American working families." Congressman Paul had thirty seconds to respond. At first, Paul, a libertarian, commented predictably, as if following a familiar script: "I want to extend the tax cut, because if you don't, you raise the taxes. But I want to pay for it, and it's not that difficult. In my proposal, in my budget, I want to cut hundreds of billions of dollars from overseas. The trust fund is gone, but how are we going to restore it? We have to quit the spending; we have to quit this being the policeman of the world; we don't need another war in Syria and another war in Iran." Then, he moved into unscripted territory and said: "Just get rid of the embassy in Baghdad. We're pretending that we're coming home from Baghdad? We built an embassy there that cost a billion dollars and we're putting 17,000 contractors in there and pretending our troops are coming home."

After that, the camera zoomed out and panned across the stage to show each of the candidates. The rules of the debate allowed for thirty-second rebuttals. But after Paul's comment came only silence. No one else had anything to say. It was as if Paul had opened a door just a crack and invited the others to enter, but instead they slammed it shut without a word.

Despite the bills proposed to enhance transparency and control of private military and security contractors; the advocates for and against them; the Wartime Contracting commissioners' eye-opening report; the work of journalists and scholars trying to sort out the complex PMSC business; the dedication of the Swiss Initiative participants; and the casualties, war profits, and power, there was still little if any public awareness about this industry. Was it possible that these companies were so well integrated into the fabric of American defense and security that there was no incentive for a dialogue? The current president was using them, actually depending on them, perhaps more than ever. Yet they were still all but invisible.

President Obama had proposed reforms in February 2009 to reduce the Pentagon's reliance on private contractors and to increase the number of personnel scrutinizing the contracts. What was called an "insourcing initiative" would reduce the number of contractors in jobs ranging from logistical support to antiterrorism training, and replace them with new full-time government employees—in fact, 33,000 by 2015. Secretary of Defense Robert M. Gates announced the plan on April 6, 2009. But only sixteen months later it fizzled. Gates told the press that he was "not satisfied with the progress made to reduce our over-reliance on contractors."

Dispelling past defeats, Representative Jan Schakowsky was still determined to expose facts about the PMSC industry, repeatedly telling the press and Congress that hiding the truth about these companies and "keeping the knowledge of this force hidden" was damaging the nation. Schakowsky, a woman with big energy, persistence, and drive, would not be deterred. She was especially concerned about the issue of casualties, having introduced legislation to require the government to collect and release the names of all contractors killed and injured. Not telling the American public about contractor casualties, she had told her colleagues back in 2007, "masks the fact that we are privatizing the military in this country."

With new reports showing that contractor casualties in 2010 had exceeded military deaths in both Iraq and Afghanistan, Schakowsky's concern deepened. And as troops exited Iraq, another issue was beginning to surface—contractors who were missing in action. By the fall of 2011, though few Americans knew, there were eight

Americans missing in action in Iraq. One was a U.S. soldier and the other seven were private contractors.

Also under the radar was the exploitation of subcontractors. On the surface, the word was that jobs with PMSCs brought big bucks and great perks. There were the stories about private contractors in Iraq making salaries far exceeding the paychecks of Uncle Sam's traditional troops. But subcontractors were in a different class, as the House Committee on Oversight and Government Reform learned in the fall of 2011. At a hearing entitled "Are Government Contractors Exploiting Workers Overseas?" testimony revealed that tens of thousands of workers hired by PMSCs as subcontractors for very low wages from Third World nations, particularly in Africa, lived in wretched housing, including barbed-wire compounds on U.S. bases, had no insurance or health-care benefits, no compensation if injured, and no access to medical services. Worse still, there were untold numbers of sexual assaults. And yet, as Representative Gerald E. Connolly, a Virginia Democrat, said, "Not a single case of human trafficking, sexual assault, wage theft or related crimes has been prosecuted by the Department of Justice. Neither the Army and Air Force Exchange Service nor any other component of DoD or the State Department has suspended or debarred a single federal contractor for [such abuses], even though they are routine."

At that hearing, both Republicans and Democrats agreed that the American taxpayer was funding work that produced profits for some companies that were guilty of exploiting workers. "These labor practices violate every human value that we have as a country. Our departments of State and Defense stand up and fight for human rights around the globe, but have turned a blind eye to these foreign workers," said Representative James Lankford, a Republican from Oklahoma. "We believe that all men and women are created equal, and the United States must not stand idly by as these injustices occur on a daily basis under our nose."

Another hidden problem was the struggles of contractor veterans. What should they even be called? Contractors injured in Iraq or Afghanistan, sometimes suffering from lifelong disabilities, were not recognized as military veterans. "Politicians pay little attention to their problems, and the military has not publicized their contributions," wrote journalist T. Christian Miller, who won a Pulitzer Prize for smartly exposing the struggles of contractor veterans. But this too was rarely, if ever, mentioned by politicians.

And yet another unrecognized casualty of the privatized wars were the numerous unresolved legal cases involving incidents of abuse and misconduct in Iraq. Delayed often by the jurisdictional complexity of these international businesses and the skill of excellent attorneys whom successful companies could now afford, lawsuits filed against PMSCs dating as far back as 2004 languished, often for many years. A judge in the District of Columbia Court of Appeals, the highest court in Washington, D.C., dismissed such a case in 2010, one that was wandering through a jurisdictional maze. The plaintiff was the father of a young girl who had been fatally shot by the employee of a PMSC one morning in Baghdad in 2007 while she was in a car riding home from church. The defendants were a company based in North Carolina under contract with USAID and a PMSC based in Dubai hired by the USAID contractor for protection. Both had offices in D.C. The father was a U.S. citizen.

There was no doubt that the girl had been shot by the employees of the PMSC. But what jurisdiction had legal authority to allow the lawsuit to move forward? The case had bounced from the U.S. District Court for the District of Columbia to the U.S. District Court for the Eastern District of North Carolina to the Superior Court of the

District of Columbia, then back to North Carolina—this time to state court—and then to the D.C. Court of Appeals, only to be dismissed there. By 2011, it seemed more like a game of hot potato than a quest for justice regarding the murder of an innocent person driving home from church.

After Kadhim Alkanani's suit was reinstated in 2010 in D.C. federal court, the judge asked Kadhim's attorneys to prove the legal rationale for trying the case there. Again, the ongoing issue was jurisdiction. The 2004 contract with the Department of Defense under which Kadhim's shooter had been employed was held by the London-based Aegis. And Aegis's American subsidiary, Aegis LLC, on K Street in D.C., did not open until 2006. Besides, it was not the legal entity under contract with the DOD when the shooting occurred in June 2005. Thus, the defense argued that trying the case in D.C., or anywhere in the United States, was not legally possible. To counter that and to prove that D.C. was where the case should be tried, in 2011 Kadhim's attorneys began to gather evidence, including phone records and travel data, to try to show how much business Aegis was doing in D.C. before the shooting. How many times did Aegis staffers travel to D.C. to attend meetings, luncheons, and dinners in an effort to procure contracts? How many other contracts did they have from U.S. agencies that might prove further presence in the nation? If the firm had secured a contract in the U.S. and profited from it, the attorneys argued, it was taking advantage of business opportunities in the U.S. and thus must be liable and accountable for what it did while conducting that business.

"What comes with opportunity are the laws," said one of Kadhim's attorneys. And as one of the lawyers representing victims of the Abu Ghraib torture incidents said: "We are hoping these cases will make a difference, serve as deterrents, draw attention to the need for heightened accountability. But by now, nearly nine years after the beginning of the [Iraq] war, we are still facing how to make companies accountable, in some cases where there is no question that the crimes took place and yet we are still struggling for justice. Where are the people of conscience on this matter?"

What concerned Schakowsky and other industry critics was that the flow of contracts to PMSCs accused of human rights violations, murders, and bribery, among other transgressions, continued at a faster pace than any resolutions of criminal allegations. Take Blackwater, for example. In December 2009, the judge had dropped all allegations against the four employees charged with the deaths of the 17 Iraqi civilians at Nisour Square in 2007, citing missteps by the Department of Justice. The State Department reportedly did threaten to deny the firm contracts as long as Erik Prince owned the company, but then in the summer of 2010, Prince put his firm, Blackwater, which by then had been renamed Xe Services LLC, up for sale. In mid-December that year, he sold Xe to an L.A.–based consortium of investors, including one who had had a close tie to Blackwater from the start. And by 2011, the case—in which prosectors argued that the contractors used grenades and machine guns in an unprovoked attack, while defense attorneys claimed that Iraqi insurgents had ambushed the contractors—was still under appeal. Meanwhile, there had been new contract awards for Xe, including one during the summer of 2010 for nearly $250 million to work for the CIA and the State Department in Afghanistan and other zones of conflict. At the time of the award, CIA Director Leon Panetta told ABC commentator Jake Tapper, on the show *This Week*, "I have to tell you that in the war zone, we continue to have needs for security. You've got a lot of forward bases. We've got a lot of attacks on some of these bases. You've got to have security. Unfortunately there are few companies that provide that kind of security. The State Department relies on them. And we rely on them to a certain extent. They [Xe, formerly Blackwater] provided a bid that underbid everyone else by about $26 million. And a panel that said that they can do the job, that they have shaped up their act. So there really was not much choice but to accept that contract."

In response to this news, Blackwater's unofficial biographer Jeremy Scahill wrote in the *Nation*, "What we are seeing clearly is the Obama administration not only using Blackwater in sensitive operations globally, but actively defending the company's continued existence as a government contractor in good standing." And, after commenting on Blackwater's payments to Democratic lobbyists in 2010, Scahill went on to say, "No one is paying attention to what should be a major story of Blackwater's thriving second marriage to the current Administration: the money trail." The *Nation* headlined the article: "Blackwater's New Sugar Daddy: The Obama Administration."

Schakowsky's drive to expose the hidden details of the industry was largely Blackwater-inspired—a drive that moved into high gear in autumn 2011 after she received a hand-delivered letter from Washington, D.C., attorney Victoria Toensing, who represented Erik Prince. In the two-page letter, Toensing accused Schakowsky of making "false and defamatory" statements against Prince in a September news article in London. The article described a new video game owned by Prince and called Blackwater. The game was set in a fictional town in North Africa, and it featured a team of Blackwater operatives depicted as heroes. According to Toensing, when the reporter asked Schakowsky to comment on the game, she said, among other things, that, "If Mr. Prince had not emigrated to the United Arab Emirates, which does not have an extradition agreement with the U.S., he too would now be facing prosecution" regarding Blackwater-related incidents.

In the letter, Toensing praised Prince for his military service with "SEAL Team 8 to Haiti, the Middle East, and the Balkans." And she noted examples of "Mr. Prince's support for human rights around the world." This included funding famine relief in Somalia and the Sudan and contributing to the building of hospitals, schools, orphanages, and churches and mosques in the Middle East and Asia. She then went on to say that Schakowsky's statement to the publication was "libelous and malicious." She characterized her earlier efforts to persuade Congress to investigate Prince as an abuse of her congressional power. She stressed the fact that Prince had never committed a crime nor had he ever been charged with one. Neither had he emigrated to the UAE; he maintained a residence in the U.S. And Toensing noted several instances when Representative Schakowsky used Blackwater as an example of problems with private security contractors.

Speaking on the House floor in late November 2011, Schakowsky described the contents of the lawyer's letter to her. Talking in a self-assured, firm tone, as if reminding her colleagues in Congress that she would not be silenced by such a letter, she called it a "heavy-handed tactic: attempted intimidation of a member of Congress. . . . I want to make it clear to Mr. Prince that I will not stop working to end our reliance on private security contractors and to investigate any and all allegations of misconduct." And she was just as outspoken in her comments about her colleagues:

> While many hours have been spent by this body debating the wars in Iraq and Afghanistan, far too little has been devoted to the United States' growing dependence on private military contractors—the weapon-carrying, for-profit security companies—who have become integral, and counterproductive, actors in our war

efforts. I believe that increased reliance on hired guns to provide security in conflict zones undermines our policy objectives. We should be concerned. Private contractors don't wear the badge of the United States. They answer to a corporation, not a uniformed commander. Our government doesn't even know how many contract personnel we've hired.

Before the end of 2011, the company changed its name again, this time to Academi, named after Plato's Academy, the first institution of higher learning in the Western world. Academi's first CEO was Ted Wright, a former executive at KBR, Inc. (successor company to Brown & Root) and the former Xe CEO. Wright wanted a different name to reflect the recent changes in the company's leadership, mainly newcomers to the board of directors and the management. These included former National Security Agency head and CIA executive Bobby Ray Inman; former U.S. Attorney General John Ashcroft; Jack Quinn, the former White House counsel to President Bill Clinton and also former chief of staff to Vice President Al Gore; and the former regulatory compliance officer for the failed insurance giant AIG. Wright also wanted the new name to help shape a low-profile "more boring" image for the company for future work, which he told the *Wall Street Journal*, might be in Iraq, "where demand for security contractors remains high." Industry critics made the predictable claim that the new name was intended to hide the past.

Image, after all, was the ruling factor. At the Pentagon during the first week of 2012, President Obama announced to the American public that he was urging Congress to accept a $500 billion cut in the U.S. military budget over the next decade. Downsizing the military, he stressed, meant that the United States was "turning a page on a decade of war" and moving into a future in which it would have a leaner military without sacrificing its superiority worldwide. This was a strong new strategy that came about, he said, largely because the post 9/11–era wars were coming to an end. Osama bin Laden was dead. The American troops in Iraq had come home. And soon, U.S. soldiers would be leaving Afghanistan. Thus, he told his audience, it was time to cut the military expenditures and change the policy.

The proposal would be hotly debated in Congress, but such a shift was inevitable. For this cut in the defense budget was not just about the end of an era of long wars in Iraq and Afghanistan, and not even just about the budget. What Obama didn't mention was that it was very much about a shift in focus from military to security, from the traditional military to a mix of Special Forces, drones, and private military and security companies that together would provide the backbone of national security and defense.

What was undisclosed was the reality that as the traditional military began to shrink, nontraditional approaches to national security and defense would flourish. Or perhaps it was just the opposite: as the PMSCs grew in strength and numbers, the traditional military could be downsized. Whichever, Obama was riding the wave of change that had already happened by 2012.

Early in the year, in the drawing room of the Special Forces Club in London, Eric Westropp discussed the future of wars and the roles of the private security companies. "[The PMSCs] will evolve into multinational and multifunctional firms so that governments and corporations will go to them as single servers and get used to relying on them. Then they'll succeed more and more, and what seems hidden now will simply be integrated so that future generations won't know the difference. Traditional militaries will become smaller and the industry will continue to grow."

16

AND NOW, THE DEBATE?

"Damn the Torpedoes, Full Speed Ahead!" was the rallying cry of Admiral David G. Farragut at the Battle of Mobile Bay during the Civil War. And in February 2012, it was the screensaver message flashing across Doug Brooks's computer at the headquarters of the International Stability Operations Association (ISOA) on I Street in Washington. From Brooks's office window on the eighth floor, he had a clear view of Farragut Square, a park that featured a statue of the famed Union admiral. As Brooks liked to tell his visitors, Farragut was the first rear admiral, vice admiral, and admiral in the U.S. Navy, especially revered for conquering pirates in the West Indies. Brooks may have known as much about Farragut as he did about the ISOA, which he not only headed but had founded. And he was equally passionate about both, for Brooks was a driven, highly enthusiastic booster whose job was to clarify the mission and capabilities of private military and security companies to the outside world—but not too much. He was, as one writer once described him, "the friendly, public face of a secretive, multibillion dollar business." And thus far, he was as successful in his realm as his hero across the park had been in his.

"The International Stability Operations Association" was the new name for the organization that used to be called the International Peace Operations Association, which Brooks had named when he started it in 2001. Changing the name was his board's decision. And though Brooks didn't advocate the change, he understood why the board did. The use of the word "peace" for a trade group composed of PMSCs was fodder for critics. "They would call it Orwellian," said Brooks.

Disaster relief—such as the work ISOA member Blackwater did during Hurricane Katrina—or landmine removal or military training, as well as peacekeeping, were all about security in a conflict-ridden world, not about war, said Brooks. Although the websites of some of its members might include a snapshot or two of gun-toting men in camouflage fatigues, the ISOA, according to Brooks, promoted ways that "private security companies" could provide much-needed services in an unstable world, even replacing U.N. peacekeepers.

Part of his spiel that day in 2012 was a familiar one. It was about how these companies could turn on a dime and go where they were needed, unlike the traditional forces of nation-states, whose deployment depended on the policies of governments and the political will of the people, and whose size could not quickly expand. And what about earthquakes, floods, and famines? As Brooks liked to say—much like Erik Prince's comment—"Fed-Ex can do things better, faster, and cheaper than the US Postal Service."

A tall man with reddish hair, perfect posture, and a constant smile, Brooks smiles even when he talks. Maybe that's because he has a lot to smile about. "The industry is here to stay. It's not a trend; it's a reality," he said in 2012. In an article in the ISOA's trade publication, the *Journal of International Peace Operations* (*JIPO*), Brooks wrote that "the private sector continues to be the nexus to success" in conflict and postconflict environments. This was good news for the man who within a decade of starting the association had brought in fifty-three member firms from across the globe, all doing quite well. Although the number of ISOA members was small compared to the hundreds, if not thousands, of private military and security firms worldwide, the membership roster nonetheless included some of the industry heavyweights, such as Triple Canopy, G4S, L-3 MPRI, SOC, DynCorp, and Academi. There were half a dozen member firms based in the UAE, mainly Dubai; others came out of the U.K., Bahrain, Cyprus, South Africa, South Korea, Kuwait, and Thailand. Aegis was not a member, for reasons Brooks did not care to discuss.

Helping its members to succeed, the ISOA retained a well-known Washington lobbying firm, J. A. Green & Company, run by Jeff Green, a specialist in defense lobbying who was former counsel to the House Armed Services Committee, a lieutenant colonel in the Air Force Reserve, and former legislative director for the Coalition Provisional Authority in Iraq. And like any industry association, the ISOA held an annual meeting for the purposes of networking and marketing, replete with speakers, mostly former high-level military, government, or NGO officials, often from the U.S. and the U.K., as well as industry insiders. At the 2011 summit, for example, which took place at the Ronald Reagan Building in Washington, the ISOA celebrated its tenth anniversary and unveiled its own code of conduct, in step with the new Swiss-sponsored International Code of

Conduct, to which by then more than 250 companies had signed on.

Brooks was particularly proud of the association's slick magazine, *JIPO*, which was more akin to *Fortune* than to *Soldier of Fortune*. There were savvy full-page ads flashing the prowess of member firms. "You Never Know What Threats Lie Ahead," read an ad for Triple Canopy. Another read, "When the stakes are highest, governments, Fortune 500 companies, and international organizations turn to Olive Group to enable their operations in developing and high risk environments."

But most of the 40 to 50 pages of *JIPO* were devoted to articles about global conflict and instability, the future of the industry, places PMSCs were working, and challenges they were facing. The focus was frequently on Africa. The writers, like the speakers at the summits, were not what one would expect for a group with members sometimes referred to in news stories as "mercenaries." For example, a postgraduate student in international human rights law at Oxford University wrote about the legal complications of using drones. Brooks himself discussed the work of industry visionaries, including one who had put together what Brooks called the "3D+3P" theory. In the past, the three D's—defense, diplomacy, and development—defined U.S. foreign-policy strategy, but in the future, wrote Brooks, there would be three D's and three P's.: President Obama's public-private partnerships. As Brooks wrote, a "3D+3P" approach would "provide greater integration and coordination with the United States's big three foreign-aid-implementing agencies—Department of Defense, State and USAID—and private sector actors." This was a "new model" that "could be the next big evolutionary step for this global industry." The private sector would be fully integrated into policies of defense, diplomacy, and development.

It was all so smooth and calm and professional in the ISOA

offices. Though still smiling, Brooks could become testy at times, especially about the M-words—both military and mercenary— when used to describe any part of his industry. (He preferred the acronym PSCs, for private security companies, of course.) And he might spend more than a few minutes complaining about books on PMSCs—even the classic texts such as Peter Singer's *Corporate Warriors* or Allison Stanger's *One Nation Under Contract.* Brooks had marked his copies, filling margins with penciled comments and tagging pages of greatest consternation with yellow Post-its. He disagreed with Singer, who had called the industry a $100 billion dollar business in 2002. His revenue figures, ten years later, were as low as $20 billion. He was also annoyed at writers who hadn't bothered to interview him for articles on the industry; that was worse than any label any writer had given him, such as "Blackwater's Man in Washington." Brooks would be more than happy to meet with anyone writing about the ISOA and its members, he said, and even happier to participate in a public debate, just to straighten out a few misperceptions, definitions, and numbers.

Barely a mile from Farragut Square, there were several legislators who were hoping for a public debate over the PMSCs. Among them was Illinois's Jan Schakowsky, who remained as frustrated as ever by the challenge of collecting basic information about the PMSCs. "There are still no good numbers," she said and without such data, the PMSCs were "masking the scope" of America's foreign policy. From her perspective by 2012, the armed sector of the business could be controlled by placing it under direct control of a new chain of U.S. command. Her biggest worry was the same as it had been since 2007. "We have here a war-making capacity in a world where there's so much instability. The mix of people with weapons and a thirst for profit could dramatically increase the likelihood of catastrophic instability, just the opposite of what they say. What is the impetus toward peace? This is a vested interest in war and conflict."

Across the Potomac in Arlington, Virginia, columnist David Isenberg also saw the merits of a debate. "The public indifference has been going on for too long," he said. Isenberg's interest in the PMSC business went back to a monograph published in 1997 by the D.C.-based Center for Defense Information. He was prescient. In it he wrote,

> In a world where there are tens of millions of soldiers serving in regular military forces, then why is the subject of mercenaries important? Simply put, at a time when there is a trend toward military downsizing worldwide, coupled with continuing and perhaps more virulent conflicts in developing nations, and a global trend towards privatization, there will be a continuing and possibly increased demand for the services of trained military personnel capable of both teaching combat skills and conducting combat. If we wish to prevent them from possibly carrying out the same sorts of atrocities that regular military forces have so often done, it is necessary to pay attention to them and to try to ensure that they adhere to the same standards of international humanitarian law by which regular military forces are expected to abide.

Fifteen years later, Isenberg was still trying to clear the fog. Like Brooks, Isenberg would not use the word "mercenary." "They aren't mercenaries and the truth is they are mostly decent people out there working hard though not necessarily in the public interest." That didn't mean that he looked at the industry through the same lens as Brooks. He was the very definition of a watchdog, which meant that he could be aggressive at times. And like everyone who delved into the private military and security sector, Isenberg was especially frustrated by trying to define precisely what the industry encompassed and to calculate accurate figures for size and revenue. "No term fully captures what they do. It helps them to be undefined. If nobody knows exactly what you do, then it's hard to protest or to object to what you do," he said.

Isenberg was careful to differentiate between the roles of watchdog and critic and did not consider himself to be a critic. "Mine is a Mr. Spock approach; I am not for them and not against them. It [the industry] is a fascinating phenomenon and I track it partly as a labor of love." Although he was unrelenting in his quest to raise the curtain on the many uses of PMSCs, the instances of misuse and waste, the contractor casualties, and America's growing dependence on them, he tried to be fair in his writings. And he firmly believed that PMSCs were permanent fixtures in America and in the global economy. Congress had missed its chance to stop them long ago, he believed. Any attempt to ban armed private contractors, as Schakowsky and colleagues might suggest, was not based on current reality but on past paradigms from a world that no longer existed. "[PMSCs] are now undifferentiated from the regular military. As I've said before, they are a fifth branch of the military or a fourth branch of government." He liked to compare the government's dependence on PMSCs to the creature clinging to human organs in the film *Alien*.

That PMSCs were a permanent fact of life was old news to Major General Ed Cardon. In February 2012, he returned for a few weeks to the United States from South Korea, where he now commanded the Army's 2nd Infantry Division. He was more aware of the dependence on PMSCs than ever before. In the previous year, the general had been one of three deputy command generals in Iraq. It had been his job to assist General Lloyd Austin in planning and executing the U.S. Army's transition out of Iraq. During that time, he had witnessed firsthand how indispensable the PMSCs had become, and because the United States was legally required to withdraw all military forces by the end of 2012, the government was forced to rely more than ever on the contractors. "Anywhere we can't use troops because of legal authority, we use PMSCs," said Cardon. "The drawdowns reshape the force. We'll contract it when we need to. Nowhere is this more evident than in replacing military support to the U.S. State Department with PMSCs."

It was time now to take measures to identify exactly where such companies were going and to accelerate all efforts to better monitor them, he said. Regarding oversight, Cardon believed that it might help if the government viewed PMSCs as weapons. Doing this could attract the kind of attention and concern the topic deserved. "The way it works is that we must use them before someone else does. In that way they are most certainly like weapons. And one way to control them would be to bring them in and use them for oversight. Buy their loyalty, in other words."

Unlike Schakowsky, General Cardon was convinced that PMSCs, armed and unarmed, were already part of the establishment. Unlike Brooks, he agreed with Singer about the size of the PMSC industry. And unlike Isenberg, he could never describe his close observations of the industry as a labor of love or even as fascinating. For him, it was a matter of survival and an obligation. Like them all, however, he was in favor of a public debate on the topic. It concerned him that so many Americans knew so little about PMSCs, especially regarding their nation's defense and security, including the industry's involvement with drones.

By 2012, there were two types of drone wars: one conducted by the U.S. military in Afghanistan and one by the CIA in places like Pakistan, Somalia, and Yemen. Soon there would be new drone bases in Ethiopia and the Arabian Peninsula among others. At the same time, the State Department would have at least two dozen unarmed drones in Iraq, for surveillance, and more in Afghanistan as the troop withdrawal began. The State Department needed drone operations for security purposes because the withdrawal of troops would end the use of armed and unarmed drones under Pentagon and CIA authority in Iraq. Indeed, drones were another example of the State Department's takeover of functions once performed only by the military.

Cardon's concern was about the role PMSCs might play in supplying the expertise to operate drones. This was a new level of depersonalized warfare. The actual killing of the enemy would be two layers removed from the citizens of the nation: a machine operated by an employee of a private company. The more the citizen was removed from combat—did not see the blood of combat, the casualties, the ramifications of war, did not feel the passion of allegiance to nation—the easier it would be for policy-makers to take the nation to war. The general, trained as he was to foresee potential dangers, said, "In one year it is hard to imagine all that has transpired. Last year [2011] only the military was talking about drones. Now everyone is. And we still don't have adequate accountability to oversee a system that can allow private contractors into the arena [with drones]. Look at what has happened in the past. The larger concern is obvious: the [PMSCs] are effectively part of policy now, but they are still invisible. And when the two worlds merge, what happens?"

A few months after Cardon's comment, one of the world's ten largest PMSCs, Academi, posted this recruitment ad on its website: "Unmanned Aerial Vehicle Operator (Tier II)" Job #1512007 out of Moyock, North Carolina. The new Academi website on which the ad was posted read: "We are a professional organization serving as a solutions provider to the U.S. government. We operate in the defense, training, logistics, and intelligence spaces, priding ourselves on providing our customers with world-class performance. We are the quiet and dedicated professionals serving the government and commercial markets."

Along with Triple Canopy, DynCorp, and numerous others, Academi was also a member of the largest drone lobby in America, the Association of Unmanned Vehicle Systems International. The American public was unaware of the role some PMSCs were playing in lobbying the FAA over drone regulations, but then, as Cardon implied, things were happening so quickly. There was even a relatively new firm based in New Mexico that was planning to sell drones directly to PMSCs. It called its product the Silent Falcon.

17

"FULL SPEED AHEAD"

In the summer of 2012, while PMSCs were quietly moving into the business of drones, the U.S. government's reliance on private military and security contractors continued to exceed the level of accountability. And yet again someone in Congress was sponsoring a bill to tug at the reins of the industry.

In early August, Representative John Tierney of Massachusetts introduced the Oversight and Accountability in Wartime Contracting Act of 2012, H.R. 6360, which created new positions in the State Department, the Pentagon, and the U.S. Agency for International Development to monitor private contractors more closely. It also demanded that U.S. contracting agencies require certain information about companies seeking contracts—including full identities, past performances, and previous corporate names. What were their "parent, subsidiary or successor entities?" Had they changed names at some point?—as was the case with Blackwater and others through the years. "We want to know the history of contractors and make sure that they can't get away just by changing a name and moving forward," Tierney told the press. "There has to be some consistency, so who were you before you were Academi, for example? And who were you before you were Blackwater or Xe?"

Tierney was the top Democrat on the Subcommittee on National Security of the House Committee on Oversight and Government Reform. In Congress since 1996, he had tried to uncover contractor abuses and to track the work of war profiteers. He was also the congressman who introduced the legislation that launched the Commission on Wartime Contracting in Iraq and Afghanistan. Three years later, he initiated a probe that uncovered an extortion racket initiated by U.S. contractors funneling funds to warlords and insurgents in Afghanistan. And in 2011 he drew attention to the State Department's private armed security forces, noting that although they were employed by the State Department, armed contractors could end up in situations requiring them to engage in combat. It was that potential scenario and the role that PMSCs under contract with the State Department would play after the troop withdrawals in both Iraq and Afghanistan that inspired his latest push for greater oversight.

Tierney was especially concerned about the government's habit of awarding contracts to companies with bad track records: a history of human rights abuses, or unresolved allegations of fraud, or longstanding active legal cases. Ironically, on the same day that H.R. 6360 was introduced, a multimillion-dollar legal settlement between the U.S. government and Blackwater, now called Academi, was announced. In a case in which the company was accused of violating arms-export controls and federal firearms rules, the company agreed to pay $7.5 million. The charges were similar to those in another case involving Blackwater, one that had resulted in a $42 million settlement in 2010. Incensed about the 2012 fine, Tierney told the press that it was simply not a big enough punishment to stop such illegal behavior in the future, whether by the former Blackwater or any other firm. "If you look at the magnitude of the problem that was there," he said, "it doesn't seem to be much more than a slap on the wrist. This was not their [former Blackwater's] first time having this kind of a problem." In a letter to the Justice Department, he wrote that the settlement did not "adequately serve the public interest or protect national security. For a company that the U.S. government previously found to be in 'systematic non-compliance' with arms export controls, and yet holds or has held billions of dollars in U.S. government contracts, it is extremely difficult to understand how it was determined that the penalty in any way fits the gravity of the determined offense."

In an interview in September, Tierney said, "This has been a repeated problem that's gone on—and it's not just Blackwater. We've had [PMSCs] taking millions of dollars from taxpayers, repeatedly making questionable decisions. If we don't hold them accountable, then it's going to keep happening." He wanted both the Pentagon and the State Department to "suspend and disbar" Academi (Blackwater's successor) to set an example. In response, a spokesman for Academi told the media that these were inherited issues that were outdated now. "Today, Academi is working to become the industry leader in governance, compliance and regulatory matters. It is fair to say—and important to note—that the company that was once known as Blackwater simply does not exist anymore in the company that is now Academi."

Barely a month after Tierney had introduced his bill, the Pentagon's Defense Intelligence Agency announced the winners of a multimillion-dollar contract for counterterrorism training of personnel leaving for overseas deployments in hostile environments. There were six: Academi, Triple Canopy, G4S, Team Crucible, Washington Security Group, and Signature Science. It was not a huge multibillion-dollar contract like the Worldwide Protective Services contract out of the State Department in 2010, but Tierney regarded it as yet another example of the critical imbalance between accountability and power. Two of the winners—Triple Canopy and G4S—had recently been caught in webs of allegations of misconduct.

Triple Canopy, which had accumulated roughly $2 billion in U.S. contracts by the time it won part of the new Pentagon contract, was facing allegations based on a whistleblower's complaint that led to the Justice Department's charges claiming the company had billed the U.S. government for hundreds of Ugandan security guards who failed to meet firearms proficiency requirements. Prosecutors claimed that the company had falsified test scores to make the workers appear to meet such requirements and that it continued to bill the government for the workers even after the government exposed the misconduct. "For a government contractor to knowingly provide deficient security services, as is alleged in this case, is unthinkable, especially in war time," an assistant attorney general at the Justice Department said at the time of the 2012 court filing. And a U.S. attorney in the Eastern District of Virginia added, "We will not tolerate government contractors anywhere in the world who seek to defraud the United States through deliberate or reckless conduct that violates contractual requirements and risks the security of government personnel."

At the same time, G4S, which by 2012 was the second-largest nongovernment employer in the world—after Walmart—and the parent company of ArmorGroup with its 9,000-strong army of guards, had had its own problems in the months leading up to the new Pentagon contract. In July, it came under fire when the news broke in London that it had recruited and trained only 4,000 of the 13,700 guards it was contracted to provide for security at the London Olympics. At the time, the policy director of the British group War on Want said, "The G4S Olympics scandal exposes the danger of the government's blind faith in the power of the market to deliver everything from policing to war." And War on Want warned, "Successive governments have ducked imposing tough regulations on the private military and security industry. Such moves will ensure that companies continue to profit from the privatisation of war whilst governments and communities will be unable to hold them to account."

Representative Tierney's attempt to make the companies and his own government accountable was based on good old-fashioned democratic intent. With the PMSCs moving into the drone business, transparency was indeed more important than ever. But whether it was Schakowsky trying to phase out the industry or Tierney trying to usher in a tighter system of controls, privatized defense and security in America was unstoppable. In only a decade, these companies had become indispensable to the national security agenda without any public discourse. At times, it seemed almost like a fictional story in which the citizens of a nation lived in two separate realities. Their government might tell them that a war was over, that troops were coming home, that defense expenditures were being cut, and the citizens of one reality would be pleased with the news. War would no longer be on their minds. But the citizens in the other reality would continue to fret about the undeclared wars of the new century. They would worry about what their fellow citizens didn't know and were unable to see. Like fog clouding a specific place, there was a barrier between the two worlds, though sometimes the mist would clear, exposing bits of truth.

In the coming months, there would be two such events. The first occurred on September 11, 2012, with the assault on the American consulate at Benghazi in Libya, resulting in the death of U.S. Ambassador J. Christopher Stevens and three others. In the aftermath of the tragedy, reporters investigating diplomatic security dug for details about private security contractors. Below is a portion of the State Department's press briefing on September 14:

> **Question:** (Inaudible) the claim was made yesterday that a company that is a spinoff of Blackwater, in fact, proposed or contracted the United States Government for this particular kind of eventuality, and it was caught up in some sort of bureaucratic—
>
> **Spokesperson Victoria Nuland:** Completely untrue with regard to Libya. I checked that this morning. At no time did we plan to hire a private security company for Libya.
>
> **Question:** You said that at no time did you have contracts with private security companies in Libya?
>
> **Nuland:** Correct.

Not correct. In February of that year the State Department had signed a contract for "Security Guards and Patrol Services" for a job described as "Local Guard Program—Benghazi, Libya." The award was for $387,413.68 initially, with an extension option that would bring the total to $783,284. However, the State Department had not listed any particular company as having received the contract. Instead the contract winner was identified as "a miscellaneous foreign awardee," bringing to mind the category of funding that the Commission on Wartime Contracting had noted in its final report in 2011, the one that showed a total expenditure of $38.5 billion out of DOD, State Department, and USAID for contracts in Iraq and Afghanistan since 2002 and the one for which the commissioners could not find an explanation or a list of companies that benefited. The contract was with Blue Mountain Group, a company based in Wales and started by two former SAS soldiers in 2001. The name of the company (and its pilgrim logo) came from a poem inscribed on the clock tower at the SAS headquarters in Hereford, England: "We are the pilgrims, master; we shall go/Always a little further; it may be/Beyond that last blue mountain barred with snow/Across that angry or that glimmering sea."

On its website, Blue Mountain noted that it provided "security solutions and training services in more than 20 countries around the world," with a client list that included the U.N. and the International Monetary Fund. "Our core expertise derives from our heritage, gained from many years' service in UK Special Forces." In Libya, Blue Mountain was one of the "very few private security companies that was authorized to operate by the Libyan authorities in partnership with a local company." The fact that the company was already working in Libya hastened the U.S. government's ability to add security in Benghazi and, as one source noted, using the miscellaneous award designation may also have speeded up the process. In other words, Blue Mountain became a quick fix. Later at a congressional hearing, a former regional security officer for the U.S. embassy in Libya would testify that contracting for the Benghazi security "was largely based on our concern of how long we would be in Benghazi. We were concerned that if we retained or brought on board full-time employees we would have to then find a position for them if that post ever went away." And what were the consequences of this quick convenience? To patrol the diplomatic compound in Benghazi, Blue Mountain hired local guards. But who were they? What were their backgrounds? What was their training? And was it possible that any of them had ties to the men who instigated the attacks?

On September 17, *Wired* magazine broke the story that the State Department had given out inaccurate information about private security contractors in Benghazi as there was indeed a PMSC under contract with the State Department for security at the Benghazi consulate. The next day, at the September 18 briefing, State Department spokesperson Victoria Nuland corrected herself.

Nuland: There was an error in what I said. The external security, external armed security, as we have been saying, outside of the perimeter, was fully handled by the Libyan side. There was no contract—contracting out of that. There was a group called Blue Mountain Group, which is a private security company with permits to operate in Libya. They were hired to provide local Libyan guards who operated inside the gate doing things like operating the security access equipment, screening the cars, that kind of thing.

Question: Just to clarify, they were contracted by the U.S. State Department or another agency—Blue Mountain?

Nuland: They were contracted by the Department.

Question: And Blue Mountain is a British company?

Nuland: I'm going to let them self-identify on that front. But the people who were hired were Libyans. . . . There's nothing else that I have that needs correcting at the moment.

In the days ahead the government repeatedly referred to two of the four men murdered at the consulate as former Navy SEALs, which they were. However, more recently in Libya, they had been private contractors working for the CIA in a sector known as the Global Response Staff, which recruited former U.S. Special Forces operatives. At least half of the work of the GRS was performed by private contractors and much of it consisted of guarding CIA spies. Clearly the role of private contractors in America's diplomatic security and its counterterrorism strategies in general was not something the State Department was eager to share with the nation in 2012.

But then, in 2013, in the months following the tenth anniversary of the Iraq invasion, another eye-opening event would expose more bits of truth. This one would bring home the issues of privatizing America's defense and security.

18

BIG BROTHER'S BIG BROTHER

On the tenth anniversary of the Iraq invasion, March 20, 2013, there was the predictable finger-pointing over the causes of going to war and there was also commentary focusing on the unprecedented role of PMSCs. "The Iraq war might best be remembered as America's most privatized military engagement to date, with contractors hired by the Pentagon actually outnumbering troops on the ground," the *Christian Science Monitor* wrote. And from an analyst for the Center for Public Integrity: "Although the war's tremendous costs helped to undermine the U.S. economy, the fighting in both Iraq and Afghanistan was a financial boon for [PMSCs]."

It was a time of reflection, as all such anniversaries are, but for anyone trying to define the scope of the "boon," it was also a time of immense frustration. No organization in the world could supply indisputable figures to define the industry, much less how much money

PMSCs had made in Iraq. Later in the year, the United Nations would issue a report claiming that this was a $244 billion industry growing at an annual rate of about 7.4 percent, that the U.S. thus far was the single biggest consumer of private military and security services, and that the Pentagon had spent $44 billion in 2012 on PMSCs in Iraq and Afghanistan. But the total cost of PMSCs in the Iraq war—that is, the cost of the bonanza that was effectively the industry's launch? This was not known.

Some commentators depended on facts out of the final report of the Commission on Wartime Contracting, which included both the Iraq and Afghanistan wars, and estimated all of the associated multi-billion-dollar costs, including the memorable detail that "between $31 billion and $60 billion" was lost to waste and fraud. The *Financial Times* wrote that Blackwater and Triple Canopy alone made "at least $3.1 billion." Other articles using the words "around," "possibly as much as," and "more than," plus that glaring $29 billion gap between the commission's two estimated totals for contractor fraud and waste, sent a message. The transparency "is very poor," wrote Linda Bilmes of the Harvard Kennedy School, who was trying to answer two big questions: How much did the Iraq War cost, including PMSCs, of course, and where exactly did the money go? The research, which required reading hundreds of thousands of contracts as well as the financial statements of thousands of companies, was especially taxing, she noted, because "many of the Pentagon's core tracking databases are dysfunctional."

Although only a partial picture was possible, the countries with the most firms operating worldwide were clearly the United States and Great Britain. There were firms also coming out of Russia, Israel, France, and Dubai, among others. And the newest nation to enter the throng was China, which, following the lead of Western companies, had started with a company consisting largely of former soldiers from China's Special Forces. Its biggest firm, Shandong Huawei Security Group, was zeroing in on opportunities overseas, especially in Africa. It was also targeting the Iraqi market, a maneuver based on the belief that there would be work after the current contractors left. And there was work in Afghanistan, where rich reserves of lithium, copper, cobalt, and other minerals were attracting Chinese mining concerns, whose workers needed protection. Well aware of the business opportunities in Africa by way of China was Erik Prince, who would soon become the chairman of Frontier Services Group, an Africa-focused security company based in Hong Kong and in business with China's largest state-owned conglomerate, CITIC Group. As the *Wall Street Journal* would note, "Beijing has titanic ambitions to tap Africa's resources—including $1 trillion in planned spending on roads, railways and airports by 2025—and Mr. Prince wants in."

By 2013, there was some consensus among experts about the biggest firms providing security and defense services globally. At the head of the list was the industry giant, Great Britain's G4S, which had a presence in at least one hundred nations. Also high up were the Australian-owned Unity Resources Group, the British firm Erinys, and the Asia Security Group, a large Afghani firm headquartered in Kabul with ties to Afghanistan's President Hamid Karzai. There was Defion Internacional, which, based in Peru, with offices in Iraq, Dubai, the Philippines, and Sri Lanka, often supplied private military personnel from Latin America to other firms, including Triple Canopy. And always listed among the top companies were Academi, DynCorp, Triple Canopy, and Aegis.

Such lists, though, were based largely on the firms that had been operating in conflict-ridden zones during the past decade and were not always helpful in assessing an industry with ever-expanding markets. For instance, South Florida, and especially Miami, had become a hub for PMSCs, "sprouting" more companies than anywhere else in the nation during the previous decade. "Camouflaged by parties and palm trees and close to troubled hot spots in the Caribbean and Latin America, Miami is a boomtown for mercenaries," wrote one journalist. One report noted at least a thousand such firms in South Florida, with many specializing in maritime security—companies with names like Armed Piracy Defense, Global Marine Security, SeaGuard Security, and Secure Waters Security Group.

Showing the tracking difficulties was the fact that only 10 of the firms on the South Florida list had signed the International Code of Conduct, which, by August 2013, 692 companies from 70 nations had signed. How to bring in more companies to agree to the Code's regulations was a challenge. At a meeting in Montreux in February, a new global industry body, the Private Security Service Providers' Association, was established—the latest development in the quest for international oversight and the third, and last, step in the Swiss Initiative. The PSSPA, as it was referred to, would certify companies and rule on allegations of human rights abuses or any alleged malfeasance. It would be based in Geneva in a massive new complex under construction to be called Maison de la Paix (House of Peace). Among the companies represented at the announcement of the new oversight plan had been G4S, Triple Canopy, and Aegis.

By the tenth anniversary of the war that had been its launching pad, Aegis was operating in twelve nations, and was especially busy with diplomatic security work and maritime security. As its website then noted, "Government and diplomatic contracts are part of the lifeblood of Aegis. Since the company was founded in 2002 we have consistently and successfully supported governments in representing themselves and their citizens across the world." Also, according to the website, the total value of Aegis's U.S. contracts in Iraq during the occupation was $1.3 billion.

Aegis had been one of the first PMSCs to fly into Libya after the victory of the NATO-led forces in 2012, to "facilitate Western business operations, meaning everything from personal protection to decent housing to building relationships with local power brokers." And in Afghanistan, it would be one of the last companies standing, so to speak. By the summer of 2013, there were more than 100,000 private contractors working for the DOD there, far exceeding the 84,000 or so military personnel. This figure did not include contractors working for USAID or the State Department, the latter of which had awarded nearly $500 million to Aegis for securing the embassy and consulates in Afghanistan. Aegis, as journalist Charles Glass wrote in a *Harper's* magazine piece in 2012, was "*the* elite private force in Afghanistan." This it would be for years to come, despite Afghan President Karzai's order to expel all PMSCs (at least fifty firms) by March 20, 2012. The order, known as Decree 62, did not include embassy security protection and thus Aegis could stay. Even the British Foreign Office, which had nearly declared war on Spicer in the 1990s, wanted Aegis to guard some of its embassies. "We've built a brand. We've built a reputation for integrity. We've dispelled all the myths about gunslingers and mercenaries and having no moral compass," Spicer told Glass, though the story wasn't over yet considering that overseeing American security in Afghanistan was a volatile mission filled with the potential for sudden crises.

It had been nine years since the headlines that marked Aegis's rise after winning the largest security contract in Iraq. Now, Spicer and his company rarely, if ever, made the news, nor did the industry he helped to launch. By 2013, these businesses sought a delicate balance between marketing their services to governments and corporate clients and keeping a low profile in the media. Clearly, they were succeeding. So little was known about them that even their growing role in diplomatic security had barely surfaced in the aftermath of the 2012 Benghazi attacks. But in late spring of 2013, another event occurred that drew far more attention to privatized security than Benghazi or the anniversary of the Iraq War.

A twenty-nine-year-old computer technician, Edward Snowden, loaded highly classified U.S. government documents onto flash drives before leaving his job at the National Security Administration's principal contractor, Booz Allen Hamilton. And at a hotel in Hong Kong he divulged top-secret information to two journalists from Britain's *Guardian,* which, on June 5, published its first exclusive based on the Snowden leaks. This was the unnerving story that exposed a secret court order forcing Verizon to release the phone records of millions of Americans to the U.S. government. The next story, on June 6, claimed that the NSA had "direct access" to data stored by Facebook, Apple, Google, and others. On June 7, President Obama defended the NSA, saying "You can't have 100% security and also then have 100% privacy and zero inconvenience." On June 9, Snowden told the world what he had done, saying, "I have no intention of hiding who I am because I know I have done nothing wrong."

Soon, in addition to the security leaks, the American public would learn a lot about Snowden's former employer. For instance, 76 percent of the 25,000 employees at Booz Allen had classified clearances—nearly half of which were top-secret. Ninety-nine percent of its income came from government contracts, and in the fiscal year ending March 2013, it reported $5.76 billion in revenue, of which $1.3 billion came from U.S. intelligence agencies, largely the NSA.

A company announcement in early 2013 had revealed two new contracts out of Homeland Security valued at $11 billion.

Booz Allen kept a low profile, and its trajectory of success, like that of many other companies, was rooted in the U.S. government's strategies in the "war on terror." In Iraq, it was under contract with the Pentagon and the Defense Information Systems Agency, as well as the Department of Homeland Security and the NSA. Well practiced in the tasks of collecting personal data, Booz Allen had once been the main contractor on a massive data collection project called Total Information Awareness, secretly established in the aftermath of 9/11 in the Pentagon's division known as DARPA (Defense Advanced Research Projects Agency). Specifically, the firm set out to collect credit card receipts and phone records of individuals identified as potential terrorists. Congress, considering the program an affront to civil liberties, effectively shuttered it. But similar work was secretly initiated at the NSA.

Although Booz Allen could not be referred to as a PMSC, it may have been the first PCSC, a private cybersecurity contractor, in what was becoming known as the cybercontractor complex. Whatever the company's label, its newsworthiness in 2013 gave the American public a glimpse at some of the basic features of the privatization revolution in their government. As threads of secrecy unraveled, Americans learned that nearly 70 percent of their nation's intelligence budget was outsourced to private firms, and at the National Security Agency, Booz Allen was conducting massive surveillance of citizens' phone calls and Internet usage, accumulating what was called "metadata" or data about data.

The Obama administration's chief intelligence officer, James R. Clapper, Jr., was a former Booz Allen executive, while the former chief intelligence officer in the Bush administration now worked at

Booz Allen. This was, as one observer said, the "revolving door in its purest form." A *New York Times* editorial pointed out the government's overreliance on contractors, noting witnesses from a 2011 congressional hearing who expressed concerns about "conflicts of interest, blurred lines of authority, and diminished accountability." It also noted that up to 500,000 private-sector employees had top-secret government clearances, which in fact made "breaches more likely." The *Times* wrote: "Outsourcing vast swaths of national security has gone on for too long with too little scrutiny."

Although academics and analysts had been exposing details about privatized defense and national security for the past decade, including scandals and alleged abuse, and congressional commissions had been begging for reforms and more transparency, the general public had remained mostly in the dark. This scandal was different. It was visceral. Commentators said that the NSA was watching people based on the premise of guilt until proven innocent. What had happened to Americans' cherished right to privacy?

President Obama announced plans to overhaul key parts of the NSA's surveillance programs, but the scandal grew, soon involving the NSA monitoring of foreign governments. And the *Wall Street Journal* revealed that the agency's battalion of private contractors had the capacity to spy on 75 percent of all U.S. Internet-based communications—far more than originally revealed. But while the nation focused on the NSA, something bigger in the realm of privacy and privatization was taking shape, something that could extend Big Brother's reach beyond emails and phone calls to monitoring Americans' daily routines and actions—and that was the domestic drone industry. The security industry that during the past decade had developed technologically and strategically for the "war on terror" was expanding to America, where a confluence of drone technologies, new surveillance strategies, and a well-practiced, entrenched PMSC sector seemed to be initiating the age of Big Brother's Big Brother.

Ironically, on the very day of the tenth anniversary of the invasion of Iraq, the Senate Committee on the Judiciary conducted a hearing called "Time Change: The Future of Drones in America: Law Enforcement and Privacy Considerations." By then, the drone business was exploding, and its proliferation was evoking reactions from human rights advocates, who worried about privacy violations; from trade regulators, who were concerned about the possibility of companies selling drones to unfriendly nations; from aviation experts, who were trying to figure out how drones could be safely introduced into U.S. airspace; and from the close observers of PMSCs, who were anxious about the drone industry developing faster than attempts at oversight and who were especially watchful regarding the union of PMSCs and drones.

There were three facts at that time that most Americans didn't know about drones: How labor intensive a military drone mission could be. How deeply involved in the drone industry private contractors were becoming. And how drones could change life in America. At the hearing, it was disclosed that in the previous decade the U.S. inventory of unmanned aerial vehicles (the formal name for drones) had grown from 167 to over 7,000 for all the military branches, and the growth rate for drone missions from 2004 projected into 2013 would be 1,200 percent. To continue at such a pace, the government was increasingly dependent on private contractors for operating drones. Drone military missions were complex operations. One twenty-four-hour Predator mission, for example, demanded 160 to 180 personnel. The larger Global Hawk drone required from 300 to 500 people. A *Los Angeles Times* reporter put such facts into perspective when he wrote, in 2011, "The Air Force is short of ground-based pilots and crews to fly the drones, intelligence analysts to scrutinize nonstop video and surveillance feeds, and technicians and mechanics to maintain the heavily used aircraft," and "with a fleet of about 230 Predators, Reapers and Global Hawks, the Air Force flies more than 50 drones around the clock over Afghanistan and other target areas. The Pentagon plans to add 730 medium and large drones in the next decade, requiring thousands more personnel."

Once again, private contractors were filling a void. And it wasn't just at the Pentagon. The State Department was calling for contract applications to provide support services for "worldwide" drones. In 2011, it had sent out requests for contractors to make and operate drones in a $1 billion program whose purpose was mainly to offer its diplomats "real-time air surveillance of fixed installations, proposed movement routes and movement operations" in "high threat environments."

The private sector was responding in several ways. Companies that manufactured drones, such as Boeing, had subsidiaries to provide the services for the drones they made. There were independent firms focusing on drone services—such as Battlespace Flight Services, which supplied drone "pilots," sensor operators, maintenance personnel, and mission planners. The multiservice, one-stop-shopping PMSCs, such as Triple Canopy, Academi, and DynCorp, had also entered the drone market. (In 2012, DynCorp, for example, teamed up with a drone manufacturer, Textron, to try to win a $1 billion five-year contract with the U.S. Air Force to maintain Predator and Reaper drones. But Battlespace won the contract.) And there were the lesser-known but long-standing firms such as the immensely influential SAIC, Science Applications International Corporation, based in McLean, Virginia, which was one of the best examples of a contractor that pivoted from Iraq to the emerging drone boom.

Hardly a household name, SAIC had nonetheless been active in the government's counterterrorism strategies for many years and "involved at every stage of the life cycle of the war in Iraq," as *Vanity Fair* magazine once noted, adding that "SAIC personnel were instrumental in pressing the case that weapons of mass destruction existed in Iraq in the first place, and that war was the only way to get rid of them. Then, as war became inevitable, SAIC secured contracts for a broad range of operations in soon-to-be-occupied Iraq. When no weapons of mass destruction were found, SAIC personnel staffed the commission that was set up to investigate how American intelligence could have been so disastrously wrong." And now, with an annual revenue of $11 billion in 2013, SAIC had a major presence in the UAV military market and was quickly capturing domestic drone markets, with a special focus on drones for the U.S.-Mexico border security.

Once again, the PMSCs were entering and locking into markets faster than safeguards and oversight could be established. At the intersection of PMSCs and drones there were big questions, especially as the business and the technology expanded to domestic markets, including surveillance. Were there once again dangers of unqualified personnel? Inadequate training? Bad behavior in the workplace? What if the contractor hired to analyze the aerial feed was not well trained or if the data and intelligence supplied by the contractor turned out to be incorrect and the drone targeted the wrong people?

By 2013, that had already happened: a Predator drone tracking suspected terrorists in central Afghanistan in December 2010 killed at least 15 innocent men, women, and children. A later investigation revealed that an Army captain had ordered the strike based partly on an erroneous analysis of the aerial feed, which had been provided by a private contractor working for SAIC. At the time, SAIC had a

$49 million contract with the U.S. Air Force to analyze aerial videos for potential drone attacks.

Along with Academi, Triple Canopy, DynCorp, and many others, SAIC was a member of the Association of Unmanned Vehicle Systems International (AUVSI), a fifteen-year-old lobby that had its roots in 1970s America, when unmanned vehicles were starting to appear. By 2011, there were more than 7,000 members in what had become a global force with a strong focus on U.S. legislation, especially urging the expansion of UAV use in U.S. airspace. The AUVSI also was in the process of creating an industry code of conduct to establish a responsible image of self-regulation and thus spur pro-industry legislation. To be sure, in February 2012, President Obama signed a new federal law ordering the Federal Aviation Administration to establish standards that would allow "the safe integration" of drones in America by September 30, 2015.

Aerospace-industry experts were predicting that in the ensuing decade, the industry would add 100,000 new jobs to the American workforce. By 2020, over 30,000 drones could be flying in the skies over America. A significant portion of those would be operated out of local police departments, which within ninety days of the 2012 law were allowed to fly drones under very rigid requirements, such as flying them under 400 feet. In anticipation of the 2015 deadline, drone manufacturers were eagerly marketing drones already used in war zones and designing new ones specifically for law enforcement use. AeroVironment, a Pasadena-based firm that supplied a significant portion of the Pentagon's UAVs and was known for its Hummingbird drone, created the Qube drone, just for police. "Rugged and reliable," wrote the company, [Qube] "fits easily in the trunk of a car, and can be assembled and ready for flight in less than five minutes, to provide a rapidly deployable eye in the sky transmitting live video directly to the operator."

In the summer of 2013, while Americans were learning about surveillance of their emails and phone calls, the government's potential surveillance capabilities were reaching new heights, so to speak, in the form of a superhigh-resolution camera mounted onto unmanned aerial vehicles. Referred to as the "Wide Area Persistent Stare," the technology offered the surveillance scope of a hundred Predator drones "staring" all at once over an area the size of a medium-sized city. ARGUS-IS was its official name—an acronym for Autonomous Real-Time Ground Ubiquitous Surveillance Imaging System. It had been developed to improve the U.S. Army's surveillance for protecting its troops. What was revolutionary was not just its wide surveillance but its high-resolution video. From as high as 17,500 feet in the air, ARGUS-IS could view objects as low as six inches from the ground. If used domestically—which according to most accounts was inevitable—such capability advanced the surveillance power of the government to an unparalleled level, which worried government watchdogs and civil liberties experts. "Even in our most pessimistic moments," said an ACLU policy analyst, "we didn't think that every street, empty lot, garden, and field would be subject to video monitoring anytime soon. But that is precisely what this technology could enable. We've speculated about self-organizing swarms of drones being used to blanket entire cities with surveillance, but this technology makes it clear that nothing that complicated is required."

A powerful aerial surveillance system that could easily be mounted on drones was especially appealing to law enforcement agencies and Homeland Security's Border Patrol division, all of which were anticipating the opening of the sky in 2015. The pent-up demand was stimulating a vast new market for unmanned aerial vehicles back home—manufactured, maintained, and operated by some of the same companies that had worked under contract in Iraq and

Afghanistan earlier. While domestic drones could facilitate heroic feats for the good of humanity, there were the ongoing issues of safety and privacy. Their use had to be controlled.

This time, unlike the explosion of PMSCs in Iraq, there was a chance to establish accountability before the gold rush began. In Iraq, an industry that instigated a major shift in how we defend and secure our nation took off before any rules or regulations were in place. The collateral damage was massive, causing death, injury, and ruination of innocent people, including the people we depended upon within our own traditional military forces, like Kadhim Al-kanani. If contractors were not held accountable from the start, what would the collateral damage look like at home?

For most Americans that summer, the NSA revelations were so shocking that they overwhelmed most other stories, including news of the $46 billion immigration reform and border security bill approved in the U.S. Senate on June 6—a potential prize for private military and security companies. Calling for "persistent surveillance" of the 2,000-mile U.S.-Mexican border, the bill would fund sophisticated surveillance systems proven useful in Iraq and Afghanistan and expand the number of 24/7 drones "guarding" the border. There would also be an increase from 20,000 to 40,000 Border Patrol agents. If the House of Representatives passed the bill and the president signed it into law, many soldiers returning from Iraq could soon be hired by PMSCs under contract to Homeland Security's Border Patrol to work as armed guards at detention centers or in prisoner transport or drone operations. But even if the bill were never to be enacted and the federal government was unable to expand its border security, the border states would likely take the initiative. Either way, the drone industry and private military and security contractors would profit immensely. The bill that summer offered a glimpse at a future in which immigration was a new frontier for PMSCs. And it brought to mind one of Reinhold Niebuhr's descriptions of irony: when "security is transmuted into insecurity because too much reliance is placed upon it."

The most frequently cited line in President Eisenhower's farewell address in 1961 is the one that introduced the American public to the potential peril in the growing bond between the military establishment and defense contractors. "In the councils of government, we must guard against the acquisition of unwarranted influence, whether sought or unsought, by the military-industrial complex." Fifty years later, the military-and-security-industrial complex, the intelligence-industrial complex, and the cybercontractor complex far exceeded the size and complexity of what had so concerned Eisenhower, thus deepening the meaning of another important if often-overlooked line in Ike's famed warning: "Crises there will continue to be. In meeting them, whether foreign or domestic, great or small, there is a recurring temptation to feel that some spectacular and costly action could become the miraculous solution to all current difficulties." The solutions for protecting America from its enemies abroad were now coming home. Was it possible that the security America so aggressively pursued, both internationally and domestically, would instead yield an age of never-ending insecurity?

To be sure, these were companies that could assist in America's quest for greater security, but they did not *belong* to America, despite the nation's decisive role in launching their industry. They belonged to whichever government, corporation, or NGO sought their services. In the early months of 2014, a reminder of the PMSCs' independence became apparent. In Iraq, where Al Qaeda forces were strengthening and violence was escalating, the Iraqi government was purchasing more than $6 billion in military equipment from the

United States—and PMSCs were once again in demand. They were training the Iraqi military to use the new Hellfire missiles or maintain the Apache attack helicopters, and they were guarding government officials. But this time their employer was the Iraqi government. When news of the latest role of PMSCs in Iraq surfaced, Christopher Shays, the former U.S. Representative from Connecticut who had served as the cochair for the Commission on Wartime Contracting, told the press, "The one thing that's a given: We can't go to war without contractors and we can't go to peace without contractors."

That was undoubtedly true. But the *we* was the entire world, not just America. Private military and security companies had become inescapable global wild cards.

ACKNOWLEDGMENTS

Writing a book demands long hours of working alone. As John Steinbeck once wrote, "Unless a writer is capable of solitude he should leave books alone and go into the theatre." Indeed, it is largely a solo performance, but there is always a support cast. I am well aware of that now because during the years of researching and writing *The Invisible Soldiers* I experienced a few personal losses, making the acknowledgment of such support all the more important.

I must first thank my editor, Bob Bender, and my agent, Alice Martell. I am honored to work with them both. *The Invisible Soldiers* is my third book with Bob Bender, whose talents I immensely respect. He is brilliant yet humble, tough yet kind. Excellence and perfection are his goals. And he cares deeply about his authors as they work to meet his high standards. Alice Martell, who is one of the most disciplined and determined humans I've ever seen in action, redefines the term "agent" and exudes endless support for those in whom she strongly believes. Thanks also to Johanna Li, at Simon & Schuster, and Stephanie Finman, at the Martell Agency. A special thanks to Jonathan Karp, President of the Simon & Schuster imprint, who truly understands what it means to be a writer and who came up with the title for this book.

I must also express my appreciation for two writers who have deeply motivated me during the years of creating this book: public intellectual and theologian Reinhold Niebuhr and historian and author Andrew Bacevich. Humility requires us to see ourselves without blinders, and Niebuhr demands that of us as citizens of a democratic nation. Bacevich shows us why we must listen to Niebuhr, whom he calls "the most clear-eyed of American prophets." I appreciate them both for their efforts to understand our nation and to inspire their readers to want to make a difference in its future.

On a more day-to-day basis, I was fortunate to be the recipient of steadfast support from my longtime friend June Zipperian, who is an excellent reader, a supreme cook, and quite brilliant. My persistent and consistent booster of spirits was Tom Scott, whose curiosity about all aspects of the privatization of defense and security on a global level was inspiring and whose support during tough times was remarkable. I also am indebted to Ann and Jim Veith for their enthusiasm and hospitality, and Alison Gibson, the research librarian whom I've described before in acknowledgments as a "national treasure." I am pleased also to thank Bob Kraft, a longtime newspaper executive, for his astute observations and his first-rate fact-checking; what a gift to be able to discuss the topic with such a fine mind. I am honored to thank Norm Pearlstine for his interest in my work and his expressions of respect at some crucial times during the writing of this book. And thank you, Nick and Nina Clooney, for the wondrous conversations and dinners that spurred me on.

My research assistants for this book were exemplary. Bridget Vis, an Internet whiz kid and a reporter par excellence, worked for me during the last two years of research, unearthing details online that assisted with my work in the field, helping to unravel a few conundrums, and keeping track of issues in this moving-target topic while I engaged in the writing. Thanks to Lisa Haitz and Elizabeth Cutting for work in the early research stages and to Wendy Beckman, a well-practiced digger, who made some discoveries that were helpful. I am grateful to Michael Yip who is so fluent in the language of story structure. Also thanks to Lee Edwards for formatting the source notes. And a very big thanks to my sister, Sarah Byers, who contributed to early research for the book and who shared the responsibilities of overseeing the care of our mother.

I am grateful to all sources, of course, and extend special thanks to those who were willing to express their thoughts with attribution. I must pay tribute here to Tom Ryan, a West Point graduate, former U.S. Army officer, and former private military contractor, who was a playwright when he died unexpectedly in 2012. I am grateful to the authors who went before me and so skillfully examined various aspects of the privatization of defense and security and whose names appear throughout the text and source notes. Thanks also to the very impressive Hall Center for the Humanities at the University of Kansas and to Victor Bailey, Dolph Simons, and Bill Tuttle for making possible my humanities fellowship during the spring of 2009. Also I thank the following: U.S. Commission on Wartime Contracting, the War on Want, the UN Working Group on Mercenaries, Human Rights First, the National Institute of Military Justice, Global Policy Forum, the U.S. Army Command and General Staff College, the International Peace Institute, Project on Government Oversight, ProPublica, Amnesty International, International Committee of the

Red Cross, the Swiss Federal Department of Foreign Affairs, the Geneva Centre for the Democratic Control of Armed Forces, Corporate Watch, the New York Public Library, the Center for Public Integrity, the Mercantile Library, U.S. Congressional Research Service, the Tabard Inn, the Eldridge Hotel, and the staff at the Excelsior Hotel.

In addition, I am grateful to the following individuals: Ann Baker, Timothy Bannon, Amanda Bennett, Anne Camm, Richard and Dianna Campbell, Jayni and Frank Carey, Scarlett Chen, Jenny Clark, Clare Coss, Pamela Fine, Henry Fortunato, Steve Gerdsen, Patti Gordy, David Gray, Tom Griffin, Bayliss Harsh, Aaron Hawthorne, Jan and Charles Ison, Crosby Kemper III, Dr. Farhang Khosh, Annie Kiefhaber, Major Odie Kokensparger, Cem and Anne Kozlu, David Lattin, Kathy and Herb Layford, Max Leone, Molly Levitt, Judith G. Levy, Gary McAvay, General Richard Mills, Patti Newberry, Bill Nichols, Patti and Buck Niehoff, Sandy Padwe, Katherine Pedigo, Dan Pinger, Dorothy Prevost, Mary Roach, Patience and Bevis Schock, Bruce Stanley, Hylda and Jerry Strange, Bob and Hope Taft, Julie Thomas, Jim Tobin, Gregory Todd, Margaret Wilson, Ted Wilson, Tom and Mary Daes Wortley, Suzie Wright, and Jeanie Wulfkuhle.

Lastly, my deepest expression of gratitude goes to my mother, who insisted that I keep moving forward on the research and writing of this book despite her position on "the exit ramp," as she called her last months of life. "Nothing can stop my exit and that must not stop your work," she said. Thank you, Elizabeth.

SOURCE NOTES ESSAY

I began the research for *The Invisible Soldiers* in London. As the author Robert Young Pelton once noted, "Britain is the perfect place to understand the mercenary and the complicated and delicate subsets of privatized warfare." The British, including journalists, human rights advocates, politicians, military experts, and private security executives, began sorting out the issues of private military companies years before the Americans. In an interview early in my research, I asked British entrepreneur Julian Radcliffe, former SAS officer and a founder of the British firm Control Risks Group, why this is true and he said, "Well, of course, that is the case. We learned long ago how to occupy a nation and had the companies to do it, and you, well, you are still learning."

For my research, I relied mostly on interviews and primary sources, including court records, letters, memos, press releases, and transcripts of congressional hearings, speeches, news programs, and government agency press briefings, as well as audits by the General Accountability Office, reports from U.S. congressional commissions, Congressional Research Service studies, United Nations reports, academic studies, financial statements, and accounts received with the help of the Freedom of Information Act. In the notes, I identify the sources for direct quotes and for much of the background material. Sometimes the information in a paragraph of text might have been derived from several sources at different times. In some instances, I have included notes that expand upon something in the narrative.

Although government reports and studies are typically tedious and dry, for the most part the sources I consulted were far from dull. For example, the Congressional Research Service reports by Moshe Schwartz were always enlightening, and the 240-page final report of the U.S. Commission on Wartime Contracting, released in August 2011, was actually a page-turner.

Some insightful journalists have covered parts of this story as it has evolved. I have immensely appreciated their analyses and have identified them in both the text and the notes. Also, in the notes, I have referred to certain websites that I found helpful. However, because the mercenary edge of the PMSC industry sometimes inspires drama, some websites and blogs brim with stories that cannot be documented. An important and reliable website is the Private Security Monitor. A joint endeavor by the University of Denver's Josef Korbel School of International Studies Sié Chéou-Kang Center for International Security and Diplomacy, and DCAF, the Center for Democratic Control of the Armed Forces in Geneva, this website is a laudable effort to connect information about the global military and security industry. Its web address is psm.du.edu. Author David

Isenberg's website for the Isenberg Institute of Strategic Satire (iissonline.net) is also helpful in following new developments in the industry. There are others, including the Business and Human Rights Resource Centre—Corporate Legal Accountability Project, which helps with tracking relevant lawsuits. And, in addition to government websites that list the latest agency contracts, there is DangerZoneJobs.com, an online resource that shows available jobs for overseas contractors and includes some of the latest military and security contracts.

I periodically quote from several authors who have examined specific aspects of the private military and security story, including its history, federal contracting, company profiles, or boots-on-the-ground experiences. These include Stephen Armstrong, Deborah Avant, Kateri Carmola, Pratap Chatterjee, Steve Fainaru, Tony Geraghty, David Isenberg, Christopher Kinsey, Rachel Maddow, Robert Young Pelton, Dina Rasor and Robert Baumann, Jeremy Scahill, Bob Shepherd, Peter W. Singer, and Allison Stanger. Equally important primary sources were the individuals I interviewed, most of whom spoke on the record and are identified. The majority of those who remained off the record agreed to be quoted but not for attribution. Only a small percentage of people provided information "not for attribution." This is, after all, an industry rooted in secrecy. The range of individuals interviewed included military scholars and three American generals; U.S. agency staffers; industry workers and leaders; mercenaries, former and current; human rights advocates; former intelligence agents; insurance providers; advocates of privatization; antimercenary campaigners; legislators and congressional researchers; and fellow journalists. I confirmed details from interviews with other sources, and enlivened details from reports with anecdotes or comments from individuals I interviewed.

The Invisible Soldiers is not a comprehensive account of the PMSC industry. Entire books could be written about the Nisour Square massacre, the struggle for industry accountability, or the legal cases languishing in the aftermath of the Iraq and Afghanistan wars, to pick just three examples. But this book, showing a trajectory from the mercenary renaissance in the second half of the twentieth century to the privatization surge in the new century and into the age of drones, is intended to provide a basic overview of an industry that affects us all and yet because of its complexity and obfuscations has not been easily accessible or understood. I have approached the subject from an objective viewpoint, neither pro- nor anti-PMSC, but with determination to bring the industry out of the shadows and begin a dialogue.

There are dedicated professionals working at PMSCs and there are exemplary firms. As the book shows, there are success stories. The use of PMSCs for armed security on ships is one; as of early 2014, it had stymied violence on the high seas. But as I hope I have shown, accountability and oversight, in both international and domestic domains, are still lacking. If this industry is indeed a permanent part of globalization and if the U.S. embraces privatized defense and security as a solution to its global challenges, then better controls must be in place soon. And if the general public is well informed about the use and impact of PMSCs in America and worldwide, then more transparency becomes more possible. A vigorous public discourse about the implications of privatizing defense and security in a democratic nation, about the significance of this industry in the larger geopolitical context, and about improving transparency, will be crucial in the years ahead. It is my hope that this book, including the notes that follow, will inspire such discourse and encourage further investigation into the PMSC industry.

NOTES

PROLOGUE

Page

1 About Kadhim: Interviews with U.S. Army Special Forces operative Kadhim
Alkanani; with Shereef Akeel, one of his attorneys; and with former U.S. soldiers.
Also, the following documents:

- International Committee of the Red Cross: Original documents, confirming
  Kadhim's exodus from Kuwait, March 12, 1991, and registration at the Arta-
  wiya Refugee Camp in Saudi Arabia, March 14, 1991.
- Official Accident Report from U.S. Department of Defense, 031900D, June, 05:
  "The incident occurred approximately 300–400 meters away from the lead bar-
  riers at ECP 1 in the right, Department of Defense only, lane. The distance inter-
  val between the US Special Forces IOVs and the Aegis [sic] trail vehicle was in
  excess of 150 meters. The occupants of USSF IOVs observed no warnings."
- Case 1:09-cv-01607-RWR: Filed 8/24/09 in U.S. District Court, District of Co-
  lumbia. Complaint and Jury Demand. Khadim [sic] Alkanani, v. Aegis Defense
  Services, LLC, Washington, D.C., Aegis Defence Services Limited, London,
  U.K., Unidentified Aegis Employees and/or Agents, London, U.K.

4 *"You have to feel something":* Interview with Kadhim.

7 *"We are Americans!":* Ibid.

7 *"The men in the SUV had to have seen us":* Ibid.

8 *"behave somewhat less like bureaucrats":* Secretary of Defense Donald Rumsfeld's speech " '21st Century Transformation' of U.S. Armed Forces," National Defense University, Fort McNair, Washington, D.C., Thursday, January 31, 2002.

10 *"The Pentagon has a new map":* Interview with Gen. Edward Cardon, Fort Leavenworth, Kansas, March 2009.

10 *"organic capacity":* Commission on Wartime Contracting in Iraq and Afghanistan, Final Report to Congress, *At What Risk? Correcting Over-reliance on Contractors in Contingency Operations,* Executive Summary, August 2011, 2.

10 About the surge of private military contractors between 2009 and 2011: Congressional Research Service (CRS), a legislative branch agency within the Library of Congress, May 2011 report by Moshe Schwartz, Department of Defense Contractors in Afghanistan and Iraq: Background and Analysis, 7.

10 About the ratios: Commission on Wartime Contracting, Final Report, 21. State and USAID federal-employee data is current as of the end of 2010, and it was collected from the U.S. State Department, June 2011.

10 About the contractor casualties: Commission on Wartime Contracting, Final Report, 31, and from the Department of Labor, Division of Longshore and Harbor Workers' Compensation, "Defense Base Act Summary," June 23, 2011. Note that the Department of Labor has a disclaimer on its website regarding the issue of accuracy in contractor casualties. "These reports do not constitute the complete or official casualty statistics of civilian contractor injuries and deaths," www.dol.gov.

10 About MIA statistics, as of May 2011: Jack Healy, "With Withdrawal Looming, Trails Grow Cold For Americans Missing in Iraq," *New York Times*, May 21, 2011. Note that by 2014, there were three private contractors still missing in action, according to the Defense Prisoner of War Missing Personnel Office of the U.S. Department of Defense.

10 *more than 90 percent of diplomatic security:* Dr. Deborah Avant, director of the Sie Cheou-Kang Center for International Security, the University of Denver. Dr. Avant oversees the Private Security Monitor, an independent research project on government contracting, part of the Swiss Initiative in Geneva. Author of

The Market for Force: The Consequences of Privatizing Security (Cambridge, U.K.: Cambridge University Press, 2001). Avant is also quoted on this in *San Diego News*, September 15, 2012. See www.utsandiego.com/news/2012/sep/15/seal-vets-drawn-government-security-contracting/?print&page=all (accessed October 2012).

10 About Department of Homeland Security spending at least half of its budget on private contractors: Allison Stanger, *One Nation Under Contract* (New Haven and London: Yale University Press, 2009), 146.

10 About the United Nations' budget for private military and security contractors: Lou Pingeot, "Contracting Insecurity: Private Military and Security Companies and the Future of One United Nations," Global Policy Forum Report, February 2014, 6.

11 About increasing numbers of PMSC contracts coming out of the Central Intelligence Agency: David Perry, "Blackwater vs. Bin Laden: The Private Sector's Role in American Counterterrorism," Department of Political Science, Carleton University, Ottawa, Canada, *Comparative Strategy* 31 (2012), 50.

11 *"The current conduct of American counterterrorism":* Ibid., 42.

11 *"Although it is not widely recognized":* From transcript of the November 2, 2011, hearing of the House Committee on Oversight and Government Reform, Subcommittee on Technology, Information Policy, Intergovernmental Relations and Procurement Reform, "Are Government Contractors Exploiting Workers Overseas?"

11 *"Think back to the Alien series":* Interview with author–military analyst–blogger David Isenberg, 2011.

12 About the figures for publicly held PMSCs: Charles J. Dunar III, Jared L. Mitchell, and Donald L. Robbins III, *Private Military Industry Analysis: Private and Public Companies*, a massive study of 585 companies conducted by the Naval Post Graduate School in Monterey, California, December 2011, 48.

12 *the DOD did not begin to gather data:* Moshe Schwartz, *The Department of Defense's Use of Private Security Contractors in Iraq and Afghanistan*, Congressional Research Service, CRS 7-5700, R40835, January 19, 2010, 1, 6.

13 *"miscellaneous foreign contractors":* Commission on Wartime Contracting in Iraq and Afghanistan, August 2011, 24.

13 *"outside the normal contract licensing protocols":* Stanger, *One Nation Under Contract*, 91.

14 *"In the past non-Americans":* Katherine McCoy, "The Role of Nationality in the Private Military and Security Labor Force," Patuxent Defense Forum, St. Mary's College of Maryland, April 9, 2008, 1.

14 *"the U.S. government often doesn't know":* Center for Public Integrity, September 2010, taken from transcript of the November 2, 2011, hearing of the House Committee on Oversight and Government Reform, "Are Government Contractors Exploiting Workers Overseas?"

14 *"a story straight out of":* Interview with Eric Westropp, London, January 2011.

PART I: TRANSFORMATION
1: BEGINNINGS

Page

19 About the SFC: Personal observations on visits to London in 2009 and 2011. The descriptions are mostly based on the 2009 visit.

20 *"Didn't he start it?":* Various cabdrivers during London research trip, 2009.

22 Membership List: categories from a club member who asked for anonymity.

23 *"the new wars":* Partly from readings in Herfried Münkler, *The New Wars* (Cambridge, UK: Polity Press, 2005). Originally published in 2001 as *Die neuen Kriege.*

24 *"one of the centers of gravity for the industry":* Club member David Lattin.

24 About "The Circuit": This is a term used by industry insiders in the U.K. and discussed in the preface in this first-person account: Bob Shepherd, *The Circuit: An Ex-SAS Soldier, A Secretive Industry, The War on Terror, A True Story* (London: Macmillan, 2008). Shepherd, a former SAS operative, became a security advisor for "The Circuit," meaning the international network of PMSCs.

24 *"particularly suited":* British Army Handbook (London: Sutton Publishing, 2003), 50, 104.

25 About the background of the industry: Culled from interviews with U.S. military experts and former British Army officers, in London, Washington, D.C., and Fort Leavenworth. And numerous readings, including the following:

- Armstrong, Stephen. *War PLC: The Rise of the New Corporate Mercenary.* London: Faber & Faber, 2008.
- Avant, Deborah. *The Market for Force: The Consequences of Privatizing Security.* Cambridge, U.K.: Cambridge University Press, 2001.

- Bloch, Jonathan, and Patrick Fitzgerald. *British Intelligence and Covert Action.* Dingle County, Kerry, Ireland: Brandon Book Publishers, 1983.
- Campbell, Duncan. "Marketing the 'New Dogs of War.'" Center for Public Integrity, October 2002.
- Geraghty, Tony. *Soldiers of Fortune: A History of the Mercenary in Modern Warfare.* New York: Pegasus Books, 2009.
- Hughes, Solomon. *War on Terror, Inc.: Corporate Profiteering From the Politics of Fear.* London: Verso, 2007.
- Isenberg, David. *Soldiers of Fortune Ltd.: A Profile of Today's Private Sector Corporate Mercenary Firms.* Washington, D.C.: Center for Defense Information Monograph, 1997. And *Shadow Force: Private Contractors in Iraq.* Westport, CT: Praeger Security International, 2009.
- Kinsey, Christopher. *Corporate Soldiers and International Security: The Rise of Private Military Companies.* London and New York: Routledge, 2006.
- Pelton, Robert Young. *Licensed to Kill: Hired Guns in the War on Terror.* New York: Three Rivers Press, 2006.
- Singer, Peter W. *Corporate Warriors.* Ithaca and London: Cornell University Press, 2002.

29 *"a rash of smaller-scale conflicts":* Avant, *The Market for Force,* 35.
29 About Halliburton and Brown & Root: Halliburton, the Houston-based oil field services company, was founded in 1919, and in 1962 it purchased Brown & Root, a construction and engineering firm, also founded in 1919 and known for its building of roads and oil rigs. Brown & Root became Halliburton's big money-maker in logistics-support contracts. Halliburton is often referred to as the cornerstone of America's privatized logistics-support sector, and that is true except that it was Halliburton's Brown & Root that had the contracts. Then in 1998, Halliburton bought Dresser Industries, a firm providing integrated services in the oil and gas industry; and one of Dresser's subsidiaries was Kellogg, an oil engineering firm. In 2002, Kellogg, Brown & Root became KBR, Inc. And in 2007 the tie between Brown & Root ended when Halliburton spun off KBR, Inc.
30 *"sending the military into war":* Rachel Maddow, *Drift: The Unmooring of American Military Power* (New York: Crown Publishers), 137.
32 *"nonstrategic interest":* Ibid., 178.
32 *"the politically correct version":* Pelton, *Licensed to Kill,* 260.

32 *"the greatest corporate assemblage"*: Isenberg, *Soldiers of Fortune Ltd.*, 14.

33 *"The privatized effort"*: Singer, *Corporate Warrior*, 6.

2: OUT OF THE SHADOWS

Page

35 About the restaurant: Author's on-site observation, 2009.

36 About the October 1995 meeting: Tim Spicer, *An Unorthodox Soldier* (Edinburgh, Scotland: Mainstream Publishing Co., 1999), 244–249. And an interview with an individual knowledgeable about the meeting, as well as Duncan Campbell's 2002 article "Marketing the Dogs of War" for the Center for Public Integrity, Stephen Armstrong's *War PLC*, Robert Young Pelton's *Licensed to Kill*, and Robert Baer's "Iraq's Mercenary King" in *Vanity Fair*, April 2007.

 NOTE: The choice of the year 1995 (as there have been references to its occurring in 1996) is based on interviews; on the reference in Spicer's book; on the date of the news article exposing the link between Heritage Oil and Executive Outcomes and issues for the British Liberal Party politician; on the dates of Sandline's beginnings; and on the first use of the term "private military company" in the media, in November 1995.

37 *"EO's Rolodex"*: Ibid., 266.

37 *"a superficial sheen of respectable leadership"*: Ibid., 267.

37 *"a properly organized, professional company marketing military skills"*: Spicer, *An Unorthodox Soldier*, 145.

37 *"There were legitimate governments"*: Ibid., 155.

38 *"took a lot of emotion out of the situation"*: Sara Pearson, public relations consultant, quoted in Campbell, "Marketing the New Dogs of War," Center for Public Integrity, October 2002, 9.

38 *The first use of the term "private military company"*: The article that described Executive Outcomes as a "private military company" was in Agence-France Presse and noted in Campbell, "Marketing the 'New Dogs of War.'" Center for Public Integrity, October 2002, 8.

38 *"the public face of a PR campaign"*: Stephen Armstrong, "The Enforcer," *The Guardian*, May 20, 2006.

39 *"The possibility of the United States"* and about the meeting at the Army War College: Thomas Ricks, *Fiasco: The American Military Adventure in Iraq* (New York: Penguin Press, 2006), 72.

39 About the figures for the occupation: Pelton, *Licensed to Kill*, 103.

40 About the two orders: James P. Pfiffner, "US Blunders in Iraq: De-Baathification and Disbanding the Army," *Intelligence and National Security* 25, no. 1 (February 2010): 76–85.

40 *40,000 schoolteachers who had joined the Party:* George Tenet, *At the Center of the Storm: My Years at the CIA* (New York: HarperCollins, 2007), 427.

40 About the statistics regarding the displaced security forces: Ricks, *Fiasco,* 162, 192.

41 *"we snatched defeat from the jaws of victory":* Ibid., 163.

41 *"the coalition will actively oppose":* L. Paul Bremer III, *My Year in Iraq* (New York: Simon & Schuster, 2006), 39.

41 About provenance of Order 2: Ibid., 57, 58, 235, and 236.

41 *"the first contractors' war":* From various sources interviewed and other writers, including Stanger, *One Nation Under Contract*, p. 99.

42 *"In a matter of months, private security":* Pelton, *Licensed to Kill,* 106.

42 About the subcontractors and internationalization of the PMSC workforce: See McCoy, "The Role of Nationality in the Private Military and Security Labor Force," 6. Pelton, *Licensed to Kill,* 105–7. Stanger, *One Nation Under Contract*, 104. David Isenberg, "The Other Side of the Global PMC Industry," Huffington Post, December 13, 2010.

44 About statistics for late 2003 in Iraq: Pelton, *Licensed to Kill,* 107.

46 *"the largest single piece":* Boston Globe, June 22, 2004.

3: A WATERSHED YEAR

Page

47 About the 2004 alerts: Robb Willer, Cornell University sociology doctoral candidate, study of twenty-six alerts, conducted in October 2004, and from individual news stories announcing the alerts.

47 *"a catastrophic attack within the U.S.":* U.S. State Department announcement on March 19, 2004. Also referred to in Anwar Iqbal, "Worldwide Caution: al Qaida Attacks Feared," United Press International, March 19, 2004.

48 *"multiple locations, multiple sources":* Ibid.

48 *"the considerable detail and quality":* Ibid.

48 *"Reports That Led to Terror":* Douglas Jehl and David Cay Johnston, *New York Times*, August 3, 2004.

48 *"Maritime terrorism is a ticking time bomb"*: Dominic Armstrong, "Insight & Opinion," *Lloyd's List*, June 22, 2004.

48 *"We believe al Qaeda and its associates"*: Stefano Ambrogi, "Experts: al Qaeda Maritime Threat Growing," Reuters, February 18, 2004.

50 *"mobile vehicle warfare"*: DOD Contract #W911SO-04-C-0003.

52 About Simon Mann and the attempted Equatorial Guinea coup, of which there are many accounts: Robert Young Pelton's account in *Licensed to Kill* is informative in Chapter Ten, "The Very Model of a Modern Major Mercenary." And Adam Roberts's book *The Wonga Coup: Guns, Thugs, and a Ruthless Determination to Create Mayhem in an Oil-Rich Corner of Africa* (New York: Public Affairs, 2006) tells the story in great detail.

4: THE FAINT HUM OF SECRECY

Page

55 *"Thanks to the contract signed"*: Remy Ourdan, "The Irresistible Rise of Lieutenant Colonel Tim Spicer in Baghdad's Private Security El Dorado," *Le Monde*, July 1, 2004.

56 *"We would draw your attention"*: Letter, from British Ministry of Defence Procurement Agency, London, sent in response to a letter from U.S. Army transportation command at Fort Eustis, Virginia, May 11, 2004.

57 *"Controversial ex-British army officer"*: *Financial Times*, June 19, 2004.

57 *"the contract could prove"*: Ibid.

57 *"colourful"*: Ibid.

57 *"a case study in what not to do"*: Peter Singer, *New York Times*, June 15, 2004.

57 *"A core problem"*: Ibid.

58 *"It's an embarrassment"*: Peter Singer, *Boston Globe*, June 22, 2004.

58 *"shockingly"*: DynCorp complaint #B-294232 filed with the GAO, and quoted in Jimmy Burns and Thomas Catan, "DynCorp Seeks to Overturn Iraq Contract," *Financial Times*, July 22, 2004.

58 *"It is inconceivable that the firm"*: Letter to Secretary of Defense Donald Rumsfeld from Republican Congressman Pete Sessions of Texas. Mary Fitzgerald, "U.S. Contract to British Firm Sparks Irish American Protest," *Washington Post*, August 9, 2004.

59 *"Dear Secretary Rumsfeld"*: Letter, signed by Senators Ted Kennedy of Massachusetts, Hillary Clinton and Charles Schumer of New York, and Chris Dodd of Connecticut, to then Secretary of Defense Rumsfeld, August 25, 2004.

61 *"Tear up that contract, Mr. Bush":* Letter to the editor. Father Sean McManus, *Washington Post*, August 9, 2004.

61 *"tender process":* Pelton, *Licensed to Kill*, 277.

61 *"The awarding of the contract":* Aegis press release, Aegis website (accessed summer 2010).

62 *"It's like a blast from the past":* Peter Singer, in Pratap Chatterjee, "Controversial Commando Wins," *CorpWatch*, June 9, 2004.

62 *"The Army never even bothered":* Charles M. Sennott, "Security Firm's $293 million Deal Under Scrutiny," *Boston Globe* (London Bureau), June 22, 2004.

62 *"security work in Africa and SE Asia":* U.S. Army spokesman Major Gary C. Tallman, a spokesman for the U.S. Army Transportation Board at Fort Eustis, Virginia, in Mary Pat Flaherty, "Iraq Work Awarded," *Washington Post*, June 16, 2004. Also, Tallman quoted in Robert Young Pelton, "Mercenary Hits Big, Thanks to the U.S.," *Los Angeles Times*, June 24, 2004.

62 *"The USG [US government] needs an organ":* Email to Deborah Avant, July 2004, from Cobus Claassens, a former EO contractor in Sierra Leone, then at the firm Southern Cross Security, in Avant, *The Market for Force*, 227, 228. About Claasens' Sierra Leone experience, see Pelton, *Licensed to Kill*, 264.

63 *"Some people have suggested":* Deborah Avant, "Armies for Hire," *Voice of America*, August 12, 2004.

63 About Spicer and Sandline, background: Obtained from his autobiography, interviews with him, and the works of other writers including Robert Young Pelton, Tony Geraghty, Stephen Armstrong, and Christopher Kinsey.

66 *"each of which achieved something":* Pelton, *Licensed to Kill*, 272.

66 *"Some people in the insurance business":* Ibid.

66 *"He told me he was":* Richard Kay, "Forsyth Is Now a Fat Cat of War," *Daily Mail*, October 25, 2005.

67 About the *Dewi Madrim* incident details: Carolin Liss, *Oceans of Crime: Maritime Piracy and Transnational Security in Southeast Asia and Bangladesh* (Singapore: Institute of Southeast Asian Studies, 2010), 105–7.

68 *"According to a new study":* The Economist, October 2, 2003.

68 *"He [Spicer] fears that":* Ibid.

68 *"Terror at Sea":* Times (London), April 26, 2004.

68 *"Terrorists May Be Rehearsing":* Ibid.

68 *"It is very easy for those":* Felix Soh, "US Terror Warning No Over-Reaction," in *The Straits Times*, August 10, 2004.

69 *"analyzing the nature of the marine terror"*: Thom Cookes, host of Australian ABC-TV show *Lateline*, September 7, 2004.

69 *"the mercenary thrown out of Papua, New Guinea"*: Cookes, Ibid.

69 *"These days"*: Ibid.

69 *"You haven't had any baggage"*: Ibid.

69 *"I am hoping that President Bush will show"*: Fr. Sean McManus, in Tom Griffin, "Spicer Contract Approved as Mercenary Links Revealed," *Irish World*, October 8, 2004.

70 *"Tony Blair's Pet Bulldog?"*: William Bowles, "Tony Blair's Pet Bulldog? The Curious Case of Colonel Tim Spicer," in online Investigating the New Imperialism, August 18, 2004.

71 *"What really happened"*: Interview with Dominick Donald, Travellers Club, London, January 2009.

71 *"In the early days of Iraq"*: This quote comes from an individual well informed in the security risk analyses of Iraq in 2004 who was interviewed in January 2011 in London. He was willing to go on the record but not for attribution. In other such instances, I have taken quotes out of the story if I could not attach a name, but in this case I did not want to deny the reader the information.

72 *"Congratulations on this assignment"*: Sir David Frost, *Breakfast with Frost*, October 3, 2004.

72 *"al-Qaeda may seek to block"*: *Lloyd's List*, December 8, 2004.

72 *"maritime insecurity"*: Ibid., December 22, 2004.

72 *"The fact that"*: Ibid., January 7, 2005.

5: RULES OF ENGAGEMENT

Page

76 *"When it arrived in Iraq"*: Industry insider in London who was in Iraq working at a PSC at the time; backed up by another private contractor and by the findings of both Robert Young Pelton in *Licensed to Kill* and Stephen Armstrong in *War PLC*.

76 *"there is no assurance that Aegis"*: Audit Report #05-005 of the Office of the Special Inspector General for Iraq Reconstruction, April 20, 2005, 1; also in Sue Pleming, "Update 1-US Audit Critical of Aegis Security Work in Iraq," *Reuters*, April 22, 2005.

77 *"failed to verify that employees"*: April 20, 2005, SIGIR Audit report, 4, 6.

77 *"police checks are difficult to obtain"*: Ibid.

77 *"fairly minor"*: Griff Witte, "Contractor, Army Office Fell Short, Audit Finds," *Washington Post*, April 23, 2005, E1.

78 *"is deeply troubling"*: Feingold, ibid.

78 *"Aegis was supposed to be providing"*: Ibid.

79 *In later years*: Interview with a contractor who now owns a private security company and asked the author not to use his name. He was in Baghdad in 2004 and 2005, and the author interviewed him jointly with a London-based journalist, at the Diplomat Hotel, Belgravia, London, January 2011.

79 About the Mystery Train video and what became known as the "Aegis Dialogues," the online commentary about the incident: Several writers have described this episode, often referred to as the "Trophy Video." Especially helpful was Tony Geraghty's excellent account in his book *Soldiers of Fortune*, 224–241. The author received a copy of all of the videos and so the descriptions are from firsthand observations.

80 *"Jesus, it must be bad if all cars"*: Geraghty, *Soldiers of Fortune*, 229.

80 *"All this plays into the hands"*: Ibid., 230.

81 *"all such incidents"*: Aegis spokesman, *Times* (London), December 1, 2005.

81 *"at least two instances of innocent"*: Ibid.

81 *"There is nothing to indicate"*: Sean Rayment, "New Iraq 'Trophy Videos' Raise Fears on Civilian Deaths," *Telegraph*, December 4, 2005.

81 *"We don't know because we never stop"*: Rod Stoner's interview on *More4 News* in London, in Geraghty, *Soldiers of Fortune*, 238, 239.

81 *"speaking to the press or disseminating"*: Ibid., 238.

81 *"living underground"*: Interview with former colleague of Stoner's, London, January 2011.

82 *"Men with Guns Are the New Dot.coms"*: Mathew Lynn, *Spectator*, November 4, 2006, 36.

84 *"If Kadhim had died"*: Interview with Shereef Akeel, Michigan attorney, autumn 2011.

6: PRIVATIZED MAYHEM

Page

85 *"We're in the wake of a speedboat"*: Interview with Ohio Representative Marcy Kaptur, spring 2010.

86 *"$292 million"*: Henry A. Waxman, *Dollars, Not Sense: Government Contracting*

Under the Bush Administration, Executive Summary, Committee on Government Reform, Special Investigations Division, June 2006.

86 *"When the [Department of Defense] refuses"*: The Green Ribbon blog, "Congresswoman Wins New Audit of Aegis Contract," May 8, 2007; *Defense Daily* 235, no. 31 (August 14), 2007.

86 *"selling out"*: Jeremy Scahill, "Pull the Plug on the Mercenary War," *The Nation*, May 14, 2007.

87 About Aegis revenues: From documents on file at the Companies House Direct in London (Britain's corporate registry). Company #04541965, for Aegis Defence Services Limited.

88 *"This is only just becoming an industry"*: James Boxell, "Aegis Defence Adds Rubicon to Its Portfolio," quoting Aegis's managing director Mark Bullough, *Financial Times*, November 4, 2005.

89 *Scott, who had served:* U.S. Government Accountability Office (GAO), B-298370; B-298490: Brian X. Scott, August 18, 2006. Decision: We deny the protests. In the end it was the GAO that allowed the government to proceed with the 2007 contract award.

90 *"a high-stakes derby"*: Alec Klein, "U.S. Army Awards Iraq Security Work To British Firm," *Washington Post*, September 14, 2007.

90 About the Nisour Square event: Factual Proffer in Support of Guilty Plea of Jeremy P. Ridgeway, in U.S. v. Jeremy P. Ridgeway, Case #08-341-01, in U.S. District Court for the District of Columbia. Filed December 4, 2008, www.justice .gov/opa/documents/us-v-ridgeway.pdf.

NOTE: A diagram of Nisour Square can be found at www.nytimes.com /interactive/2007/09/21/world/middleeast/0921-blackwater-nisour-square.html.

91 About Nisour Square, names of victims: Estate of Mushtaq Karim Abd Al-Razzaq et al v. XE et al, in U.S. District Court Southern District of California (San Diego), Case #3:09-cv-00626-LAB-BLM. Filed March 26, 2009. Newspaper accounts about the tragedy include Sudarsan Raghavan, "Tracing the Paths of 5 Who Died in a Storm of Gunfire," *Washington Post*, October 4, 2007; *New York Times*, September 21, 2007; and Jeremy Scahill, "Blackwater's Youngest Victim," *The Nation*, January 28, 2010.

92 *"posed no threat to the convoy"*: Estate of Mushtaq Karim Abd Al-Razzaq et al v. XE et al.

93 *"may often be forced"*: Ibid.

93 *"about 15 layers of regulatory control"*: Times (London), October 15, 2007.

PART II: REACTION
7: SOUNDING THE ALARM

Page

98 *"Over the past 25 years"*: From the transcript of the hearing conducted in Washington, D.C., at the Rayburn House Office Building on October 2, two weeks after Nisour Square, in Room 2143 at 10:12 A.M., the U.S. House of Representatives Committee on Oversight and Government Reform, 3.

99 *"We thank you for that service"*: Ibid., 4.

99 *"We are trying to do"*: Ibid., 3.

99 *"In recent days"*: Ibid., 4, 5.

100 *"This didn't happen out on a mission"*: Ibid., 5.

101 *"become an inescapable fact of modern life"*: Ranking member Davis, ibid., 6.

101 *"Blackwater has protected dozens, if not hundreds"*: Ibid., 7.

102 *"the liberal cause du jour"*: North Carolina House Republican Patrick T. McHenry, ibid., 9.

102 *"our team/their team"*: Ohio Republican Michael Turner, ibid., 43.

103 *"Eighty-four percent of the shooting"*: Ohio Democrat Dennis Kucinich, 27.

103 *"if war is privatized and private contractors"*: Kucinich, ibid., 28.

103 *"the random death of an innocent Iraqi"* and the June 25, 2005 incident: Ibid., 32.

103 About the November 27, 2004 incident: Ibid., 86.

104 *"You are an X-wing fighter"*: During Blackwater plane crash, November 27, 2004, ibid., 16.

104 *"background and experience shortfalls"*: Email sent from site manager to Blackwater executive, ibid., 17.

105 *"Mike, like Mr. Prince, was a CEO"*: Ibid.

105 *"Mr. Prince, Colonel McMahon is asking"*: Ibid.

105 *"Were any sanctions placed on the company"*: Ibid., 18, 19.

106 *"weapons were discharged in"*: Ibid., 14.

107 *"Everything Blackwater's men did"*: Erik Prince, *Civilian Warriors: The Inside Story of Blackwater and the Unsung Heroes of the War on Terror* (New York: Penguin, 2013), 235.

107 *"got its 100 percent survival rate"*: Ibid., 163.

107 *"and other nefarious forces"*: Transcript from October 2, 2007 hearing, 40.

107 *"If the [U.S.] government doesn't want"*: Ibid., 41.

108 *"I want to let everyone know"*: October 2 hearing transcript, 69.

8: "A REMARKABLY UNPRECEDENTED EXPERIMENT"

Page

109 About Jan Schakowsky: Interview with Schakowsky, Rayburn Office Building, Washington, D.C., February 2012.

110 About Colombia trip: "Joint Statement of Representatives Jan Schakowsky and Jim McGovern from Bogotá, Colombia," a press release out of Schakowsky's office, February 21, 2001.

110 *"privateer mercenaries":* Jeremy Bigwood, "DynCorp in Colombia: Outsourcing the Drug War," *Corp Watch,* May 25, 2001.

110 *"American taxpayers already pay $300 billion":* Schakowsky quote, ibid.

111 *"Are we outsourcing in order to avoid":* Ibid.

112 *"There were wake-up calls":* Interview with Schakowsky.

112 About laws: Especially helpful, for both MEJA and the Uniform Code of Military Justice, were the following: "The Long Arm of the Law: The Military Extraterritorial Jurisdiction Act," www.questia.com, a Free Online Library (accessed September 2012); Elizabeth K. Waits, "Avoiding the 'Legal Bermuda Triangle': The Military Extraterritorial Jurisdiction Act's Unprecedented Expansion of U.S. Criminal Jurisdiction Over Foreign Nationals," *Arizona Journal of International & Comparative Law* 23, no. 6 (2006): 493–518; David Isenberg, *Shadow Force: Private Security Contractors in Iraq* (Westport, Conn., and London: Praeger Security International, 2009); interviews with Asher Hildebrand, who worked in North Carolina Representative David Price's office and was especially helpful in pulling together the threads of this quite complicated tapestry.

113 *"The Iraq and Afghanistan Contractors Sunshine Act":* H.R. 897, introduced February 7, 2007.

114 *"restore the responsibility of the American military":* Jan Schakowsky, press release, H.R. 4102, October 2007.

115 *"Mr. Prince, in your testimony":* U.S. House of Representatives Committee on Oversight and Government Reform, Hearing Transcript, October 2, 2007.

118 *"I'm no hero":* Prince, *Civilian Warriors,* 170.

118 About the number of hearings: There are several numbers for the total number of hearings. I counted seven and the professor from Carlton University did too: David Perry, "Blackwater vs. Bin Laden: The Private Sector's Role in American Counterterrorism," *Comparative Strategy* 31, no. 1 (2012), 43.

118 *"grave concerns":* Isenberg, *Shadow Force,* 134.

119 *"designated by the Secretary of Defense":* Perry, "Blackwater vs. Bin Laden," 46.

120 About Swiss Initiative background: Interviews in London and in Geneva, 2011.

9: CONQUERING CHAOS

Page

123 About the Eden Palace: Observation of author when conducting interviews in Geneva, July 2011.

123 About the Swiss Initiative and *The Montreux Document on Private Military and Security Companies*: From interviews with participants in the Swiss Initiative as well as the detailed description in the Federal Department of Foreign Affairs of the Government of Switzerland, September 17, 2008. Also from the document itself, *Montreux Document on Pertinent International Legal Obligations and Good Practices for States Related to Operations of Private Military and Security Companies During Armed Conflict* (Montreux, Switzerland, Swiss Initiative, in Cooperation with the International Committee of the Red Cross, on Private Military and Security Companies," September 17, 2008). And a few more informative works on the topic, including:

- Doug Brooks, "The Swiss Show Some Initiative," *Journal of International Peace Operations*, no. 6 (May–June 2008).
- Colum Lynch, "UN Embraces Private Military Contractors," Global Policy Forum, *Foreign Policy Magazine*, January 17, 2010.
- Andre du Plessis, "The Global Code of Conduct for Private Security Companies: Why It Matters to Humanitarian Organisations," *Humanitarian Exchange Magazine*, www.odihpn.org/report.asp?id=3122 (accessed January 2011).
- Amnesty International, "Amnesty International Public Statement on the Montreux Document on Pertinent International Legal Obligations and Good Practices for States Related to the Operations of Private Military and Security Companies During Armed Conflict," October 2008, www.amnestyusa.org /document.php?id=ENGIOR300102008.

124 *"a new archetype":* Ibid.

124 *"toolkit," "bible," "milestone":* James Cockayne, "Regulating Private Military and Security Companies: The Content, Negotiation, Weaknesses and Promise of the Montreux Document," *Journal of Conflict & Security Law* 13, no. 3 (2009): 401–28.

126 *"expression to the consensus":* Press release issued by the Federal Department of Foreign Affairs, Switzerland, September 17, 2008.

126 *"[Montreux] was about recognizing"*: Interview with Anne-Marie Buzatu, Geneva, July 2011.

126 *"It all worked well"*: Ibid.

126 About the history of DCAF: Interviews, and report by the director from Geneva Centre for the Democratic Control of Armed Forces (covering the period January 1999 to March 2001), 2001.

127 *"The privatization of military and security services"*: "Private Military Companies," DCAF Backgrounder Series, April 2006.

129 *"What we wanted to do from the start"*: Interview with Buzatu.

130 *"confusion among terms"*: Anne Marie Buzatu, speech given at Montreux, Switzerland, April 14, 2008.

131 *"far from providing insurance against sudden death"*: James Glanz and Andrew W. Lehren, "Use of Contractors Added to War's Chaos in Iraq," *New York Times,* October 23, 2010.

132 Erinys shooting in October 2007: Mark Townsend, "Iraq Victims Sue UK Security Firm," *The Observer,* January 10, 2009.

132 Killing of four young Iraqis in October 2007: "Shot on Their Way Home from Church." The Guardian Australia Culture Blog, October 16, 2007.

132 *"still in the development phase"*: Interview with Julian Radcliffe, London, January 2011.

132 The ethics committees: Interview with head of the British Association of Private Security Companies, Andy Bearpark, London, January 2011.

132 About Eric Westropp: Interviews in London, 2009 and 2011.

133 *"Eric is the one who is always"*: A long-time acquaintance and former colleague, 2011.

134 *"a way to conquer the chaos"*: Westropp, interviews.

134 *"It will happen eventually"*: Ibid.

135 *"The CEO of Aegis Defense Services"*: Letter to a Chicago, Illinois, constituent from then Senator Barack Obama, November 27, 2005; Tom Griffin, "Irish Urge Obama to Keep Promise on Spicer," *Irish Echo,* December 15, 2005.

135 *"From this war's very beginning"*: Statement from then New York Senator Hillary Clinton, out of Clinton campaign, "Senator Clinton Cosponsors Legislation to Ban Use of Private Security Contractors in Iraq and Afghanistan," February 28, 2008.

136 *"There is room for private contractors"*: *Military Times,* July 2, 2008.

137 About the Obama-Goodman exchange: Cooper Union in NYC after Obama gave a speech there, on March 28, 2008.

137 *"bordering on inherently governmental functions":* Walter Pincus, "Despite Concerns, Pentagon Seeks Civilian Firm to Oversee Contractors," *Washington Post,* December 19, 2008.

138 *"to specialize in peacemaking, peacekeeping":* Andrew Bacevich, *The Limits of Power: The End of American Exceptionalism* (New York: Henry Holt & Co., 2008; with Afterword, 2009), 143.

138 *"Rather than transforming the armed forces":* Ibid.

139 *"thousands of contract security forces":* Transcript from January 10, 2007, hearing at the Senate Armed Services Committee, Gen. David H. Petraeus statements to the committee. www.gpo.gov/fdsys/pkgCHRG-110shrg42309/html (accessed August 2013).

139 *"assets available to him to supplement":* Walter Pincus, "Security Contracts to Continue in Iraq: New Top Commander Counts Hired Guards Among His Assets," January 2007, *Washington Post,* February 4, 2007, A19.

10: THE GENERAL AND KADHIM

Page

141 *"unprecedented inclusion of private military companies":* "Private Military Companies (PMC) Case Study," by Section 16—PMC Pilot Study Group at the U.S. Army Command and General Staff College, Fort Leavenworth, Kansas, 2009, 4.

141 *the U.S. force in Afghanistan:* James Glanz, "Contractors Outnumber U.S. Troops in Afghanistan," *New York Times,* September 2, 2009, A8.

141 About the percentage of defense contractors supplying services: Allison Stanger, *One Nation Under Contract: The Outsourcing of American Power and the Future of Foreign Policy* (London: Yale University Press, 2009), 87.

142 *"Some nation could hire":* Interview with Gen. Edward Cardon, Command and General Staff College at Fort Leavenworth, March 2009.

142 About Fort Leavenworth: The author visited Fort Leavenworth several times during the spring of 2009.

142 *"Leavenworth is where military doctrine is written":* Robert D. Kaplan, "Fort Leavenworth and the Eclipse of Nationhood," *Atlantic Monthly,* September 1996, 2.

144 *"has altered irrevocably the American way of war":* Deborah C. Kidwell, *Public War, Private Fight? The United States and Private Military Companies,* Global

War on Terrorism, Occasional Paper 12 (Fort Leavenworth, Kans.: Combat Studies Institute Press, 2005), 65.

144 *"PMCs lack the exemplary performance record"*: Ibid., 67.

144 *"Does the current extensive use"*: Ibid.

145 *"Walmarts of war"*: Discussion with one of the Leavenworth Study participants, who spoke on record without attribution. Note that the author met with participants of the study, all career military, on several occasions, and each asked not to be named.

145 *"Have we circumvented the ability to have"*: Discussion with participant in the study.

146 *"What concerns me are the paradoxes"*: Discussion with participant in the study.

147 *"symmetrical conflicts between states"*: Interview with Gen. Edward Cardon, Command and General Staff College, Fort Leavenworth, March 2009.

148 *"the nation state, with its slow ability"*: Ibid.

148 *"update the DOD doctrine"*: Moshe Schwartz, *Department of Defense Contractors in Iraq and Afghanistan: Background and Analysis*, Congressional Research Service, August 13, 2009, 16.; Moshe Schwartz, *The Department of Defense's Use of Private Security Contractors in Iraq and Afghanistan*," Congressional Research Service, January 19, 2010, "Summary," 1.

149 *"blowing through intersections"*: (CNN Executive Producer) Suzanne Simmons, *Master of War: Blackwater USA's Erik Prince and the Business of War* (New York: HarperCollins, 2009), 161.

150 *"core US military missions"*: Thom Shanker and David S. Cloud, "Pentagon to Raise Importance of 'Stability' Efforts in War," *New York Times*, November 20, 2005.

150 *"Once the Iraq and Afghanistan"*: Sean McFate, "US Africa Command: Next Step OR Next Stumble? *African Affairs* (U.S. Institute of Peace), December 24, 2007, 7.

151 like *"seeing the sun after many days of darkness"*: Interview with Kadhim Alkanani, Fort Worth, Texas, 2011.

151 *"One of our own gets shot"*: Interview with Shereef Akeel, 2011.

151 *"unidentified agents acted negligently"*: Case 1:09-cv-01607-RWR, filed 8/24/09 in U.S. District Court, District of Columbia, 2.

152 *"I tried not to judge"*: Interview with Kadhim Alkanani, 2011.

154 *"One wonders if the Olympic"*: David Isenberg, Huffington Post blog, May 21, 2010.

11: "WHAT'S ALL THE FUSS ABOUT?"

Page

156 *"The spread of sporadic small-scale wars"*: Martin van Creveld, *The Transformation of War* (New York: Simon & Schuster, 1991), 207.

157 *"The private military sector is distinctive"*: Stanger, *One Nation Under Contract*, 91. Note that several good examples of the challenges of tracking the contracts, such as the $50 million lid for reporting to Congress, are in Stanger, 91–92.

158 *"moved from the periphery of international politics"*: Fabien Mathieu and Nick Dearden, *Corporate Mercenaries: The Threat of Private Military and Security Companies* (London: War on Want, 2006), 2.

159 *"If the government does propose"*: Tim Hancock (campaigns director), *The Guardian*, April 23, 2009.

159 *"The government proposal that mercenary groups"*: Paddy McGuffin, "Scandal of Britain's Hired Guns," *Morning Star* (a London-based tabloid), May 11, 2009.

160 *"Behind [this] is the old colonial structure"*: Elizabeth Rubin, "An Army of One's Own," *Harper's* magazine, February 1997.

161 About privatization of the military being a strategy in the last years of apartheid in South Africa: Deborah Avant, *Market for Force,* 158–59.

161 *"mercenary activity"*: Mathieu and Dearden, *Corporate Mercenaries*, 18–19.

161 *"highlighted the government's inability"*: "Privatized War and Its Price," *New York Times*, editorial, January 10, 2010.

162 *"I have watched the discussions"*: Dominick Donald, *After the Bubble*, Whitehall Paper 66 (London: The Royal United Services Institute for Defence and Security Studies, 2006), ix. His point of view, from an interview in London in 2009.

163 *"Since privatization is intimately connected"*: Stanger, *One Nation Under Contract,* 33.

163 *"taking on a different shape"*: Ibid., 7.

164 *"As private security companies"*: Aegis Defence Services, www.aegisworld.com (accessed spring 2010).

164 *"A first step towards regulation"*: Spicer, *An Unorthodox Soldier*, 25.

166 *"Tim Spicer is the future of warfare"*: Stephen Armstrong, "The Enforcer," *The Guardian*, May 20, 2006.

166 *"the closest thing to the father"*: Armstrong, *War PLC*, 51.

166 *"The American companies came later"*: Interview with Tim Spicer, Washington, D.C., January 2010.

166 *"At first, they were accused"*: Ibid.

167 *"Military expeditionary operations"*: Ibid.

168 The British edition of the third volume of Sword of Honour is entitled *Unconditional Surrender*.

168 *"much more concerned about his regiment"*: Ibid.

12: A THICKET OF IRONIES

Page

169 *"If virtue becomes vice"*: Reinhold Niebuhr, *The Irony of American History* (New York: Charles Scribner's Sons, 1952), xxiv.

170 *"a mercenary outfit"*: Newspaper headlines in Switzerland.

170 *"governments that were Western-Allied governments"*: Kristi Clemens Rogers testimony before the Commission on Wartime Contracting hearing "Private Security Contractors in Iraq: Where Are We Going?" June 21, 2010.

170 *"Everyone was busy"*: Interview with Rep. Marcy Kaptur in Ohio, 2010.

171 *"a blandly named cut-out"*: Spencer Ackerman, wired.com, February 24, 2010. Details about IDS's geneaology in this article and also in Jeff Stein's "Blackwater Firm Partners with State Dept., CIA Insiders," *Washington Post*, October 1, 2010.

171 *"setting up shell companies"*: Senate Armed Services Committee hearing, February, 24, 2010.

171 *"Do we check these things out?"*: Ibid.

173 *In the report:* 2009 Report from the Special Inspector General for Iraq Reconstruction, *Oversight of Aegis's Performance on Security Services Contracts in Iraq with the Department of Defense*, SIGIR-09-010, January 14, 2009, Executive Summary; Robert O'Harrow, Jr., "Government Inc." *Washington Post*, January 15, 2009.

173 *"Dogs of War"*: David Isenberg, UPI, January 30, 2009.

173 *"considered to be a model contractor"*: Ibid.

PART III: EXPANSION
13: SHELL GAMES

Page

178 *"anarchist literature"*: Zane Fischer, "Welcome to Terror Town" *Santa Fe Reporter*, November 5, 2003.

178 *"the realistic environment of the FBI's Hogan's Alley"*: Ibid.

179 About the Aegis contract: Matthew Potter, "New Mexico Tech's Investment in Realistic Training Leads to Protection Contract Support," *Defense Procurement News*, March 14, 2011.

180 *"Securing Our Country"*: Special Operations Consulting, "Training," www.soc-usa.com (accessed December 2011).

180 *"I can report that, as promised"*: President Barack Obama speech, October 21, 2011, reported in various news outlets by the Associated Press, October 21, 2011.

181 *"a backdoor way of continuing"*: Jeremy Scahill, "Iraq Withdrawal? Obama and Clinton Expanding US Paramilitary Force in Iraq," *The Nation*, July 22, 2010.

181 *"When President Obama tells the American people"*: Hearing transcript, U.S. Rep. Jason Chaffetz, Utah Republican, at a hearing of the House Committee on Oversight and Government Reform, Subcommittee on National Security, Homeland Defense and Foreign Operations, 112th Congress, First Session, October 12, 2011, 2.

181 About U.S. Army helicopters: NPR commentator Tom Bowman, May 17, 2011.

182 *"What is clear from the current State Department"*: Scahill, "Iraq Withdrawal?"

182 *"items of equipment only available"*: Written request from Undersecretary of State Patrick Kennedy to Ashton Carter, the Defense Department's Undersecretary for Acquisition and Technology, April 7, 2010.

182 *"I understand the department will employ a number of contractors"*: John Tierney, House Committee on Oversight hearing transcript, October 12, 2011, 4, 5.

183 *"So, as the defense department winds down"*: Jason Chaffetz, ibid.

183 NOTE: in 2012, DynCorp would hire more than 4,000 veterans, according to a DynCorp International press release on April 30, 2013, bringing the total it had hired in response to the White House initiative to 7,300.

184 *"people acting in the name of the U.S."*: Spokesman for the Commission on Wartime Contracting, quoted in R.M. Schneiderman, "Mercenaries to Fill Void Left by U.S. Army," *Newsweek*, August 10, 2010.

184 *"a large permanent and ever-expanding"*: Bacevich, *The Limits of Power,* 85.

184 *"to control the information provided to the American people"*: Ibid.

184 *"If we don't act today"*: Discussion between Arthur Schlesinger and author on preventive war, 2005.

185 *"for the United States war"*: Bacevich, *The Limits of Power,* 118.

185 *"The potential for the disastrous"*: Dwight D. Eisenhower, Farewell Address, January 17, 1961.

185 *"Contractors represent more than half"*: Commission on Wartime Contracting, Final Report, "Foreword."

185 *"Delay and denial are not good options"*: Ibid.

186 *"the rubber hits the road day"*: David Isenberg, "War and Private Contractors: Can't Live with Them, Can't Live Without Them," Huffington Post, September 2, 2011.

186 *"Clearly, if one could bring back"*: Ibid.

187 *"significant additional waste"*: Commission on Wartime Contracting, Final Report, 7.

187 *"The extensive use of contractors"*: Ibid., 30.

188 *"undoubtedly higher"*: Ibid., 31.

189 *"Because the U.S. government"*: Ibid., 33.

189 *"will remain a significant element"*: Ibid., 13.

189 *"forced to treat contractors as the default option"*: Ibid., 2.

190 *"not getting into the business of training mercenaries"*: Suzanne Barteau, "Tech Gets Piece of $10 billion WPS Contract," in *El Defensor Chieftain*, March 12, 2011.

14: BEYOND IRAQ

Page

191 *"The U.S. government assumes no responsibility"*: Baghdad embassy, www.iraq.usembassy.gov, with the list for all of the companies (accessed summer 2012).

192 *"mercenaries in armed conflict"*: Sixty-sixth General Assembly, Third Committee, 37th Meeting (PM), October 31, 2011; Jt Nguyen, "Countries Facing Strife Relying More on Hired Guns," *Deutsche Presse-Agentur*, November 2, 2011.

193 *"an onslaught of human rights problems"*: Nguyen, "Countries Facing Strife."

193 *"He [Starr] wanted you to know"*: U.N. spokesman Farhan Haq, in 2009, for Gregory Starr, in Colum Lynch, "UN Embraces Private Military Contractors," *Foreign Policy Magazine*, January 17, 2010.

194 *"we care about you"*: Interview with Jean-Marie Guehenno, U.N. peacekeeping official and French diplomat, ibid.

194 *"will have to turn to the private sector"*: Lynch, "UN Embraces Private Military Contractors," 51.

194 *"quietly turning to private security"*: Ibid.

194 About U.N. increase in private security spending: Lou Pingeot, "Contracting

Insecurity: Private Military and Security Companies and the Future of the United Nations," Global Policy Forum, February 2014, 6.

194 *"security services," "not an exact,"* and *"rapid increase":* Ibid., 6.

195 *"the use of privately contracted":* A memo from U.S. Secretary of State Hillary Clinton, issued on October 27, 2011, in Robert Young Pelton, "US to Promote Use of Armed Guards on Vessels: Sec of State Hillary Clinton Orders Embassies to Sell the Use of Contractors," SomaliaReport, November 4, 2011. Note that at the end of the article, the Somalia Report stated that it was "neither a proponent or opponent on the use of armed guards aboard ships because the industry generally does not want to have lethal force on board, but a quick glance of our list of October pirate attacks and how they were deterred tells a tale that cannot be ignored."

195 *"With so much water to patrol":* Andrew J. Shapiro, assistant secretary of state, Bureau of Political-Military Affairs, U.S. Department of State, spoke to the Defense Trade Advisory Group, November 9, 2011, www.state.gov (accessed January 2012).

196 *"If the government cannot protect its citizens":* Julian Aguilar, "Texas OKs Private Border Security Contractor," *Texas Tribune,* August 11, 2011.

197 *"I love my country":* President of the International Security Agency, ibid.

197 *"Our practice":* Ibid.

197 *"former military with at least four years of service":* International Security Agency, www.intersec.org (accessed winter 2012).

198 *"Let's be clear here":* Press release, office of Governor Rick Perry, August 11, 2011.

198 About other firms involved in such work: One was Serco, a U.K. firm with a division in Reston, Virginia. Serco listed immigration enforcement in its $10 billion portfolio, along with nuclear weapons maintenance, operation of ballistic-missile early-warning systems, air transport, air traffic control at eighty or more international airports worldwide, surveillance, and two "immigration removal centers" in the U.K. Yet another was a Florida-based company, GEO Group, which attributed part of its 40 percent increase in second-quarter profits for 2011 to new immigration security contracts.

201 *"When police officers are dressed like soldiers":* Editorial, *Atlantic Monthly,* November 2011.

202 *"the incubation of new and more powerful capabilities":* Barrett Brown. "A Virtual Secret State: The Military-Industrial Complex 2.0," *The Guardian,* October 9, 2011.

15: RIDING THE WAVE

Page

203 About the debate: "Republican Debate, Transcript, Iowa, December 10, 2011, Co-sponsored by ABC News, ABC5/WOI-DT and the Iowa Republican Party." Transcript provided by ABC.

204 *"it would add as much as $1,000"*: Diane Sawyer, ibid.

204 *"I want to extend the tax cut"*: Ron Paul, ibid.

205 *"insourcing initiative"*: David Berteau, Joachim Hofbauer, Jesse Ellman, Gregory Kiley, Guy Ben-Ari, "DoD Workforce Cost Realism Assessment," Center for Strategic and International Studies, May 2011.

205 *"not satisfied with the progress"*: Robert Brodsky, "Government Executive" articles, August 10, 2010. www.govexec.com/defense/2010/08/pentagon-abandons-insourcing-effort/3211/ (accessed August 2012).

205 *"keeping the knowledge of this force hidden"*: Interview with Jan Schakowsky, 2012.

205 *"masks the fact that we are privatizing the military"*: Ibid.

205 About MIA statistics, as of May 2011: Jack Healy, "With Withdrawal Looming, Trails Grow Cold for Americans Missing in Iraq," *New York Times*, May 21, 2011.

206 *"Are Government Contractors Exploiting Workers Overseas?"*: Government hearing, U.S. House of Representatives, Committee on Oversight and Government Reform, Subcommittee on Technology, Information Policy, "Intergovernmental Relations and Procurement Reform," Hearing #112-93, November 2, 2011.

206 *"Not a single case of human trafficking"*: U.S. Rep. Gerald E. Connolly of Virginia, ibid.

206 *"These labor practices violate every human value"*: James Lankford, U.S. Representative from Oklahoma. Rep. Lankford's statement, from which this was taken: "This violates everything in the American value: that we value the individual person. It is a person created in God's image and has inalienable rights no matter what country they are from, they are to be honored as an individual in the middle of all that and to know that our State Department, which stands for human rights around the world, has indentured servitude happening in our embassies is deplorable to me. This is the group that is standing up for American values worldwide. Yet, when these individuals return back to their home countries, all they can speak of is I worked for a year for nothing and lived in these deplorable conditions. This

violates everything about who we are and what we do." www.lankford.house.gov (accessed August 2012).

NOTE: What follows are more sources for contractor deaths and injuries, to offer perspective. Keep in mind that these cover DOD contracts and do not necessarily include contractors working for other agencies, such as the State Department and USAID. And as noted in the Prologue notes, it was the Commission on Wartime Contracting that revealed the moment when the contractors' casualties in Iraq exceeded troop casualties as noted in the following: Commission on Wartime Contracting, Final Report, 31. Also useful is the Department of Labor, Division of Longshore and Harbor Workers' Compensation, "Defense Base Act Summary," June 23, 2011. Note that the Department of Labor has a disclaimer on its website regarding the issue of accuracy in contractor casualties, *"These reports do not constitute the complete or official casualty statistics of civilian contractor injuries and deaths."* www.dol.gov.

- From the Office of Workers' Compensation Programs of the U.S. Department of Labor: reports that since September of 2001, and as of June, 30, 2012 *3,066 contractors* under the Defense of Base Act have been killed and lists injuries by time lost. www.dol.gov/owcp/dlhwc/dbaallnation6-30-12.htm#.UNYXO5P jmFc.

- From ProPublica, map of injuries and deaths to civilian contractors in Iraq and Afghanistan by U.S. state from the Department of Labor in 2008. www .propublica.org/special/map-injuries-and-deaths-to-civilian-contractors-by-state-614.

- From a presentation compiled by Amada Benavides de Pérez about the DOD's use of PSCs in Afghanistan and Iraq with information from Moshe Schwartz circa February 2011: "According to DOD, from June 2009 to November 2010, 319 private security contractor personnel working for DOD have been killed in action in Afghanistan, compared to 626 U.S. troops killed in action over the same period. Compared to troops, a PSC employee working for DOD in Afghanistan is 2.75 times more likely to be killed in action than uniformed personnel." psm.du.edu/media/documents/international_regulation/united_nations /human_rights_council_and_ga/open_ended_we/session_1/presentations/un _open_ended_we_session_1_benavides_26_ May_2011.pdf.

207 *"Politicians pay little attention":* T. Christian Miller, "Contractors in Iraq Are Hidden Casualties of War," October 2009, www.propublica.org/article/kbr-contractor-struggles-after-Iraq-injuries-1006 (accessed June 2013).

207 About the case in which a private contractor fatally shot a woman in Baghdad in 2007: Jalal Askander v. Research Triangle Institute, International, and Unity Resources Group, L.L.C: U.S. District Court for the District of Columbia, April 2008. Superior Court of the District of Columbia, Civil Division. Complaint and Jury Demand, August 2010. See also "In Death of Iraqi Woman, D.C. Appeals Court Considers Jurisdiction," *Legal Times*, November 7, 2011; and "Failure to Serve Sends Father of Slain Iraqi Woman Back to Square One," *Legal Times*, November 22, 2011.

208 *"What comes with opportunity are the laws":* Interview with Shereef Akeel, 2011.

208 *"We are hoping these cases will make a difference":* Ibid.

209 About the four Blackwater employees charged: In 2011, an appeals court would reinstate it and on October 17, 2013, the Justice Department brought new charges. Then, in April of 2014, a U.S. District judge in Washington called for an investigation of the State Department over years of delays in prosecuting the Blackwater security guards for the shootings at Nisour Square. The guards were scheduled to go on trial on June 11, 2014.

209 *"I have to tell you that in the war zone":* CIA Director Leon Panetta, to ABC's *This Week* commentator Jake Tapper, for story "CIA Defends Blackwater Contractor," June 27, 2010. Tapper also interviewed Jan Schakowsky, who said: "I'm just mystified why any branch of the government would decide to hire Blackwater, such a repeat offender. We're talking about murder, a company with a horrible reputation that really jeopardizes our mission in so many different, different ways."

210 *"What we are seeing clearly":* Jeremy Scahill, "Blackwater's New Sugar Daddy: The Obama Administration," *The Nation*, June 28, 2010.

210 *"false and defamatory":* Letter, statements, written by Washington, D.C., attorney Victoria Toensing on behalf of Erik Prince, to Rep. Jan Schakowsky, October 7, 2011.

210 *"If Mr. Prince had not emigrated":* Ibid.

211 *"heavy-handed tactic":* Rep. Jan Schakowsky, on the floor of the U.S. House of Representatives, transcript of hearing, November 30, 2011.

211 *"While many hours have been spent":* Ibid.

212 *"more boring":* Nathan Hodge, "Company Once Known as Blackwater Ditches Xe for Yet Another New Name," *Wall Street Journal*, December 12, 2011.

212 *"turning a page":* ABC News, January 6, 2012.

213 *"[The PMSCs] will evolve":* Interview with Eric Westropp, January 2012.

16: AND NOW, THE DEBATE?

Page

215 *"Damn the Torpedoes, Full Speed Ahead!":* Screensaver in Doug Brooks's office in Washington, D.C., February 2012. Note that the ISOA office, by 2014, had moved to Vienna, Virginia.

216 *"the friendly, public face":* Bruce Falconer, "Blackwater's Man in Washington," *Mother Jones,* September 25, 2007.

216 *"They would call it Orwellian":* Interview with Doug Brooks.

216 *"FedEx can do things better":* Ibid.

217 *"The industry is here to stay":* Ibid.

217 *"the private sector continues to be":* Doug Brooks, "The Future of the Stability Operations Industry: Defining Stability Operations in a Changing World," *Journal of International Peace Operations,* March–April (2011), 8.

217 About ISOA members: By 2014 Aegis still not listed on the roster.

218 *"You Never Know What Threats Lie Ahead":* Ad for Triple Canopy, ibid., 7.

218 *"When the stakes are highest":* Ad for Olive Group, in ISOA, Annual Summit Guide, 2011.

218 *This was a "new model":* Brooks, "The Future of the Stability Operations Industry," 8.

219 *"Blackwater's Man in Washington":* Falconer, 25.

219 *"There are still no good numbers":* Interview with U.S. Rep. Jan Schakowsky, 2012.

220 *"The public indifference":* Interview with David Isenberg, 2012.

220 *"In a world where there are":* David Isenberg, *Soldiers of Fortune Ltd.,* 2.

220 *"They aren't mercenaries":* David Isenberg interview.

221 *"No term fully captures":* Ibid.

221 *"Mine is a Mr. Spock approach":* Ibid.

221 *"[PMSCs] are now undifferentiated":* Ibid.

222 *"Anywhere we can't use troops":* Interview with Gen. Edward Cardon, Washington, D.C., February 2012.

222 *"The way it works is that":* Ibid.

223 *"In one year it is hard to imagine":* Ibid.

223 *"We are a professional organization":* Academi posting for a job for Unmanned Aerial Vehicle Operator (Tier II), Job #1512007, www.academi.com (accessed March 2013).

NOTE: Triple Canopy receiving drone contracts. See www.triplecanopy.com /assets/GSA_Schedule_Terms_and_Conditions.pdf (December 1, 2009–November 30, 2014), Federal Supply Services.

224 About the drone lobby AUVSI, Association for Unmanned Vehicle Systems International: The list of members can be found at www.auvsi.org/membershipand chapters/corporatemembers (accessed June 2013).

224 About Silent Falcon: The advertisement for the product manufactured by Silent Falcon UAS Technologies, "Fly Silent, Fly Longer, See More," March, 2013, on its website, www.silentfalconuas.com/Silent-Falcon. And see www.forbes.com /sites/davidferris/2012/08/16/this-solar-powered-drone-will-watch-you-all-day (accessed April 2012).

17: "FULL SPEED AHEAD"

Page

225 *"parent, subsidiary or successor entities?":* H.R. 6360, "Oversight and Accountability in Wartime Contracting Act of 2012," August 7, 2012.

226 *"We want to know the history of contractors":* Leigh Munsil, "Mass. Congressman Eyes Ban of Former Blackwater," *Politico*, September 12, 2012.

227 About the $42 million settlement: James Risen, "Blackwater Reaches Deal in U.S. Export Violations," *New York Times*, August 20, 2010.

227 *"If you look at the magnitude of the problem":* Ibid.

227 *"adequately serve the public interest":* U.S. Rep. John Tierney letter to the Justice Department, September 11, 2012.

227 *"This has been a repeated problem":* Munsil, "Mass. Congressman Eyes Ban of Former Blackwater," POLITICO, September 12, 2012.

227 *"Today, Academi is working to become":* Academi press release, published in numerous news outlets.

228 *"For a government contractor to knowingly provide":* Stuart F. Delery, acting assistant attorney general for the Civil Division of the Department of Justice, commenting in a press release on U.S. ex rel. Badr v. Triple Canopy, Inc., filed in the U.S. District Court for the Eastern District of Virginia in Alexandria, October 31, 2012.

228 *"We will not tolerate government contractors":* Neil H. MacBride, U.S. attorney for the Eastern District of Virginia, ibid. The case was dismissed in June of 2013, and under appeal by September that year. Website sources for quotes and more information on the case: www.justice.gov/opa/pr/2012/October

/12-civ-1300.html; pogoblog.typepad.com/pogo/2012/11/government-sues-triple-canopy-for-iraq-contract-fraud.html; www.fairfaxtimes.com/article/20121116/NEWS/711169732/1064/fairfax-law-firm-represents-whistleblower-from-reston-company&template=fairfaxTimes.

228 About G4S and London Olympics: Adam Taylor, "How the Plan to Privatize London Olympic Security Turned into a Disaster," *Business Insider*, July 18, 2012.

229 *"The G4S Olympics scandal exposes":* Ruth Tanner, War on Want campaigns and policy director, "G4S Olympics Games Security Row Sparks Call for Mercenary Regulation," Isenberg Institute of Strategic Satire, July 17, 2012.

229 *"Successive governments have ducked":* War on Want petition, "Regulate Private Security Contractors Now," July 2012.

230 *"(Inaudible) the claim was made yesterday":* Transcript, U.S. State Department press briefing, September 14, 2012.

231 *The contract was with Blue Mountain Group: Award ID SAQMMA12COOO92 for Security Guards and Patrol Services:* Judicial Watch v. U.S. Department of State (No. 1:13-cv-00243). Its official description was from the Federal Procurement Data System website at www.fpds.gov. More details about the "miscellaneous foreign contractors" fund are in the Commission on Wartime Contracting, Final Report, August 2011, 24. And a news article referring to the miscellaneous category and noting that the company was not on the State Department's master list of contract awardees is: Tabassum Zakana, Susan Cornwell, and Hadeel Al Shalchi, "For Benghazi diplomatic security, U.S. relied on small British firm," *Reuters*, October 17, 2012.

231 *"We are the pilgrims, master":* Blue Mountain Group, www.bluemountaingroup.co.uk (accessed September 2012).

231 *"security solutions and training services":* Ibid.

231 *"very few private security companies":* Intelligence Online, no. 672, September 20, 2012 (originally in same publication, December 16, 2011).

231 *"was largely based on our concern":* Tabassum Zakana, Susan Cornwell, and Hadeel Al Shalchi, "For Benghazi diplomatic security, U.S. relied on British firm," *Reuters*, October 17, 2012.

232 *"There was an error in what I said":* Victoria Nuland, spokesperson, U.S. State Department, press briefing transcript, September 18, 2012.

233 About Global Response Staff: Greg Miller and Julie Tate, "CIA's Global Response Staff Emerging from Shadows After Incidents in Libya and Pakistan," *Washington Post*, December 26, 2012.

18: BIG BROTHER'S BIG BROTHER

Page

235 *"The Iraq war might best be remembered":* Molly Dunigan, "A Lesson From Iraq War," *Christian Science Monitor,* March 19, 2013.

235 *"Although the war's tremendous costs helped":* "Invasion of Iraq, 10 Years Later," Center for Public Integrity, March 19, 2013.

236 About the report: out of the United Nations working group in the use of mercenaries, November 4, 2013.

236 *"between $31 billion":* Commission on Wartime Contracting, Final Report, 32.

236 *"at least $3.1 billion": Financial Times,* March 20, 2013.

236 *"is very poor":* Linda Bilmes, "Who Profited from the Iraq War?" *Newsletter of Economists for Peace & Security* 24, no. 1 (March 2012), www.epsusa.org /publications/newsletter/2012/mar2012/Bilmes.html (accessed April 2013).

Note that statistics for PMSCs in Iraq and Afghanistan in March 2013 can be found in: "Warfighter Support: DOD Needs Additional Steps to Fully Integrate Operational Contract Support into Contingency Planning," GAO Report, GAO-13-212, February 2013.

236 About China: Interview with industry insider based in London; and Andrew Erickson, and Gabe Collins, "Enter China's Security Firms," *East Asia Security: China,* February 21, 2012.

NOTE: For more about China and the private military and security industry, see thediplomat.com/2012/02/21/enter-china%E2%80%99s-security-firms. Note also that during the 2013 Sudan hostage crisis, the *Wall Street Journal* reported that the Sudanese troops that engaged in the rescue effort were joined by a dozen armed Chinese private security contractors. While that article and coverage of the issue in the Chinese media didn't identify where the contractors came from, there's a strong likelihood they were drawn from the same pool of former security-forces personnel that Shandong Huawei recruits from and perhaps even came from the company.

237 About Erik Prince in China and *"Beijing has titanic ambitions":* David Feith, "The Weekend Interview with Erik Prince," in the *Wall Street Journal,* January 25–26, 2014.

237 About the top ten: There are companies that specialize in particular military or security services, and there are companies like G4S and Academi (formerly Blackwater) that are considered the defense and security department stores, offering a broad range from counterterrorism to combat to intelligence-gathering to security

risk consulting to video feed analysis for drones to armed security for embassies, ships, and oil rigs. Thus, to put together a top-ten list is not an easy task. This one was originally compiled by DARPA (Defense Advanced Research Projects Agency) and factors in size of company, range of services, range of contracting sources (that is, nations, NGOs, and corporations), and future prospects. It is international in scope, and it represents the broad range of the companies that serve the market for privatized defense and security. There are other lists, such as the Wartime Contracting Commission's Final Report, which includes companies supplying services and providing weapons and equipment but is limited to contracts in Iraq and Afghanistan. And there are websites with lists—for example, www.sipri .org/research/armaments/production/researchissues/pmsc, which has a list of types of PMSC work and sorts out which companies do which type of work, as well as the Congressional Research Service reports, which have included lists, but these focus on U.S. contracts only. Also, the International Code of Conduct website keeps track of registered signatory companies and thus offers a good glimpse at the hundreds of companies defined as private military or private security or private military and security. By the end of 2013, there were more than 700 signatories.

238 *"Camouflaged by parties":* Michael E. Miller, "Miami Mercenaries: International Security Business Is Booming in South Florida," *Miami New Times,* August 1, 2013, 1.

238 About the "PSSPA" and the oversight mechanism of the International Code of Conduct for Private Security Service Providers: "International Code of Conduct for Private Security Service Providers—Consensus on Oversight Mechanism," news release, February 22, 2013, out of the Federal Department of Foreign Affairs of the government of Switzerland. By January 2014, no companies had been disciplined yet, according to sources in Geneva.

238 *"Government and diplomatic contracts":* From the Aegis website, www.aegisworld .com (last accessed April 2014).

239 *"facilitate Western business operations":* Aegis in Libya. Charles Glass, "The Warrior Class: A Golden Age for the Freelance Soldier," *Harper's,* April 2012.

239 "the *elite private force in Afghanistan":* Ibid.

239 *"We've built a brand":* Ibid.

240 About Snowden and the NSA: From coverage of the story in the *New York Times, Corporate Watch, Bloomberg Businessweek, Wall Street Journal, Washington Post, Guardian,* and *Bloomberg News* as well as David Perry's "Blackwater vs. Bin Laden: The Private Sector's Role in American Counterterrorism."

242 *"revolving door in its purest form":* Richard Eskow, "Big Money and the NSA Scandal . . . How Dangerous Is the 'Security/Digital Complex'?" Campaign for America's Future, June 10, 2013. www.ourfuture.org/blog (accessed July 2013).

242 *"breaches more likely":* Editorial Board of the *New York Times*, "Prying Private Eyes," June 19, 2013.

242 About the agency's battalion: "NSA surveillance covers 75% U.S. Internet Traffic," *Wall Street Journal,* August 20, 2013.

243 *"Time Change":* Hearing, "Time Change: The Future of Drones in America: Law Enforcement and Privacy Considerations," U.S. Senate Committee on the Judiciary, March 20, 2013, from www.judiciary.senate.gov/hearings/hearing .cfm?id=d27f2c4073b40a8e678e4a9f6f36acec (accessed April 2013).

243 The U.S. inventory growth from 167 to over 7,000: Ibid.

243 About how labor-intensive drone missions can be: Keric D. Clanahan, "Drone-Sourcing United States Air Force Unmanned Aircraft Systems, Inherently Governmental Functions, and the Role of Contractors," *Federal Circuit Bar Journal,* May 4, 2012.

243 *"The Air Force is short of ground-based pilots":* David S. Cloud, "Civilian Contractors Playing Key Operations," *Los Angeles Times*, December 29, 2011; and David S. Cloud, "Contractors' Role Grows in Drone Missions, Worrying Some in the Military," *Los Angeles Times*, December 30, 2011.

244 *"real-time air surveillance":* Keric D. Clanahan, "Drone-Sourcing? United States Air Force Unmanned Aircraft Systems, Inherently Governmental Functions, and the Role of Contractors," *Federal Circuit Bar Journal,* May 4, 2012, 21.

Note also: understandingempire.wordpress.com/2012/01/03/contractors-play-key-role-in-drone-wars. "Our No. 1 manning problem in the Air Force is manning our unmanned platforms"—Gen. Philip M. Breedlove, Air Force vice chief of staff.

244 About the DynCorp/Textron pursuit of contract and Battlespace winning it: www .washingtonpost.com/business/economy/retired-veterans-beat-textron-for-nearly-1-billion-military-drone-contract/2012/12/18/c0f707f0-4 4b3-11e2-8061-253bccfc 7532_story.html (accessed April 2013).

245 *"involved at every stage":* Donald L. Bartlett and James B. Steele, "Washington's $8 Billion Shadow," *Vanity Fair*, March 2007.

245 About the December 2010 deaths from the drone strike in central Afghanistan: David S. Cloud, "Contractors' Role Grows in Drone Missions, Worrying Some in the Military," *Los Angeles Times*, December 30, 2011, 1.

246 *"the safe integration":* Nick Wingfield and Somini Sengupta, "Drones Set Sights on U.S. Skies," *New York Times*, February 17, 2012.

246 About police departments that have drones as of the summer of 2012 and the companies supplying them: www.businessinsider.com/us-police-drones-2012-7?op=1 (accessed July 2013).

246 *"Rugged and reliable":* www.avinc.com/uas/small_uas/qube (accessed June 2013).

247 *"Wide Area Persistent Stare":* Jay Stanley, "Drone 'Nightmare Scenario' Now Has a Name: ARGUS," www.aclu.org/print/blog/technology-and-liberty-free-speech-national-security/drone (accessed June 2013); and "BAE Systems Newsroom, 8 February 2010," www.baesystems.com (accessed June 2013).

247 *ARGUS-IS:* Ibid.

247 *"Even in our most pessimistic moments":* Jay Stanley, ibid.

249 *"security is transmuted into":* Niebuhr, *The Irony of American History*, xxiv.

249 *"In the councils of government":* Dwight D. Eisenhower, Farewell Address, January 17, 1961.

249 About the $6 billion in military equipment: From Dion Nissenbaum, "Role of U.S. Contractors Grows as Iraq Fights Insurgents," *Wall Street Journal*, February 3, 2014, online.wsj.com/news/articles (last accessed April 2014).

250 *"The one thing that's a given":* Dan Lamothe, "Ghosts of Baghdad: America's Army of Contractors Hasn't Gone Anywhere. They Just Work for the Iraqi Government," in blog.foreignpolicy.com, January 23, 2014.

SOURCE NOTES ESSAY

Page

255 *"Britain is the perfect place to understand":* Robert Young Pelton, *Licensed to Kill* (New York: Three Rivers Press, 2006), 252.

255 *"Well, of course, that is the case":* Interview with Julian Radcliffe, 2009.

INDEX

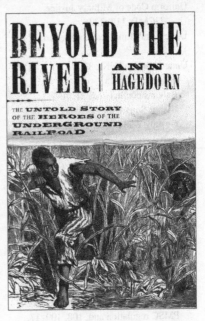